PRIVACY AND IDENTITY PROTECTION

CONSUMER PRIVACY IN THE 21ST CENTURY

BEST PRACTICES FOR BUSINESSES AND POLICYMAKERS

PRIVACY AND IDENTITY PROTECTION

Additional books in this series can be found on Nova's website
under the Series tab.

Additional E-books in this series can be found on Nova's website
under the E-book tab.

BUSINESS ISSUES, COMPETITION AND ENTREPRENEURSHIP

Additional books in this series can be found on Nova's website
under the Series tab.

Additional E-books in this series can be found on Nova's website
under the E-book tab.

PRIVACY AND IDENTITY PROTECTION

CONSUMER PRIVACY IN THE 21ST CENTURY

BEST PRACTICES FOR BUSINESSES AND POLICYMAKERS

LARRY A. SCHWARTZ
EDITOR

nova publishers
New York

For permission to use material from this book please contact us:
Telephone 631-231-7269; Fax 631-231-8175
Web Site: http://www.novapublishers.com

Library of Congress Cataloging-in-Publication Data

ISBN: 978-1-62417-252-6

Published by Nova Science Publishers, Inc. † New York

CONTENTS

PREFACE

In today's world of smart phones, smart grids, and smart cars, companies are collecting, storing, and sharing more information about consumers than ever before. Although companies use this information to innovate and deliver better products and services to consumers, they should not do so at the expense of consumer privacy. This book provides an overview for how companies can act now to implement best practices to protect consumers' private information. These best practices would include making privacy the "default setting" for commercial data practices and give consumers greater control over the collection and use of their personal data through simplified choices and increased transparency. Implementing these best practices will enhance trust and stimulate commerce.

Chapter 1 – In today's world of smart phones, smart grids, and smart cars, companies are collecting, storing, and sharing more information about consumers than ever before. Although companies use this information to innovate and deliver better products and services to consumers, they should not do so at the expense of consumer privacy.

With this Report, the Commission calls on companies to act now to implement best practices to protect consumers' private information. These best practices include making privacy the "default setting" for commercial data practices and giving consumers greater control over the collection and use of their personal data through simplified choices and increased transparency. Implementing these best practices will enhance trust and stimulate commerce. This Report follows a preliminary staff report that the Federal Trade Commission ("FTC" or "Commission") issued in December 2010. The preliminary report proposed a framework for protecting consumer privacy in the 21st Century. Like this Report, the framework urged companies to adopt the following practices, consistent with the Fair Information Practice Principles first articulated almost 40 years ago:

- **Privacy by Design:** Build in privacy at every stage of product development;
- **Simplified Choice for Businesses and Consumers:** Give consumers the ability to make decisions about their data at a relevant time and context, including through a Do Not Track mechanism, while reducing the burden on businesses of providing unnecessary choices; and
- **Greater Transparency:** Make information collection and use practices transparent.

The Commission received more than 450 public comments in response to the preliminary report from various stakeholders, including businesses, privacy advocates, technologists and individual consumers. A wide range of stakeholders, including industry, supported the principles underlying the framework, and many companies said they were already following them. At the same time, many commenters criticized the slow pace of self-regulation, and argued that it is time for Congress to enact baseline privacy legislation. In this Report, the Commission addresses the comments and sets forth a revised, final privacy framework that adheres to, but also clarifies and fine-tunes, the basic principles laid out in the preliminary report.

Since the Commission issued the preliminary staff report, Congress has introduced both general privacy bills and more focused bills, including ones addressing Do Not Track and the privacy of teens. Industry has made some progress in certain areas, most notably, in responding to the preliminary report's call for Do Not Track. In other areas, however, industry progress has been far slower. Thus, overall, consumers do not yet enjoy the privacy protections proposed in the preliminary staff report.

The Administration and certain Members of Congress have called for enactment of baseline privacy legislation. The Commission now also calls on Congress to consider enacting baseline privacy legislation and reiterates its call for data security legislation. The Commission is prepared to work with Congress and other stakeholders to craft such legislation. At the same time, the Commission urges industry to accelerate the pace of self-regulation.

The remainder of this Executive Summary describes key developments since the issuance of the preliminary report, discusses the most significant revisions to the proposed framework, and lays out several next steps.

Chapter 2 – Trust is essential to maintaining the social and economic benefits that networked technologies bring to the United States and the rest of the world. With the confidence that companies will handle information about them fairly and responsibly, consumers have turned to the Internet to express their creativity, join political movements, form and maintain friendships, and engage in commerce. The Internet's global connectivity means that a single innovator's idea can grow rapidly into a product or service that becomes a daily necessity for hundreds of millions of consumers. American companies lead the way in providing these technologies, and the United States benefits through job creation and economic growth as a result. Our continuing leadership in this area depends on American companies' ability to earn and maintain the trust of consumers in a global marketplace.

Privacy protections are critical to maintaining consumer trust in networked technologies. When consumers provide information about themselves—whether it is in the context of an online social network that is open to public view or a transaction involving sensitive personal data—they reasonably expect companies to use this information in ways that are consistent with the surrounding context. Many companies live up to these expectations, but some do not. Neither consumers nor companies have a clear set of ground rules to apply in the commercial arena. As a result, it is difficult today for consumers to assess whether a company's privacy practices warrant their trust.

The consumer data privacy framework in the United States is, in fact, strong. This framework rests on fundamental privacy values, flexible and adaptable common law protections and consumer protection statutes, Federal Trade Commission (FTC) enforcement, and policy development that involves a broad array of stakeholders. This framework has encouraged not only social and economic innovations based on the Internet but also vibrant discussions of how to protect privacy in a networked society involving civil society, industry, academia, and the government. The current framework, however, lacks two elements: a clear statement of basic privacy principles that apply to the commercial world, and a sustained commitment of all stakeholders to address consumer data privacy issues as they arise from advances in technologies and business models.

To address these issues, the Administration offers *Consumer Data Privacy in a Networked World.* At the center of this framework is a Consumer Privacy Bill of Rights, which embraces privacy principles recognized throughout the world and adapts them to the dynamic environment of the commercial Internet. The Administration has called for Congress to pass legislation that applies the Consumer Privacy Bill of Rights to commercial sectors that are not subject to existing Federal data privacy laws. The Federal Government will play a role in convening discussions among stakeholders—companies, privacy and consumer advocates, international partners, State Attorneys General, Federal criminal and civil law enforcement representatives, and academics—who will then develop codes of conduct that implement the Consumer Privacy Bill of Rights. Such practices, when publicly and affirmatively adopted by companies subject to Federal Trade Commission jurisdiction, will be legally enforceable by the FTC. The United States will engage with our international partners to create greater interoperability among our respective privacy frameworks. This will provide more consistent protections for consumers and lower compliance burdens for companies.

Of course, this framework is just a beginning. Starting now, the Administration will work with and encourage stakeholders, including the private sector, to implement the Consumer Privacy Bill of Rights. The Administration will also work with Congress to write these flexible, general principles into law. The Administration is ready to do its part as a convener to achieve privacy protections that preserve consumer trust and promote innovation.

Chapter 3 – The market for mobile applications has experienced explosive growth over the past three and a half years. When Apple's iTunes App Store and Google's Android Market first launched in 2008, smartphone users could choose from about 600 apps. Today, there are more than 500,000 apps in the Apple App store and 380,000 apps in the Android Market, which consumers can access from a variety of mobile devices, including smartphones and tablets. Consumers have downloaded these apps more than 28 billion times, and young children and teens are increasingly embracing smartphone technology for entertainment and educational purposes. As consumers increasingly rely on their mobile devices for multiple activities, the quantity and diversity of mobile apps continue to expand.

This rapidly growing market provides enormous opportunities and benefits for app users of all ages, but raises questions about users' privacy, especially when the users are children and teens. Mobile apps can capture a broad range of user information from the device automatically – including the user's precise geolocation, phone number, list of contacts, call logs, unique device identifiers, and other information stored on the mobile device – and can share this data with a large number of possible recipients. These capabilities can provide beneficial services to consumers – for example, access to maps and directions, and the ability to play interactive games with other users – but they also can be used by apps to collect detailed personal information in a manner parents cannot detect.

Protecting children's privacy is one of the Commission's top priorities. In order to better understand and evaluate the emerging app market and the products and services it offers to children, Federal Trade Commission staff designed and conducted a survey of the apps offered for children in the two largest U.S. app stores, the Android Market and the Apple App store. Staff focused in particular on the types of apps offered to children; the age range of the intended audience; the disclosures provided to users about the apps' data collection and sharing practices; the availability of interactive features, such as connecting with social media; and the app store ratings and parental controls offered for these systems. This report highlights the lack of information available to parents prior to downloading mobile apps for their children, and calls on industry to provide greater transparency about their data practices.

Staff searched the app stores using the word "kids," and examined hundreds of pages promoting apps, which ranged from alphabet and word games, math and number games, and memory games to books and stories, flash cards, and puzzles. Most of the apps' descriptions specifically indicated that the apps were intended for use by children, and some promoted use by children of certain ages, stating, for example, "teach young children, ages 2 to 5." Prices ranged from free to $9.99, but most apps were $0.99 or less, and free apps were overwhelmingly the most frequently downloaded.

While staff encountered a diverse pool of apps for kids created by hundreds of different developers, staff found little, if any, information in the app marketplaces about the data collection and sharing practices of these apps. Staff found almost no relevant language regarding app data collection or sharing on the Apple app promotion pages, and minimal information (beyond the general "permission" statements required on the Android operating system) on just three of the Android promotion pages. In most instances, staff was unable to determine from the promotion pages whether the apps collected any data at all, let alone the type of data collected, the purpose of the collection, and who collected or obtained access to the data.

As part of its mission to protect children, the Commission vigorously enforces the Children's Online Privacy Protection Act ("COPPA") and the FTC's implementing Rule, which require operators of online services (including interactive mobile apps) directed to children under age 13 to provide notice and obtain parental consent before collecting items of "personal information" from children. Since collecting the data for this survey, the FTC settled its first COPPA enforcement action against a mobile app developer and issued a Notice of Proposed Rulemaking to amend the Commission's COPPA Rule. Those initiatives, along with this report, are a warning call to industry that it must do more to provide parents with easily accessible, basic information about the mobile apps that their children use.

Most of the apps in the study appear to be intended for children's use, and many may, in fact, be "directed to children" within the meaning of COPPA. This survey focused on the disclosures provided to users regarding their data practices; it did not test whether the selected apps actually collected, used, or disclosed personal information from children. Over the next six months, staff will conduct an additional review to determine whether there are COPPA violations and whether enforcement is appropriate. Staff also will evaluate whether the industry is moving forward to address the disclosure issues raised in this report.

In: Consumer Privacy in the 21st Century
Editor: Larry A. Schwartz

ISBN: 978-1-62417-252-6

Chapter 1

PROTECTING CONSUMER PRIVACY IN AN ERA OF RAPID CHANGE: RECOMMENDATIONS FOR BUSINESSES AND POLICYMAKERS*

Federal Trade Commission

EXECUTIVE SUMMARY

In today's world of smart phones, smart grids, and smart cars, companies are collecting, storing, and sharing more information about consumers than ever before. Although companies use this information to innovate and deliver better products and services to consumers, they should not do so at the expense of consumer privacy.

With this Report, the Commission calls on companies to act now to implement best practices to protect consumers' private information. These best practices include making privacy the "default setting" for commercial data practices and giving consumers greater control over the collection and use of their personal data through simplified choices and increased transparency. Implementing these best practices will enhance trust and stimulate commerce. This Report follows a preliminary staff report that the Federal Trade Commission ("FTC" or "Commission") issued in December 2010. The preliminary report proposed a framework for protecting consumer privacy in the 21st Century. Like this Report, the framework urged companies to adopt the following practices, consistent with the Fair Information Practice Principles first articulated almost 40 years ago:

- **Privacy by Design:** Build in privacy at every stage of product development;
- **Simplified Choice for Businesses and Consumers:** Give consumers the ability to make decisions about their data at a relevant time and context, including through a Do Not Track mechanism, while reducing the burden on businesses of providing unnecessary choices; and
- **Greater Transparency:** Make information collection and use practices transparent.

---

* This is an edited, reformatted and augmented version of Federal Trade Commission, dated March 2012.

The Commission received more than 450 public comments in response to the preliminary report from various stakeholders, including businesses, privacy advocates, technologists and individual consumers. A wide range of stakeholders, including industry, supported the principles underlying the framework, and many companies said they were already following them. At the same time, many commenters criticized the slow pace of self-regulation, and argued that it is time for Congress to enact baseline privacy legislation. In this Report, the Commission addresses the comments and sets forth a revised, final privacy framework that adheres to, but also clarifies and fine-tunes, the basic principles laid out in the preliminary report.

Since the Commission issued the preliminary staff report, Congress has introduced both general privacy bills and more focused bills, including ones addressing Do Not Track and the privacy of teens. Industry has made some progress in certain areas, most notably, in responding to the preliminary report's call for Do Not Track. In other areas, however, industry progress has been far slower. Thus, overall, consumers do not yet enjoy the privacy protections proposed in the preliminary staff report.

The Administration and certain Members of Congress have called for enactment of baseline privacy legislation. The Commission now also calls on Congress to consider enacting baseline privacy legislation and reiterates its call for data security legislation. The Commission is prepared to work with Congress and other stakeholders to craft such legislation. At the same time, the Commission urges industry to accelerate the pace of self-regulation.

The remainder of this Executive Summary describes key developments since the issuance of the preliminary report, discusses the most significant revisions to the proposed framework, and lays out several next steps.

Developments Since Issuance of the Preliminary Report

In the last 40 years, the Commission has taken numerous actions to shape the consumer privacy landscape. For example, the Commission has sued dozens of companies that broke their privacy and security promises, scores of telemarketers that called consumers on the Do Not Call registry, and more than a hundred scammers peddling unwanted spam and spyware. Since it issued the initial staff report, the Commission has redoubled its efforts to protect consumer privacy, including through law enforcement, policy advocacy, and consumer and business education. It has also vigorously promoted self-regulatory efforts.

On the law enforcement front, since December 2010, the Commission:

- Brought enforcement actions against Google and Facebook. The orders obtained in these cases require the companies to obtain consumers' affirmative express consent before materially changing certain of their data practices and to adopt strong, company-wide privacy programs that outside auditors will assess for 20 years. These orders will protect the more than one billion Google and Facebook users worldwide.
- Brought enforcement actions against online advertising networks that failed to honor opt outs. The orders in these cases are designed to ensure that when consumers choose to opt out of tracking by advertisers, their choice is effective.

- Brought enforcement actions against mobile applications that violated the Children's Online Privacy Protection Act as well as applications that set default privacy settings in a way that caused consumers to unwittingly share their personal data.
- Brought enforcement actions against entities that sold consumer lists to marketers in violation of the Fair Credit Reporting Act.
- Brought actions against companies for failure to maintain reasonable data security.
On the policy front, since December 2010, the FTC and staff:
- Hosted two privacy-related workshops, one on child identity theft and one on the privacy implications of facial recognition technology.
- Testified before Congress ten times on privacy and data security issues.
- Consulted with other federal agencies, including the Federal Communications Commission, the Department of Health and Human Services, and the Department of Commerce, on their privacy initiatives. The Commission has supported the Department of Commerce's initiative to convene stakeholders to develop privacy-related codes of conduct for different industry sectors.
- Released a survey of data collection disclosures by mobile applications directed to children.
- Proposed amendments to the Children's Online Privacy Protection Act Rule.

On the education front, since December 2010, the Commission:

- Continued outreach efforts through the FTC's consumer online safety portal, OnGuardOnline.gov, which provides information in a variety of formats – articles, games, quizzes, and videos – to help consumers secure their computers and protect their personal information. It attracts approximately 100,000 unique visitors per month.
- Published new consumer education materials on identity theft, Wi-Fi hot spots, cookies, and mobile devices.
- Sent warning letters to marketers of mobile apps that do background checks on individuals, educating them about the requirements of the Fair Credit Reporting Act.

To promote self-regulation, since December 2010, the Commission:

- Continued its call for improved privacy disclosures and choices, particularly in the area of online behavioral tracking. In response to this call, as well as to Congressional interest:
- A number of Internet browser vendors developed browser-based tools for consumers to request that websites not track their online activities.
- The World Wide Web Consortium, an Internet standard setting organization, is developing a universal web protocol for Do Not Track.
- The Digital Advertising Alliance ("DAA"), a coalition of media and marketing organizations, has developed a mechanism, accessed through an icon that consumers can click, to obtain information about and opt out of online behavioral advertising. Additionally, the DAA has committed to preventing the use of consumers' data for

secondary purposes like credit and employment and honoring the choices about tracking that consumers make through the settings on their browsers.

- Participated in the development of enforceable cross-border privacy rules for businesses to harmonize and enhance privacy protection of consumer data that moves between member countries of the forum on Asia Pacific Economic Cooperation.

The Final Report

Based upon its analysis of the comments filed on the proposed privacy framework, as well as commercial and technological developments, the Commission is issuing this final Report. The final framework is intended to articulate best practices for companies that collect and use consumer data. These best practices can be useful to companies as they develop and maintain processes and systems to operationalize privacy and data security practices within their businesses.

The final privacy framework contained in this Report is also intended to assist Congress as it considers privacy legislation. To the extent the framework goes beyond existing legal requirements, the framework is not intended to serve as a template for law enforcement actions or regulations under laws currently enforced by the FTC.

While retaining the proposed framework's fundamental best practices of privacy by design, simplified choice, and greater transparency, the Commission makes revised recommendations in three key areas in response to the comments.

First, the Commission makes changes to the framework's scope. The preliminary report proposed that the privacy framework apply to all commercial entities that collect or use consumer data that can be reasonably linked to a specific consumer, computer, or other device.

To address concerns about undue burdens on small businesses, the final framework does not apply to companies that collect only non-sensitive data from fewer than 5,000 consumers a year, provided they do not share the data with third parties.

Commenters also expressed concern that, with improvements in technology and the ubiquity of public information, more and more data could be "reasonably linked" to a consumer, computer or device, and that the proposed framework provided less incentive for a business to try to de-identify the data it maintains. To address this issue, the Report clarifies that data is not "reasonably linkable" to the extent that a company: (1) takes reasonable measures to ensure that the data is de-identified; (2) publicly commits not to try to reidentify the data; and (3) contractually prohibits downstream recipients from trying to re-identify the data.

Second, the Commission revises its approach to how companies should provide consumers with privacy choices. To simplify choice for both consumers and businesses, the proposed framework set forth a list of five categories of "commonly accepted" information collection and use practices for which companies need not provide consumers with choice (product fulfillment, internal operations, fraud prevention, legal compliance and public purpose, and first-party marketing). Several business commenters expressed concern that setting these "commonly accepted practices" in stone would stifle innovation.

Other commenters expressed the concern that the "commonly accepted practices" delineated in the proposed framework were too broad and would allow a variety of practices to take place without consumer consent. In response to these concerns, the Commission sets forth a modified approach that focuses on the context of the consumer's interaction with the business. Under this approach, companies do not need to provide choice before collecting and using consumers' data for practices that are consistent with the context of the transaction, consistent with the company's relationship with the consumer, or as required or specifically authorized by law.

Although many of the five "commonly accepted practices" identified in the preliminary report would generally meet this standard, there may be exceptions. The Report provides examples of how this new "context of the interaction" standard would apply in various circumstances.

Third, the Commission recommends that Congress consider enacting targeted legislation to provide greater transparency for, and control over, the practices of information brokers. The proposed framework recommended that companies provide consumers with reasonable access to the data the companies maintain about them, proportionate to the sensitivity of the data and the nature of its use. Several commenters discussed in particular the importance of consumers' ability to access information that information brokers have about them.

These commenters noted the lack of transparency about the practices of information brokers, who often buy, compile, and sell a wealth of highly personal information about consumers but never interact directly with them. Consumers are often unaware of the existence of these entities, as well as the purposes for which they collect and use data.

The Commission agrees that consumers should have more control over the practices of information brokers and believes that appropriate legislation could help address this goal. Any such legislation could be modeled on a bill that the House passed on a bipartisan basis during the 111th Congress, which included a procedure for consumers to access and dispute personal data held by information brokers.

Implementation of the Privacy Framework

While Congress considers privacy legislation, the Commission urges industry to accelerate the pace of its self-regulatory measures to implement the Commission's final privacy framework. Although some companies have excellent privacy and data security practices, industry as a whole must do better. Over the course of the next year, Commission staff will promote the framework's implementation by focusing its policymaking efforts on five main action items, which are highlighted here and discussed further throughout the report.

- **Do Not Track:** As discussed above, industry has made significant progress in implementing Do Not Track. The browser vendors have developed tools that consumers can use to signal that they do not want to be tracked; the Digital Advertising Alliance ("DAA") has developed its own icon-based tool and has committed to honor the browser tools; and the World Wide Web Consortium ("W3C") has made substantial progress in creating an international standard for Do Not Track. However, the work is not done. The Commission will work with these groups to complete implementation of an easy-to use, persistent, and effective Do Not Track system.

- **Mobile:** The Commission calls on companies providing mobile services to work toward improved privacy protections, including the development of short, meaningful disclosures. To this end, FTC staff has initiated a project to update its business guidance about online advertising disclosures. As part of this project, staff will host a workshop on May 30, 2012 and will address, among other issues, mobile privacy disclosures and how these disclosures can be short, effective, and accessible to consumers on small screens. The Commission hopes that the workshop will spur further industry self-regulation in this area.
- **Data Brokers:** To address the invisibility of, and consumers' lack of control over, data brokers' collection and use of consumer information, the Commission supports targeted legislation – similar to that contained in several of the data security bills introduced in the 112th Congress – that would provide consumers with access to information about them held by a data broker. To further increase transparency, the Commission calls on data brokers that compile data for marketing purposes to explore creating a centralized website where data brokers could (1) identify themselves to consumers and describe how they collect and use consumer data and (2) detail the access rights and other choices they provide with respect to the consumer data they maintain.
- **Large Platform Providers:** To the extent that large platforms, such as Internet Service Providers, operating systems, browsers, and social media seek, to comprehensively track consumers' online activities, it raises heightened privacy concerns. To further explore privacy and other issues related to this type of comprehensive tracking, FTC staff intends to host a public workshop in the second half of 2012.
- **Promoting Enforceable Self-Regulatory Codes:** The Department of Commerce, with the support of key industry stakeholders, is undertaking a project to facilitate the development of sector-specific codes of conduct. FTC staff will participate in that project. To the extent that strong privacy codes are developed, the Commission will view adherence to such codes favorably in connection with its law enforcement work. The Commission will also continue to enforce the FTC Act to take action against companies that engage in unfair or deceptive practices, including the failure to abide by self-regulatory programs they join.

FINAL FTC PRIVACY FRAMEWORK AND IMPLEMENTATION RECOMMENDATIONS

The final privacy framework is intended to articulate best practices for companies that collect and use consumer data. These best practices can be useful to companies as they develop and maintain processes and systems to operationalize privacy and data security practices within their businesses. The final privacy framework contained in this report is also intended to assist Congress as it considers privacy legislation. To the extent the framework goes beyond existing legal requirements, the framework is not intended to serve as a template for law enforcement actions or regulations under laws currently enforced by the FTC.

Scope

Final Scope: The framework applies to all commercial entities that collect or use consumer data that can be reasonably linked to a specific consumer, computer, or other device, unless the entity collects only non-sensitive data from fewer than 5,000 consumers per year and does not share the data with third parties.

Privacy by Design

Baseline Principle: Companies should promote consumer privacy throughout their organizations and at every stage of the development of their products and services.

A. The Substantive Principles

Final Principle: Companies should incorporate substantive privacy protections into their practices, such as data security, reasonable collection limits, sound retention and disposal practices, and data accuracy.

B. Procedural Protections to Implement the Substantive Principles

Final Principle: Companies should maintain comprehensive data management procedures throughout the life cycle of their products and services.

Simplified Consumer Choice

Baseline Principle: Companies should simplify consumer choice.

A. Practices That Do Not Require Choice

Final Principle: Companies do not need to provide choice before collecting and using consumer data for practices that are consistent with the context of the transaction or the company's relationship with the consumer, or are required or specifically authorized by law.

To balance the desire for flexibility with the need to limit the types of practices for which choice is not required, the Commission has refined the final framework so that companies engaged in practices consistent with the context of their interaction with consumers need not provide choices for those practices.

B. Companies Should Provide Consumer Choice for Other Practices

Final Principle: For practices requiring choice, companies should offer the choice at a time and in a context in which the consumer is making a decision about his or her data. Companies should obtain affirmative express consent before (1) using consumer data in a materially different manner than claimed when the data was collected; or (2) collecting sensitive data for certain purposes.

The Commission commends industry's efforts to improve consumer control over online behavioral tracking by developing a Do Not Track mechanism, and encourages continued improvements and full implementation of those mechanisms.

Transparency

Baseline Principle: Companies should increase the transparency of their data practices.

A. Privacy Notices

Final Principle: Privacy notices should be clearer, shorter, and more standardized to enable better comprehension and comparison of privacy practices.

B. Access

Final Principle: Companies should provide reasonable access to the consumer data they maintain; the extent of access should be proportionate to the sensitivity of the data and the nature of its use.

The Commission has amplified its support for this principle by including specific recommendations governing the practices of information brokers.

C. Consumer Education

Final Principle: All stakeholders should expand their efforts to educate consumers about commercial data privacy practices.

Legislative Recommendations

The Commission now also calls on Congress to consider enacting baseline privacy legislation and reiterates its call for data security and data broker legislation. The Commission is prepared to work with Congress and other stakeholders to craft such legislation. At the same time, the Commission urges industry to accelerate the pace of self-regulation.

FTC Will Assist with Implementation in Five Key Areas

As discussed throughout the Commission's final Report, there are a number of specific areas where policy makers have a role in assisting with the implementation of the self-regulatory principles that make up the final privacy framework. Areas where the FTC will be active over the course of the next year include the following:

1. Do Not Track

Industry has made significant progress in implementing Do Not Track. The browser vendors have developed tools that consumers can use to signal that they do not want to be tracked; the DAA has developed its own icon-based tool and has committed to honor the browser tools; and the W3C has made substantial progress in creating an international standard for Do Not Track. However, the work is not done. The Commission will work with these groups to complete implementation of an easy-to use, persistent, and effective Do Not Track system.

2. Mobile

The Commission calls on companies providing mobile services to work toward improved privacy protections, including the development of short, meaningful disclosures. To this end, FTC staff has initiated a project to update its business guidance about online advertising disclosures. As part of this project, staff will host a workshop on May 30, 2012 and will address, among other issues, mobile privacy disclosures and how these disclosures can be short, effective, and accessible to consumers on small screens. The Commission hopes that the workshop will spur further industry self-regulation in this area.

3. Data Brokers

To address the invisibility of, and consumers' lack of control over, data brokers' collection and use of consumer information, the Commission supports targeted legislation – similar to that contained in several of the data security bills introduced in the 112th Congress – that would provide consumers with access to information about them held by a data broker. To further increase transparency, the Commission calls on data brokers that compile data for marketing purposes to explore creating a centralized website where data brokers could (1) identify themselves to consumers and describe how they collect and use consumer data and (2) detail the access rights and other choices they provide with respect to the consumer data they maintain.

4. Large Platform Providers

To the extent that large platforms, such as Internet Service Providers, operating systems, browsers, and social media, seek to comprehensively track consumers' online activities, it raises heightened privacy concerns. To further explore privacy and other issues related to this type of comprehensive tracking, FTC staff intends to host a public workshop in the second half of 2012.

5. Promoting Enforceable Self-Regulatory Codes

The Department of Commerce, with the support of key industry stakeholders, is undertaking a project to facilitate the development of sector-specific codes of conduct. FTC staff will participate in that project. To the extent that strong privacy codes are developed, the Commission will view adherence to such codes favorably in connection with its law enforcement work. The Commission will also continue to enforce the FTC Act to take action against companies that engage in unfair or deceptive practices, including the failure to abide by self-regulatory programs they join. In all other areas, the Commission calls on individual companies, trade associations, and self-regulatory bodies to adopt the principles contained in the final privacy framework, to the extent they have not already done so. For its part, the FTC will focus its policy efforts on the five areas identified above, vigorously enforce existing laws, work with industry on self-regulation, and continue to target its education efforts on building awareness of existing data collection and use practices and the tools to control them.

I. INTRODUCTION

In December 2010, the Federal Trade Commission ("FTC" or "Commission") issued a preliminary staff report to address the privacy issues associated with new technologies and business models.[1] The report outlined the FTC's 40-year history of promoting consumer privacy through policy and enforcement work, discussed the themes and areas of consensus that emerged from the Commission's "Exploring Privacy" roundtables, and set forth a proposed framework to guide policymakers and other stakeholders regarding best practices for consumer privacy. The proposed framework called on companies to build privacy protections into their business operations (*i.e.*, adopt "privacy by design"[2]), offer simplified choice mechanisms that give consumers more meaningful control, and increase the transparency of their data practices.

The preliminary report included a number of questions for public comment to assist and guide the Commission in developing a final privacy framework. The Commission received more than 450 comments from a wide variety of interested parties, including consumer and privacy advocates, individual companies and trade associations, academics, technologists, and domestic and foreign government agencies. Significantly, more than half of the comments came from individual consumers. The comments have helped the Commission refine the framework to better protect consumer privacy in today's dynamic and rapidly changing marketplace.

In this Final Report, the Commission adopts staff's preliminary framework with certain clarifications and revisions. The final privacy framework is intended to articulate best practices for companies that collect and use consumer data. These best practices can be useful to companies as they develop and maintain processes and systems to operationalize privacy and data security practices within their businesses. The final privacy framework contained in this Report is also intended to assist Congress as it considers privacy legislation. To the extent the framework goes beyond existing legal requirements, the framework is not intended to serve as a template for law enforcement actions or regulations under laws currently enforced by the FTC.

The Report highlights the developments since the FTC issued staff's preliminary report, including the Department of Commerce's parallel privacy initiative, proposed legislation, and actions by industry and other stakeholders. Next, it analyzes and responds to the main issues raised by the public comments. Based on those comments, as well as marketplace developments, the Report sets forth a revised privacy framework and legislative recommendations. Finally, the Report outlines a series of policy initiatives that FTC staff will undertake in the next year to assist industry with implementing the final framework as best practices.

II. Background

A. FTC Roundtables and Preliminary Staff Report

Between December 2009 and March 2010, the FTC convened its "Exploring Privacy" roundtables.[3] The roundtables brought together stakeholders representing diverse interests to evaluate whether the FTC's existing approach to protecting consumer privacy was adequate in light of 21st Century technologies and business models. From these discussions, as well as submitted materials, a number of themes emerged. First, the collection and commercial use of consumer data in today's society is ubiquitous and often invisible to consumers. Second, consumers generally lack full understanding of the nature and extent of this data collection and use and, therefore, are unable to make informed choices about it. Third, despite this lack of understanding, many consumers are concerned about the privacy of their personal information. Fourth, the collection and use of consumer data has led to significant benefits in the form of new products and services. Finally, the traditional distinction between personally identifiable information and "anonymous" data has blurred.

Participants also pointed to shortcomings in existing frameworks that have attempted to address privacy concerns. The "notice-and-choice model," which encouraged companies to develop privacy policies describing their information collection and use practices, led to long, incomprehensible privacy policies that consumers typically do not read, let alone understand.[4] The "harm-based model," which focused on protecting consumers from specific harms – physical security, economic injury, and unwarranted intrusions into their daily lives – had been criticized for failing to recognize a wider range of privacy-related concerns, including reputational harm or the fear of being monitored.[5] Participants noted that both of these privacy frameworks have struggled to keep pace with the rapid growth of technologies and business models that enable companies to collect and use consumers' information in ways that often are invisible to consumers.[6]

Building on the record developed at the roundtables and on its own enforcement and policymaking expertise, FTC staff proposed for public comment a framework for approaching privacy. The proposed framework included three major components. It called on companies to treat privacy as their "default setting" by implementing "privacy by design" throughout their regular business operations. The concept of privacy by design includes limitations on data collection and retention, as well as reasonable security and data accuracy. By considering and addressing privacy at every stage of product and service development, companies can shift the burden away from consumers who would otherwise have to seek out privacy-protective practices and technologies. The proposed framework also called on companies to simplify consumer choice by presenting important choices – in a streamlined way – to consumers at the time they are making decisions about their data. As part of the call for simplified choice, staff asked industry to develop a mechanism that would allow consumers to more easily control the tracking of their online activities, often referred to as "Do Not Track." Finally, the framework focused on improving consumer understanding of commercial data practices ("transparency") and called on companies – both those that interact directly with consumers and those that lack a consumer interface – to improve the transparency of their practices. As discussed below, the Commission received a large number of thoughtful and informative comments regarding each of the framework's elements. These comments have allowed the Commission to refine the framework and to provide further guidance regarding its implementation.

B. Department of Commerce Privacy Initiatives

In a related effort to examine privacy, in May 2010, the Department of Commerce ("DOC" or "Commerce") convened a public workshop to discuss how to balance innovation, commerce, and consumer privacy in the online context.[7] Based on the input received from the workshop, as well as related research, on December 16, 2010, the DOC published for comment a strategy paper outlining privacy recommendations and proposed initiatives.[8]

Following the public comment period, on February 23, 2012, the Administration issued its final "White Paper" on consumer privacy. The White Paper recommends that Congress enact legislation to implement a Consumer Privacy Bill of Rights based on the Fair Information Practice Principles ("FIPPs").[9] In addition, the White Paper calls for a multistakeholder process to determine how to apply the Consumer Privacy Bill of Rights in different business contexts. Commerce issued a Notice of Inquiry on March 5, 2012, asking for public input on both the process for convening stakeholders on this project, as well as the proposed subject areas to be discussed.[10]

Staff from the FTC and Commerce worked closely to ensure that the agencies' privacy initiatives are complementary. Personnel from each agency actively participated in both the DOC and FTC initiatives, and have also communicated regularly on how best to develop a meaningful, effective, and consistent approach to privacy protection. Going forward, the agencies will continue to work collaboratively to guide implementation of these complementary privacy initiatives.

C. Legislative Proposals and Efforts by Stakeholders

Since Commission staff released its preliminary report in December 2010, there have been a number of significant legislative proposals, as well as steps by industry and other stakeholders, to promote consumer privacy.

1. Do Not Track

The preliminary staff report called on industry to create and implement a mechanism to allow consumers to control the collection and use of their online browsing data, often referred to as "Do Not Track." Bills introduced in the House and the Senate specifically address the creation of Do Not Track mechanisms, and, if enacted, would mandate that the Commission promulgate regulations to establish standards for a Do Not Track regime.[11]

In addition to the legislative proposals calling for the creation of Do Not Track, staff's preliminary report recommendation triggered significant progress by various industry sectors to develop tools to allow consumers to control online tracking. A number of browser vendors – including Mozilla, Microsoft, and Apple – announced that the latest versions of their browsers permit consumers to instruct websites not to track their activities across websites.[12] Mozilla has also introduced a mobile browser for Android devices that enables Do Not Track.[13] The online advertising industry has also established an important program. The Digital Advertising Alliance ("DAA"), an industry coalition of media and marketing associations, has developed an initiative that includes an icon embedded in behaviorally targeted online ads.[14] When consumers click on the icon, they can see information about how the ad was targeted and delivered to them and they are given the opportunity to opt out of such targeted advertising. The program's recent growth and implementation has been significant. In addition, the DAA has committed to preventing the use of consumers' data for secondary purposes like credit and employment decisions. The DAA has also agreed to honor the choices about tracking that consumers make through settings on their web browsers. This will provide consumers two ways to opt out: through the DAA's icon in advertisements or through their browser settings. These steps demonstrate the online advertising industry's support for privacy and consumer choice.

Finally, the World Wide Web Consortium ("W3C")[15] convened a working group to create a universal standard for Do Not Track. The working group includes DAA member companies, other U.S. and international companies, industry groups, and consumer groups. The W3C group has made substantial progress toward a standard that is workable in the desktop and mobile settings, and has published two working drafts of its standard documents. The group's goal is to complete a consensus standard in the coming months.

2. Other Privacy Initiatives

Beyond the Do Not Track developments, broader initiatives to improve consumer privacy are underway in Congress, Federal agencies, and the private sector. For example, Congress is considering several general privacy bills that would establish a regulatory framework for protecting consumer privacy by improving transparency about the commercial uses of personal information and providing consumers with choice about such use.[16] The bills would also provide the Commission rulemaking authority concerning, among other things, notice, consent, and the transfer of information to third parties.

In the House of Representatives, Members have introduced bipartisan legislation to amend the Children's Online Privacy Protection Act[17] ("COPPA") and establish other protections for children and teens.[18] The bill would prohibit the collection and use of minors' information for targeted marketing and would require websites to permit the deletion of publicly available information of minors. Members of Congress also introduced a number of other bills addressing data security and data breach notification in 2011.[19]

Federal agencies have taken significant steps to improve consumer privacy as well. For its part, since issuing the preliminary staff report, the FTC has resolved seven data security cases,[20] obtained orders against Google, Facebook, and online ad networks,[21] and challenged practices that violate sector-specific privacy laws like the Fair Credit Reporting Act ("FCRA") and COPPA.[22]

The Commission has also proposed amendments to the COPPA Rule to address changes in technology. The comment period on the Proposed Rulemaking ran through December 23, 2011, and the Commission is currently reviewing the comments received.[23] Additionally, the Commission has hosted public workshops on discrete privacy issues such as child identity theft and the use of facial recognition technology.

Other federal agencies have also begun examining privacy issues. In 2011, the Federal Communications Commission ("FCC") hosted a public forum to address privacy concerns associated with location-based services.[24] The Department of Health and Human Services ("HHS") hosted a forum on medical identity theft, developed a model privacy notice for personal health records,[25] and is developing legislative recommendations on privacy and security for such personal health records. In addition, HHS recently launched an initiative to identify privacy and security best practices for using mobile devices in health care settings.[26]

The private sector has taken steps to enhance user privacy and security as well. For example, Google and Facebook have improved authentication mechanisms to give users stronger protection against compromised passwords.[27]

Also, privacy-enhancing technologies such as the HTTPS Everywhere browser add-on have given users additional tools to encrypt their information in transit.[28] On the mobile front, the Mobile Marketing Association released its Mobile Application Privacy Policy.[29]

This document provides guidance on privacy principles for application ("app") developers and discusses how to inform consumers about the collection and use of their data.

Despite these developments, as explained below, industry still has more work to do to promote consumer privacy.

III. MAIN THEMES FROM COMMENTERS

The more than 450 comments filed in response to the preliminary staff report addressed three overarching issues: how privacy harms should be articulated; the value of global interoperability of different privacy regimes; and the desirability of baseline privacy legislation to augment self-regulatory efforts. Those comments, and the Commission's analysis, are discussed below.

A. Articulation of Privacy Harms

There was broad consensus among commenters that consumers need basic privacy protections for their personal information. This is true particularly in light of the complexity of the current personal data ecosystem. Some commenters also stated that the Commission should recognize a broader set of privacy harms than those involving physical and economic injury.[30] For example, one commenter cited complaints from consumers who had been surreptitiously tracked and targeted with prescription drug offers and other health-related materials regarding sensitive medical conditions.[31]

At the same time, some commenters questioned whether the costs of broader privacy protections were justified by the anticipated benefits.[32] Relatedly, many commenters raised concerns about how wider privacy protections would affect innovation and the ability to offer consumers beneficial new products and services.[33]

The Commission agrees that the range of privacy-related harms is more expansive than economic or physical harm or unwarranted intrusions and that any privacy framework should recognize additional harms that might arise from unanticipated uses of data. These harms may include the unexpected revelation of previously private information, including both sensitive information (*e.g.*, health information, precise geolocation information) and less sensitive information (*e.g.*, purchase history, employment history) to unauthorized third parties.[34] As one example, in the Commission's case against Google, the complaint alleged that Google used the information of consumers who signed up for Gmail to populate a new social network, Google Buzz.[35] The creation of that social network in some cases revealed previously private information about Gmail users' most frequent email contacts. Similarly, the Commission's complaint against Facebook alleged that Facebook's sharing of users' personal information beyond their privacy settings was harmful.[36] Like these enforcement actions, a privacy framework should address practices that unexpectedly reveal previously private information even absent physical or financial harm, or unwarranted intrusions.[37]

In terms of weighing costs and benefits, although it recognizes that imposing new privacy protections will not be costless, the Commission believes doing so not only will help consumers but also will benefit businesses by building consumer trust in the marketplace. Businesses frequently acknowledge the importance of consumer trust to the growth of digital commerce[38] and surveys support this view. For example, in the online behavioral advertising area, a recent survey shows that consumers feel better about brands that give them transparency and control over advertisements.[39]

Companies offering consumers information about behavioral advertising and the tools to opt out of it have also found increased customer engagement. In its comment, Google noted that visitors to its Ads Preference Manager are far more likely to edit their interest settings and remain opted in rather than to opt out.[40] Similarly, another commenter conducted a study showing that making its customers aware of its privacy and data security principles – including restricting the sharing of customer data, increasing the transparency of data practices, and providing access to the consumer data it maintains – significantly increased customer trust in its company.[41]

In addition, some companies appear to be competing on privacy. For example, one company offers an Internet search service that it promotes as being far more privacy-sensitive than other search engines.[42] Similarly, in response to Google's decision to change its privacy policies to allow tracking of consumers across different Google products, Microsoft encouraged consumers to switch to Microsoft's more privacy-protective products and services.[43]

The privacy framework is designed to be flexible to permit and encourage innovation. Companies can implement the privacy protections of the framework in a way that is proportional to the nature, sensitivity, and amount of data collected as well as to the size of the business at issue. For example, the framework does not include rigid provisions such as specific disclosures or mandatory data retention and destruction periods. And, as discussed below, the framework streamlines communications for businesses and consumers alike by requiring consumer choice mechanisms only for data practices that are inconsistent with the context of a particular transaction or the business relationship with the consumer.[44]

B. Global Interoperability

Reflecting differing legal, policy, and constitutional regimes, privacy frameworks around the world vary considerably. Many commenters cited the value to both consumers and businesses of promoting more consistent and interoperable approaches to protecting consumer privacy internationally. These commenters stated that consistency between different privacy regimes reduces companies' costs, promotes international competitiveness, and increases compliance with privacy standards.[45]

The Commission agrees there is value in greater interoperability among data privacy regimes as consumer data is increasingly transferred around the world. Meaningful protection for such data requires convergence on core principles, an ability of legal regimes to work together, and enhanced cross-border enforcement cooperation. Such interoperability is better for consumers, whose data will be subject to more consistent protection wherever it travels, and more efficient for businesses by reducing the burdens of compliance with differing, and sometimes conflicting, rules. In short, as the Administration White Paper notes, global interoperability "will provide more consistent protections for consumers and lower compliance burdens for companies."[46]

Efforts underway around the world to re-examine current approaches to protecting consumer privacy indicate an interest in convergence on overarching principles and a desire to develop greater interoperability. For example, the Commission's privacy framework is consistent with the nine privacy principles set forth in the 2004 Asia-Pacific Economic Cooperation ("APEC") Privacy Framework. Those principles form the basis for ongoing APEC work to implement a cross-border privacy rules system to facilitate data transfers among the 21 APEC member economies, including the United States.[47] In 2011, the Organization for Economic Cooperation and Development ("OECD") issued a report re-examining its seminal 1980 Privacy Guidelines in light of technological changes over the past thirty years.[48] Further, the European Commission has recently proposed legislation updating its 1995 data protection directive and proposed an overhaul of the European Union approach that focuses on many of the issues raised elsewhere in this report as well as issues relating to international transfers and interoperability.[49] These efforts reflect a commitment to many of the high-level principles embodied in the FTC's framework – increased transparency and consumer control, the need for privacy protections to be built into basic business practices, and the importance of accountability and enforcement. They also reflect a shared international interest in having systems that work better with each other, and are thus better for consumers.

C. Legislation to Augment Self-Regulatory Efforts

Numerous comments, including those from large industry stakeholders, consumer and privacy advocates, and individual consumers supported some form of baseline privacy legislation that incorporates the FIPPs.[50] Business commenters noted that legislation would help provide legal certainty,[51] serve as a key mechanism for building trust among customers,[52] and provide a way to fill gaps in existing sector-based laws.[53] Consumer and privacy advocates cited the inability of self-regulation to provide comprehensive and long-lasting protection for consumers.[54] One such commenter cited the fact that many self-regulatory initiatives that arose in response to the Commission's 2000 recommendation for privacy legislation were short-lived and failed to provide long-term privacy protections for consumers.[55]

At the same time, a number of commenters raised concerns about government action beyond providing guidance for self-regulatory programs.[56] Some cautioned the FTC about taking an approach that might impede industry's ability to innovate and develop new products and services in a rapidly changing marketplace. Others noted that a regulatory approach could lead to picking "winners and losers" among particular technologies and business models and called for a technology-neutral approach.[57] Commenters also argued that it might be impractical to craft omnibus standards or rules that would apply broadly across different business sectors.[58]

The Commission agrees that, to date, self-regulation has not gone far enough. In most areas, with the notable exception of efforts surrounding Do Not Track, there has been little self-regulation. For example, the FTC's recent survey of mobile apps marketed to children revealed that many of these apps fail to provide any disclosure about the extent to which they collect and share consumers' personal data.[59] Similarly, efforts of the data broker industry to establish self-regulatory rules concerning consumer privacy have fallen short.[60] These examples illustrate that even in some well-established markets, basic privacy concepts like transparency about the nature of companies' data practices and meaningful consumer control are absent. This absence erodes consumer trust.

There is also widespread evidence of data breaches and vulnerabilities related to consumer information.[61] Published reports indicate that some breaches may have resulted from the unintentional release of consumer data, for which companies later apologized and took action to address.[62] Other incidents involved planned releases or uses of data by companies that ultimately did not occur due to consumer and public backlash.[63] Still other incidents involved companies' failure to take reasonable precautions and resulted in FTC consent decrees. These incidents further undermine consumer trust, which is essential for business growth and innovation.[64]

The ongoing and widespread incidents of unauthorized or improper use and sharing of personal information are evidence of two points. First, companies that do not intend to undermine consumer privacy simply lack sufficiently clear standards to operate and innovate while respecting the expectations of consumers. Second, companies that do seek to cut corners on consumer privacy do not have adequate legal incentives to curtail such behavior.

To provide clear standards and appropriate incentives to ensure basic privacy protections across all industry sectors, in addition to reiterating its call for federal data security legislation,[65] the Commission calls on Congress to consider enacting baseline privacy legislation that is technologically neutral and sufficiently flexible to allow companies to continue to innovate. The Commission is prepared to work with Congress and other stakeholders to craft such legislation.

In their comments, many businesses indicated that they already incorporate the FIPPS into their practices. For these companies, a legislative mandate should not impose an undue burden and indeed, will "level the playing field" by ensuring that all companies are required to incorporate these principles into their practices.

For those companies that are not already taking consumer privacy into account – either because of lack of understanding or lack of concern – legislation should provide clear rules of the road. It should also provide adequate deterrence through the availability of civil penalties and other remedies.[66] In short, legislation will provide businesses with the certainty they need to understand their obligations and the incentive to meet those obligations, while providing consumers with confidence that businesses will be required to respect their privacy. This approach will create an environment that allows businesses to continue to innovate and consumers to embrace those innovations without sacrificing their privacy.[67] The Commission is prepared to work with Congress and other stakeholders to formulate baseline privacy legislation.

While Congress considers such legislation, the Commission urges industry to accelerate the pace of its self-regulatory measures to implement the Commission's final privacy framework. Over the course of the next year, Commission staff will promote the framework's implementation by focusing its policymaking efforts on five main action items, which are highlighted here and discussed further throughout the report.

- **Do Not Track:** As discussed above, industry has made significant progress in implementing Do Not Track. The browser vendors have developed tools that consumers can use to signal that they do not want to be tracked; the DAA has developed its own icon-based tool and has committed to honor the browser tools; and the W3C has made substantial progress in creating an international standard for Do Not Track. However, the work is not done. The Commission will work with these groups to complete implementation of an easy-to use, persistent, and effective Do Not Track system.

- **Mobile:** The Commission calls on companies providing mobile services to work toward improved privacy protections, including the development of short, meaningful disclosures. To this end, FTC staff has initiated a project to update its business guidance about online advertising disclosures.[68] As part of this project, staff will host a workshop on May 30, 2012 and will address, among other issues, mobile privacy disclosures and how these disclosures can be short, effective, and accessible to consumers on small screens. The Commission hopes that the workshop will spur further industry self-regulation in this area.
- **Data Brokers:** To address the invisibility of, and consumers' lack of control over, data brokers' collection and use of consumer information, the Commission supports targeted legislation – similar to that contained in several of the data security bills introduced in the 112th Congress – that would provide consumers with access to information about them held by a data broker.[69] To further increase transparency, the Commission calls on data brokers that compile data for marketing purposes to explore creating a centralized website where data brokers could (1) identify themselves to consumers and describe how they collect and use consumer data and (2) detail the access rights and other choices they provide with respect to the consumer data they maintain.
- **Large Platform Providers:** To the extent that large platforms, such as Internet Service Providers ("ISPs"), operating systems, browsers, and social media, seek to comprehensively track consumers' online activities, it raises heightened privacy concerns. To further explore privacy and other issues related to this type of comprehensive tracking, FTC staff intends to host a public workshop in the second half of 2012.
- **Promoting enforceable self-regulatory codes:** The Department of Commerce, with the support of key industry stakeholders, is undertaking a project to facilitate the development of sector-specific codes of conduct. FTC staff will participate in that project. To the extent that strong privacy codes are developed, the Commission will view adherence to such codes favorably in connection with its law enforcement work. The Commission will also continue to enforce the FTC Act to take action against companies that engage in unfair or deceptive practices, including the failure to abide by self-regulatory programs they join.

IV. PRIVACY FRAMEWORK

In addition to the general comments described above, the Commission received significant comments on the scope of the proposed framework and each individual element. Those comments, as well as several clarifications and refinements based on the Commission's analysis of the issues raised, are discussed below.

A. Scope

> **Proposed Scope:** The framework applies to all commercial entities that collect or use consumer data that can be reasonably linked to a specific consumer, computer, or other device.

A variety of commenters addressed the framework's proposed scope. Some of these commenters supported an expansive reach while others proposed limiting the framework's application to particular types of entities and carving out certain categories of businesses. Commenters also called for further clarification regarding the type of data the framework covers and staff's proposed "reasonably linked" standard.

1. Companies Should Comply with the Framework Unless They Handle Only Limited Amounts of Non-Sensitive Data That Is Not Shared with Third Parties

Numerous commenters addressed whether the framework should apply to entities that collect, maintain, or use limited amounts of data. Several companies argued that the burden the framework could impose on small businesses outweighed the reduced risk of harm from the collection and use of limited amounts of non-sensitive consumer data.[70] These commenters proposed that the framework not apply to entities that collect or use non-sensitive data from fewer than 5,000 individuals a year where the data is used for limited purposes, such as internal operations and first-party marketing.[71] As additional support for this position, these commenters noted that proposed privacy legislation introduced in the 111th Congress contained an exclusion to this effect.[72]

Although one consumer and privacy organization supported a similar exclusion,[73] others expressed concern about exempting, *per se*, any types of businesses or quantities of data from the framework's scope.[74] These commenters pointed to the possibility that excluded companies would sell the data to third parties, such as advertising networks or data brokers.

The Commission agrees that the first-party collection and use of non-sensitive data (*e.g.*, data that is not a Social Security number or financial, health, children's, or geolocation information) creates fewer privacy concerns than practices that involve sensitive data or sharing with third parties.[75] Accordingly, entities that collect limited amounts of non-sensitive consumer data from under 5,000 consumers need not comply with the framework, as long as they do not share the data with third parties. For example, consider a cash-only curb-side food truck business that offers to send messages announcing when it is in a given neighborhood to consumers who provide their email addresses. As long as the food truck business does not share these email addresses with third parties, the Commission believes that it need not provide privacy disclosures to its customers. This narrow exclusion acknowledges the need for flexibility for businesses that collect limited amounts of non-sensitive information. It also recognizes that some business practices create fewer potential risks to consumer information.

2. The Framework Sets Forth Best Practices and Can Work in Tandem with Existing Privacy and Security Statutes

The proposed framework's applicability to commercial sectors that are covered by existing laws generated comments primarily from representatives of the healthcare and financial services industries. These commenters noted that statutes such as the Health

Insurance Portability and Accountability Act ("HIPAA"), the Health Information Technology for Economic and Clinical Health Act ("HITECH"), and the GrammLeach-Bliley Act ("GLBA") already impose privacy protections and security requirements through legal obligations on companies in these industries.[76] Accordingly, these commenters urged the Commission to avoid creating duplicative or inconsistent standards and to clarify that the proposed framework is intended to cover only those entities that are not currently covered by existing privacy and security laws. Another commenter, however, urged government to focus on fulfilling consumer privacy expectations across all sectors, noting that market evolution is blurring distinctions about who is covered by HIPAA and that consumers expect organizations to protect their personal health information, regardless of any sector-specific boundaries.[77]

The Commission recognizes the concern regarding potentially inconsistent privacy obligations and notes that, to the extent Congress enacts any of the Commission's recommendations through legislation, such legislation should not impose overlapping or duplicative requirements on conduct that is already regulated.[78] However, the framework is meant to encourage best practices and is not intended to conflict with requirements of existing laws and regulations. To the extent that components of the framework exceed, but do not conflict with existing statutory requirements, entities covered by those statutes should view the framework as best practices to promote consumer privacy. For example, it may be appropriate for financial institutions covered by GLBA to incorporate elements of privacy by design, such as collection limitations, or to improve transparency by providing reasonable access to consumer data in a manner that does not conflict with their statutory obligations. In any event, the framework provides an important baseline for entities that are not subject to sector-specific laws like HIPAA or GLBA.[79]

3. The Framework Applies to Offline as Well as Online Data

In addressing the framework's applicability to "all commercial entities," numerous commenters discussed whether the framework should apply to both online and offline data. Diverse commenters expressed strong support for a comprehensive approach applicable to both online and offline data practices.[80] Commenters noted that as a practical matter, many companies collect both online and offline data.[81]

Commenters also listed different offline contexts in which entities collect consumer data. These include instances where a consumer interacts directly with a business, such as through the use of a retail loyalty card, or where a non-consumer facing entity, such as a data broker, obtains consumer data from an offline third-party source.[82] One commenter noted that, regardless of whether an entity collects or uses data from an online or an offline source, consumer privacy interests are equally affected.[83] To emphasize the importance of offline data protections, this commenter noted that while the behavioral advertising industry has started to implement self-regulatory measures to improve consumers' ability to control the collection and the use of their online data, in the offline context such efforts by data brokers and others have largely failed.[84]

By contrast, a financial industry organization argued that the FTC should take a more narrow approach by limiting the scope of the proposed framework in a number of respects, including its applicability to offline data collection and use.[85] This commenter stated that some harms in the online context may not exist offline and raised concern about the framework's unintended consequences. For example, the commenter cited the significant costs that a requirement to provide consumers with access to data collected about them would impose on companies that collect and maintain data in paper rather than electronic form. Another commenter cited the costs of providing privacy disclosures and choices in an offline environment.[86]

The Commission notes that consumers face a landscape of virtually ubiquitous collection of their data. Whether such collection occurs online or offline does not alter the consumer's privacy interest in his or her data. For example, the sale of a consumer profile containing the consumer's purchase history from a brickand-mortar pharmacy or a bookstore would not implicate fewer privacy concerns simply because the profile contains purchases from an offline retailer rather than from an online merchant. Accordingly, the framework applies in all commercial contexts, both online and offline.

4. The Framework Applies to Data That Is Reasonably Linkable to a Specific Consumer, Computer, or Device

The scope issue that generated the most comments, from a wide range of interested parties, was the proposed framework's applicability to "consumer data that can be reasonably linked to a specific consumer, computer, or other device."

A number of commenters supported the proposed framework's application to data that, while not traditionally considered personally identifiable, is linkable to a consumer or device. In particular, several consumer and privacy groups elaborated on the privacy concerns associated with supposedly anonymous data and discussed the decreasing relevance of the personally identifiable information ("PII") label.[87] These commenters pointed to studies demonstrating consumers' objections to being tracked, regardless of whether the tracker explicitly learns a consumer name, and the potential for harm, such as discriminatory pricing based on online browsing history, even without the use of PII.[88]

Similarly, the commenters noted, the ability to re-identify "anonymous" data supports the proposed framework's application to data that can be reasonably linked to a consumer or device. They pointed to incidents, identified in the preliminary staff report, in which individuals were re-identified from publicly released data sets that did not contain PII.[89] One commenter pointed out that certain industries extensively mine data for marketing purposes and that re-identification is a commercial enterprise.[90] This adds to the likelihood of data re-identification.

Some industry commenters also recognized consumers' privacy interest in data that goes beyond what is strictly labeled PII.[91] Drawing on the FTC's roundtables as well as the preliminary staff report, one such commenter noted the legitimate interest consumers have in controlling how companies collect and use aggregated or de-identified data, browser fingerprints,[92] and other types of non-PII.[93] Another company questioned the notion of distinguishing between PII and non-PII as a way to determine what data to protect.[94] Supporting a scaled approach rather than a bright line distinction, this commenter noted that all data derived from individuals deserves some level of protection.[95]

Other commenters representing industry opposed the proposed framework's application to non-PII that can be reasonably linked to a consumer, computer, or device.[96] These commenters asserted that the risks associated with the collection and use of data that does not contain PII are simply not the same as the risks associated with PII. They also claimed a lack of evidence demonstrating that consumers have the same privacy interest in non-PII as they do with the collection and use of PII. Instead of applying the framework to non-PII, these commenters recommended the Commission support efforts to de-identify data.

Overall, the comments reflect a general acknowledgment that the traditional distinction between PII and non-PII has blurred and that it is appropriate to more comprehensively examine data to determine the data's privacy implications.[97] However, some commenters, including some of those cited above, argued that the proposed framework's "linkability" standard is potentially too open-ended to be practical.[98] One industry organization asserted, for instance, that if given enough time and resources, any data may be linkable to an individual.[99] In addition, commenters stated that requiring the same level of protection for all data would undermine companies' incentive to avoid collecting data that is more easily identified or to take steps to de-identify the data they collect and use.[100] Other commenters argued that applying the framework to data that is potentially linkable could conflict with the framework's privacy by design concept, as companies could be forced to collect more information about consumers than they otherwise would in order to be able to provide those consumers with effective notice, choice, or access.[101] To address these concerns, some commenters proposed limiting the framework to data that is actually linked to a specific consumer, computer, or device.[102]

One commenter recommended that the Commission clarify that the reasonably linkable standard means non-public data that can be linked with *reasonable effort*.[103] This commenter also stated that the framework should exclude data that, through contract or by virtue of internal controls, will not be linked with a particular consumer. Taking a similar approach, another commenter suggested that the framework should apply to data that is reasonably likely to relate to an identifiable consumer.[104] This commenter also noted that a company could commit through its privacy policy that it would only maintain or use data in a de-identified form and that such a commitment would be enforceable under Section 5 of the FTC Act.[105]

The Commission believes there is sufficient support from commenters representing an array of perspectives – including consumer and privacy advocates as well as of industry representatives – for the framework's application to data that, while not yet linked to a particular consumer, computer, or device, may reasonably become so. There is significant evidence demonstrating that technological advances and the ability to combine disparate pieces of data can lead to identification of a consumer, computer, or device even if the individual pieces of data do not constitute PII.[106] Moreover, not only is it possible to re-identify nonPII data through various means,[107] businesses have strong incentives to actually do so.

In response to the comments, to provide greater certainty for companies that collect and use consumer data, the Commission provides additional clarification on the application of the reasonable linkability standard to describe how companies can take appropriate steps to minimize such linkability. Under the final framework, a company's data would not be reasonably linkable to a particular consumer or device to the extent that the company implements three significant protections for that data.

First, the company must take reasonable measures to ensure that the data is de-identified. This means that the company must achieve a reasonable level of justified confidence that the data cannot reasonably be used to infer information about, or otherwise be linked to, a particular consumer, computer, or other device. Consistent with the Commission's approach in its data security cases,[108] what qualifies as a reasonable level of justified confidence depends upon the particular circumstances, including the available methods and technologies. In addition, the nature of the data at issue and the purposes for which it will be used are also relevant. Thus, for example, whether a company publishes data externally affects whether the steps it has taken to de-identify data are considered reasonable. The standard is not an absolute one; rather, companies must take reasonable steps to ensure that data is de-identified.

Depending on the circumstances, a variety of technical approaches to de-identification may be reasonable, such as deletion or modification of data fields, the addition of sufficient "noise" to data, statistical sampling, or the use of aggregate or synthetic data.[109] The Commission encourages companies and researchers to continue innovating in the development and evaluation of new and better approaches to de-identification. FTC staff will continue to monitor and assess the state of the art in de-identification.

Second, a company must publicly commit to maintain and use the data in a de-identified fashion, and not to attempt to re-identify the data. Thus, if a company does take steps to re-identify such data, its conduct could be actionable under Section 5 of the FTC Act.

Third, if a company makes such de-identified data available to other companies – whether service providers or other third parties – it should contractually prohibit such entities from attempting to re-identify the data. The company that transfers or otherwise makes the data available should exercise reasonable oversight to monitor compliance with these contractual provisions and take appropriate steps to address contractual violations.[110]

FTC staff's letter closing its investigation of Netflix, arising from the company's plan to release purportedly anonymous consumer data to improve its movie recommendation algorithm, provides a good illustration of these concepts. In response to the privacy concerns that FTC staff and others raised, Netflix revised its initial plan to publicly release the data. The company agreed to narrow any such release of data to certain researchers. The letter details Netflix's commitment to implement a number of "operational safeguards to prevent the data from being used to re-identify consumers."[111] If it chose to share such data with third parties, Netflix stated that it would limit access "only to researchers who contractually agree to specific limitations on its use."[112]

Accordingly, as long as (1) a given data set is not reasonably identifiable, (2) the company publicly commits not to re-identify it, and (3) the company requires any downstream users of the data to keep it in de-identified form, that data will fall outside the scope of the framework.[113]

This clarification of the framework's reasonable linkability standard is designed to help address the concern that the standard is overly broad. Further, the clarification gives companies an incentive to collect and use data in a form that makes it less likely the data will be linked to a particular consumer or device, thereby promoting privacy. Additionally, by calling for companies to publicly commit to the steps they take, the framework promotes accountability.[114] Consistent with the discussion above, the Commission restates the framework's scope as follows.

Final Scope: The framework applies to all commercial entities that collect or use consumer data that can be reasonably linked to a specific consumer, computer, or other device, unless the entity collects only non-sensitive data from fewer than 5,000 consumers per year and does not share the data with third parties.

B. Privacy by Design

Baseline Principle: Companies should promote consumer privacy throughout their organizations and at every stage of the development of their products and services.

The preliminary staff report called on companies to promote consumer privacy throughout their organizations and at every stage of the development of their products and services. Although many companies already incorporate substantive and procedural privacy protections into their business practices, industry should implement privacy by design more systematically. A number of commenters, including those representing industry, supported staff's call that companies "build in" privacy, with several of these commenters citing to the broad international recognition and adoption of privacy by design.[115] The Commission is encouraged to see broad support for this concept, particularly in light of the increasingly global nature of data transfers.

In calling for privacy by design, staff advocated for the implementation of substantive privacy protections – such as data security, limitations on data collection and retention, and data accuracy – as well as procedural safeguards aimed at integrating the substantive principles into a company's everyday business operations. By shifting burdens away from consumers and placing obligations on businesses to treat consumer data in a responsible manner, these principles should afford consumers basic privacy protections without forcing them to read long, incomprehensible privacy notices to learn and make choices about a company's privacy practices. Although the Commission has not changed the proposed "privacy by design" principles, it responds to a number of comments, as discussed below.

1. The Substantive Principles: Data Security, Reasonable Collection Limits, Sound Retention Practices, and Data Accuracy

Proposed Principle: Companies should incorporate substantive privacy protections into their practices, such as data security, reasonable collection limits, sound retention practices, and data accuracy.

a. Should Additional Substantive Principles Be Identified?

Responding to a question about whether the final framework should identify additional substantive protections, several commenters suggested incorporating the additional principles articulated in the 1980 OECD Privacy Guidelines.[116] One commenter also proposed adding the "right to be forgotten," which would allow consumers to withdraw data posted online about themselves at any point.[117] This concept has gained importance as people post more information about themselves online without fully appreciating the implications of such data sharing or the persistence of online data over time.[118] In supporting an expansive view of privacy by design, a consumer advocacy group noted that the individual elements and principles of the proposed framework should work together holistically.[119]

In response, the Commission notes that the framework already embodies all the concepts in the 1980 OECD privacy guidelines, although with some updates and changes in emphasis. For example, privacy by design includes the collection limitation, data quality, and security principles. Additionally, the framework's simplified choice and transparency components, discussed below, encompass the OECD principles of purpose specification, use limitation, individual participation, and openness. The framework also adopts the OECD principle that companies must be accountable for their privacy practices. Specifically, the framework calls on companies to implement procedures – such as designating a person responsible for privacy, training employees, and ensuring adequate oversight of third parties – to help ensure that they are implementing appropriate substantive privacy protections. The framework also calls on industry to increase efforts to educate consumers about the commercial collection and use of their data and the available privacy tools. In addition, there are aspects of the proposed "right to be forgotten" in the final framework, which calls on companies to (1) delete consumer data that they no longer need and (2) allow consumers to access their data and in appropriate cases suppress or delete it.[120]

All of the principles articulated in the preliminary staff report are intended to work together to shift the burden for protecting privacy away from consumers and to encourage companies to make strong privacy protections the default. Reasonable collection limits and data disposal policies work in tandem with streamlined notices and improved consumer choice mechanisms. Together, they function to provide substantive protections by placing reasonable limits on the collection, use, and retention of consumer data to more closely align with consumer expectations, while also raising consumer awareness about the nature and extent of data collection, use, and third-party sharing, and the choices available to them.

b. Data Security: Companies Must Provide Reasonable Security for Consumer Data

It is well settled that companies must provide reasonable security for consumer data. The Commission has a long history of enforcing data security obligations under Section 5 of the FTC Act, the FCRA and the GLBA. Since 2001, the FTC has brought 36 cases under these laws, charging that businesses failed to appropriately protect consumers' personal information. Since issuance of the preliminary staff report alone, the Commission has resolved seven data security actions against resellers of sensitive consumer report information, service providers that process employee data, a college savings program, and a social media service.[121] In addition to the federal laws the FTC enforces, companies are subject to a variety of other federal and state law obligations. In some industries, such as banking, federal regulators have given additional guidance on how to define reasonable security.[122]

The Commission also promotes better data security through consumer and business education. For example, the FTC sponsors OnGuard Online, a website to educate consumers about basic computer security.[123] Since the Commission issued the preliminary staff report there have been over 1.5 million unique visits to OnGuard Online and its Spanish-language counterpart Alerta en Línea. The Commission's business outreach includes general advice about data security as well as specific advice about emerging topics.[124]

The Commission also notes that the private sector has implemented a variety of initiatives in the security area, including the Payment Card Institute Data Security Standards for payment card data, the SANS Institute's security policy templates, and standards and best practices guidelines for the financial services industry provided by BITS, the technology policy division of the Financial Services Roundtable.[125] These standards can provide useful guidance on appropriate data security measures that organizations should implement for specific types of consumer data or in specific industries. The Commission further calls on industry to develop and implement best data security practices for additional industry sectors and other types of consumer data.

Because this issue is important to consumers and because businesses have existing legal and self-regulatory obligations, many individual companies have placed great emphasis and resources on maintaining reasonable security. For example, Google has cited certain security features in its products, including default SSL encryption for Gmail and security features in its Chrome browser.[126] Similarly, Mozilla has noted that its cloud storage system encrypts user data using SSL communication.[127] Likewise, Twitter has implemented encryption by default for users logged into its system.[128] The Commission commends these efforts and calls on companies to continue to look for additional ways to build data security into products and services from the design stage.

Finally, the Commission reiterates its call for Congress to enact data security and breach notification legislation. To help deter violations, such legislation should authorize the Commission to seek civil penalties.

c. Reasonable Collection Limitation: Companies Should Limit Their Collection of Data

The preliminary staff report called on companies to collect only the data they need to accomplish a specific business purpose. Many commenters expressed support for the general principle that companies should limit the information they collect from consumers.[129] Despite the broad support for the concept, however, many companies argued for a flexible approach based on concerns that allowing companies to collect data only for existing business needs would harm innovation and deny consumers new products and services.[130] One commenter cited Netflix's video recommendation feature as an example of how secondary uses of data can create consumer benefits. The commenter noted that Netflix originally collected information about subscribers' movie preferences in order to send the specific videos requested, but later used this information as the foundation for generating personalized recommendations to its subscribers.[131]

In addition, commenters raised concerns about who decides what a "specific business purpose" is.[132] For example, one purpose for collecting data is to sell it to third parties in order to monetize a service and provide it to consumers for free. Would collecting data for this purpose be a specific business purpose? If not, is the only alternative to charge consumers for the service, and would this result be better for consumers?

As an alternative to limiting collection to accomplish a "specific business purpose," many commenters advocated limiting collection to business purposes *that are clearly articulated.* This is akin to the Fair Information Practice Principle of "purpose specification," which holds that companies should specify to consumers all of the purposes for which information is collected at the time of collection. One commenter supported purpose specification statements in general categories to allow innovation and avoid making privacy policies overly complex.[133]

The Commission recognizes the need for flexibility to permit innovative new uses of data that benefit consumers. At the same time, in order to protect consumer privacy, there must be some reasonable limit on the collection of consumer data. General statements in privacy policies, however, are not an appropriate tool to ensure such a limit because companies have an incentive to make vague promises that would permit them to do virtually anything with consumer data.

Accordingly, the Commission clarifies the collection limitation principle of the framework as follows: Companies should limit data collection to that which is consistent with the context of a particular transaction or the consumer's relationship with the business, or as required or specifically authorized by law.[134] For any data collection that is inconsistent with these contexts, companies should make appropriate disclosures to consumers at a relevant time and in a prominent manner – outside of a privacy policy or other legal document. This clarification of the collection limitation principle is intended to help companies assess whether their data collection is consistent with what a consumer might expect; if it is not, they should provide prominent notice and choice. (For a further discussion of this point, see *infra* Section IV.C.2.) This approach is consistent with the Administration's Consumer Privacy Bill of Rights, which includes a Respect for Context principle that limits the use of consumer data to those purposes consistent with the context in which consumers originally disclosed the data.[135]

One example of a company innovating around the concept of privacy by design through collection limitation is the Graduate Management Admission Council ("GMAC"). This entity previously collected fingerprints from individuals taking the Graduate Management Admission Test. After concerns were raised about individuals' fingerprints being cross-referenced against criminal databases, GMAC developed a system that allowed for collection of palm prints that could be used solely for test-taking purposes.[136] The palm print technology is as accurate as fingerprinting but less susceptible to "function creep" over time than the taking of fingerprints, because palm prints are not widely used as a common identifier. GMAC received a privacy innovation award for small businesses for its work in this area.

d. Sound Data Retention: Companies Should Implement Reasonable Data Retention and Disposal Policies

Similar to the concerns raised about collection limits, many commenters expressed concern about limiting retention of consumer data, asserting that such limits would harm innovation. Trade associations and businesses requested a flexible standard for data retention to allow companies to develop new products and other uses of data that provide benefits to consumers.[137] One company raised concerns about prescriptive retention periods, arguing that retention standards instead should be based on business need, the type and location of data at issue, operational issues, and legal requirements.[138] Other commenters noted that retention limits should be sufficiently flexible to accommodate requests from law enforcement or other legitimate business purposes, such as the need of a mortgage banker to retain information about a consumer 's payment history.[139] Some commenters suggested that the Commission's focus should be on data security and proper handling of consumer data, rather than on retention limits.[140]

In contrast, some consumer groups advocated specific retention periods. For example, one such commenter cited a proposal made by a consortium of consumer groups in 2009 that companies that collect data for online behavioral advertising should limit their retention of the data to three months and that companies that retained their online behavioral advertising data for only 24 hours may not need to obtain consumer consent for their data collection and use.[141] Others stated that it might be appropriate for the FTC to recommend industry-specific retention periods after a public consultation.[142]

The Commission confirms its conclusion that companies should implement reasonable restrictions on the retention of data and should dispose of it once the data has outlived the legitimate purpose for which it was collected.[143] Retention periods, however, can be flexible and scaled according to the type of relationship and use of the data; for example, there may be legitimate reasons for certain companies that have a direct relationship with customers to retain some data for an extended period of time. A mortgage company will maintain data for the life of the mortgage to ensure accurate payment tracking; an auto dealer will retain data from its customers for years to manage service records and inform its customers of new offers. These long retention periods help maintain productive customer relationships. This analysis does not, however, apply to all data collection scenarios. A number of commenters noted that online behavioral advertising data often becomes stale quickly and need not be retained long.[144] For example, a consumer researching hotels in a particular city for an upcoming vacation is unlikely to be interested in continuing to see hotel advertisements after the trip is completed. Indefinite retention of data about the consumer's interest in finding a hotel for a particular weekend serves little purpose and could result in marketers sending the consumer irrelevant advertising.

In determining when to dispose of data, as well as limitations on collection described above, companies should also take into account the nature of the data they collect. For example, consider a company that develops an online interactive game as part of a marketing campaign directed to teens. The company should first assess whether it needs to collect the teens' data as part of the game, and if so, how it could limit the data collected, such as by allowing teens to create their own username instead of using a real name and email address. If the company decides to collect the data, it should consider disposing of it even more quickly than it would if it collected adults' data. Similarly, recognizing the sensitivity of data such as a particular consumer 's real time location, companies should take special care to delete this data as soon as possible, consistent with the services they provide to consumers.

Although restrictions may be tailored to the nature of the company's business and the data at issue, companies should develop clear standards and train its employees to follow them. Trade associations and self-regulatory groups also should be more proactive in providing guidance to their members about retention and data destruction policies. Accordingly, the Commission calls on industry groups from all sectors – the online advertising industry, online publishers, mobile participants, social networks, data brokers and others – to do more to provide guidance in this area. Similarly, the Commission generally supports the exploration of efforts to develop additional mechanisms, such as the "eraser button" for social media discussed below,[145] to allow consumers to manage and, where appropriate, require companies to delete the information consumers have submitted.

e. Accuracy: Companies Should Maintain Reasonable Accuracy of Consumers' Data

The preliminary staff report called on companies to take reasonable steps to ensure the accuracy of the data they collect and maintain, particularly if such data could cause significant harm or be used to deny consumers services. Similar to concerns raised about collection limits and retention periods, commenters opposed rigid accuracy standards,[146] and noted that the FCRA already imposes accuracy standards in certain contexts.[147] One commenter highlighted the challenges of providing the same levels of accuracy for non-identifiable data versus data that is identifiable.[148]

To address these challenges, some commenters stated that a sliding scale approach should be followed, particularly for marketing data. These commenters stated that marketing data is not used for eligibility purposes and that, if inaccurate, the only harm a consumer may experience is an irrelevant advertisement.[149] Providing enhanced accuracy standards for marketing data would raise additional privacy and data security concerns,[150] as additional information may need to be added to marketing databases to increase accuracy.[151]

The Commission agrees that the best approach to improving the accuracy of the consumer data companies collect and maintain is a flexible one, scaled to the intended use and sensitivity of the information. Thus, for example, companies using data for marketing purposes need not take special measures to ensure the accuracy of the information they maintain. Companies using data to make decisions about consumers' eligibility for benefits should take much more robust measures to ensure accuracy, including allowing consumers access to the data and the opportunity to correct erroneous information.[152]

Final Principle: Companies should incorporate substantive privacy protections into their practices, such as data security, reasonable collection limits, sound retention and disposal practices, and data accuracy.

2. Companies Should Adopt Procedural Protections to Implement the Substantive Principles

Proposed Principle: Companies should maintain comprehensive data management procedures throughout the life cycle of their products and services.

In addition to the substantive principles articulated above, the preliminary staff report called for organizations to maintain comprehensive data management procedures, such as designating personnel responsible for employee privacy training and regularly assessing the privacy impact of specific practices, products, and services. Many commenters supported this call for accountability within an organization.[153] Commenters noted that privacy risk assessments promote accountability, and help identify and address privacy issues.[154] One commenter stated that privacy risk assessments should be an ongoing process, and findings should be used to update internal procedures.[155] The Commission agrees that companies should implement accountability mechanisms and conduct regular privacy risk assessments to ensure that privacy issues are addressed throughout an organization.

The preliminary staff report also called on companies to "consider privacy issues systemically, at all stages of the design and development of their products and services." A range of commenters supported the principle of "baking" privacy into the product development process.[156] One commenter stated that this approach of including privacy considerations in the product development process was preferable to requiring after-the-fact reviews.[157] Another argued that privacy concerns should be considered from the outset, but observed that such concerns should continue to be evaluated as the product, service, or feature evolves.[158]

The Commission's recent settlements with Google and Facebook illustrate how the procedural protections discussed above might work in practice.[159] In both cases, the Commission alleged that the companies deceived consumers about the level of privacy afforded to their data.

The FTC's orders will require the companies to implement a comprehensive privacy program reasonably designed to address privacy risks related to the development and management of new and existing products and services and to protect the privacy and confidentiality of "covered information," defined broadly to mean *any* information the companies collect from or about a consumer.

The privacy programs that the orders mandate must, at a minimum, contain certain controls and procedures, including: (1) the designation of personnel responsible for the privacy program; (2) a risk assessment that, at a minimum, addresses employee training and management and product design and development; (3) the implementation of controls designed to address the risks identified; (4) appropriate oversight of service providers; and (5) evaluation and adjustment of the privacy program in light of regular testing and monitoring.[160] Companies should view the comprehensive privacy programs mandated by these consent orders as a roadmap as they implement privacy by design in their own organizations.

As an additional means of implementing the substantive privacy by design protections, the preliminary staff report advocated the use of privacy-enhancing technologies ("PETs") – such as encryption and anonymization tools – and requested comment on implementation of such technologies. One commenter stressed the need for "privacy-aware design," calling for techniques such as obfuscation and cryptography to reduce the amount of identifiable consumer data collected and used for various products and services.[161] Another stressed that PETs are a better approach in this area than rigid technical mandates.[162]

The Commission agrees that a flexible, technology-neutral approach towards developing PETs is appropriate to accommodate the rapid changes in the marketplace and will also allow companies to innovate on PETs. Accordingly, the Commission calls on companies to continue to look for new ways to protect consumer privacy throughout the life cycle of their products and services, including through the development and deployment of PETs.

Finally, Commission staff requested comment on how to apply the substantive protections articulated above to companies with legacy data systems.

Many commenters supported a phase-out period for legacy data systems, giving priority to systems that contain sensitive data.[163] Another commenter suggested that imposing strict access controls on legacy data systems until they can be updated would enhance privacy.[164] Although companies need to apply the various substantive privacy by design elements to their legacy data systems, the Commission recognizes that companies need a reasonable transition period to update their systems. In applying the substantive elements to their legacy systems, companies should prioritize those systems that contain sensitive data and they should appropriately limit access to all such systems until they can update them.

Final Principle: Companies should maintain comprehensive data management procedures throughout the life cycle of their products and services.

Data Collection and Disposal Case Study: Mobile

The rapid growth of the mobile marketplace illustrates the need for companies to implement reasonable limits on the collection, transfer, and use of consumer data and to set policies for disposing of collected data. The unique features of a mobile phone – which is highly personal, almost always on, and travels with the consumer – have facilitated unprecedented levels of data collection. Recent news reports have confirmed the extent of this ubiquitous data collection.

Researchers announced, for example, that Apple had been collecting geolocation data through its mobile devices over time, and storing unencrypted data files containing this information on consumers' computers and mobile devices.[1] The Wall Street Journal has documented numerous companies gaining access to detailed information – such as age, gender, precise location, and the unique ID associated with a particular mobile device – that can then be used to track and predict consumer behavior.[2] Not surprisingly, consumers are concerned: for example, a recent Nielsen study found that a majority of smartphone app users worry about their privacy when it comes to sharing their location through a mobile device.[3] The Commission calls on companies to limit collection to data they need for a requested service or transaction. For example, a wallpaper app or an app that tracks stock quotes does not need to collect location information.[4] The extensive collection of consumer information – particularly location information – through mobile devices also heightens the need for companies to implement reasonable policies for purging data.[5] Without data retention and disposal policies specifically tied to the stated business purpose for the data collection, location information could be used to build detailed profiles of consumer movements over time that could be used in ways not anticipated by consumers.[6] Location information is particularly useful for uniquely identifying (or re-identifying) individuals using disparate bits of data.[7] For example, a consumer can use a mobile application on her cell phone to "check in" at a restaurant for the purpose of finding and connecting with friends who are nearby. The same consumer might not expect the application provider to retain a history of restaurants she visited over time. If the application provider were to share that information with third parties, it could reveal a predictive pattern of the consumer's movements thereby exposing the consumer to a risk of harm such as stalking.[8] Taken together, the principles of reasonable collection limitation and disposal periods help to minimize the risks that information collected from or about consumers could be used in harmful or unexpected ways. With respect to the particular concerns of location data in the mobile context, the Commission calls on entities involved in the mobile ecosystem to work together to establish standards that address data collection, transfer, use, and disposal, particularly for location data. To the extent that location data in particular is collected and shared with third parties, entities should work to provide consumers with more prominent notice and choices about such practices. Although some in the mobile ecosystem provide notice about the collection of geolocation data, not all companies have adequately disclosed the frequency or extent of the collection, transfer, and use of such data.

Notes

[1] *See* Jennifer Valentino-Devries, *Study: iPhone Keeps Tracking Data*, WALL ST. J., Apr. 21, 2011, *available at* http://online.wsj.com/article/SB10001424052748704570 704576275323811369758.html.

[2] *See, e.g.*, Robert Lee Hotz, *The Really Smart Phone*, WALL ST. J., Apr. 22, 2011, *available at* http://online.wsj.com/ article/SB10001424052748704547604576263 261679848814.html (describing how researchers are using mobile data to predict consumers' actions); Scott Thurm & Yukari Iwatane Kane, *Your Apps are Watching You*, WALL ST. J., Dec. 18, 2010, *available at* http://online.wsj.com/article/ SB100014240527487043680045 760277 51867039730. html (documenting the data collection that occurs through many popular smartphone apps).

[3] *Privacy Please! U.S. Smartphone App Users Concerned with Privacy When It Comes to Location*, NIELSENWIRE BLOG (Apr. 21, 2011), http://blog.nielsen.com/ nielsenwire/online_mobile/privacy-please-u-s-smartphone-app-usersconcerned-with-privacy-when-it-comes-to-location/; *see also* Ponemon Institute, *Smartphone Security: Survey of U.S. Consumers* 7 (Mar. 2011), *available at* http://aa-download.avg.com/ filedir/other/Smartphone.pdf (reporting that 64% of consumers worry about their location being tracked when using their smartphones).

[4] Similarly, the photo-sharing app Path faced widespread criticism for uploading its users' iPhone address books without their consent. *See, e.g.*, Mark Hachman, *Path Uploads Your Entire iPhone Contact List By Default*, PC MAGAZINE, Feb. 7, 2012, *available at* http://www.pcmag.com/article2/ 0,2817,2399970,00.asp.

[5] The Commission is currently reviewing its COPPA Rule, including the application of COPPA to geolocation information. *See* FTC, Proposed Rule and Request for Public Comment, Children's Online Privacy Protection Rule, 76 Fed. Reg. 59,804 (Sept. 15, 2011), *available at* http://www.gpo.gov/fdsys/pkg/FR-2011-09-27/pdf/2011- 24314. pdf.

[6] *See* ACLU of Northern California, *Location-Based Services: Time for a Privacy Check-In*, 14-15 (Nov. 2010), *available at* http://dotrights.org/sites/default/files/lbs-white-paper.pdf.

[7] *Comment of Electronic Frontier Foundation*, cmt. #00400, at 3.

[8] *Cf. U.S. v. Jones*, 565 U.S. 132 S. Ct. 945, 955 (2012) (Sotomayor, J., concurring) (noting that "GPS monitoring generates a precise, comprehensive record of a person's public movements that reflects a wealth of detail about her familial, political, professional, religious, and sexual associations").

C. Simplified Consumer Choice

Baseline Principle: Companies should simplify consumer choice.

As detailed in the preliminary staff report and in submitted comments, many consumers face challenges in understanding the nature and extent of current commercial data practices and how to exercise available choices regarding those practices. This challenge results from a number of factors including: (1) the dramatic increase in the breadth of consumer data collection and use, made possible by an ever-increasing range of technologies and business models; (2) the ability of companies, outside of certain sector-specific laws, to collect and use data without first providing consumer choice; and (3) the inadequacy of typical privacy policies as a means to effectively communicate information about the privacy choices that are offered to consumers.

To reduce the burden on those consumers who seek greater control over their data, the proposed framework called on companies that collect and use consumer data to provide easy-to-use choice mechanisms that allow consumers to control whether their data is collected and how it is used. To ensure that choice is most effective, the report stated that a company should provide the choice mechanism at a time and in a context that is relevant to consumers – generally at the point the company collects the consumer's information. At the same time, however, in recognition of the benefits of various types of data collection and use, the proposed framework identified certain "commonly accepted" categories of commercial data practices that companies can engage in without offering consumer choice.

Staff posed a variety of questions and received numerous comments regarding the proposed framework's simplified consumer choice approach. Two trade organizations argued that the framework should identify those practices for which choice is appropriate rather than making choice the general rule, subject to exceptions for certain practices.[165] The majority of commenters, however, did not challenge the proposed framework's approach of setting consumer choice as the default.[166] Instead, these commenters focused on the practicality of staff's "commonly accepted" formulation.[167] For example, several commenters questioned whether the approach was sufficiently flexible to allow for innovation.[168] Others discussed whether specific practices should fall within the categories enumerated in the preliminary staff report.[169] In addition, numerous commenters addressed the appropriate scope of the first-party marketing category and how to define specific business models. With respect to those practices that fall outside the "commonly accepted" categories, commenters also addressed the mechanics of providing choice at the relevant time and what types of practices require enhanced choice.

Consistent with the discussion and analysis set forth below, the Commission retains the proposed framework's simplified choice model. Establishing consumer choice as a baseline requirement for companies that collect and use consumer data, while also identifying certain practices where choice is unnecessary, is an appropriately balanced model. It increases consumers' control over the collection and use of their data, preserves the ability of companies to innovate new products and services, and sets clear expectations for consumers and industry alike. In order to better foster innovation and take into account new technologies and business models, however, the Commission is providing further clarification of the framework's simplified choice concept.

1. Practices That Do Not Require Choice

> **Proposed Principle:** Companies do not need to provide choice before collecting and using consumers' data for commonly accepted practices, such as product fulfillment.

The preliminary staff report identified five categories of data practices that companies can engage in without offering consumer choice, because they involve data collection and use that is either obvious from the context of the transaction or sufficiently accepted or necessary for public policy reasons. The categories included: (1) product and service fulfillment; (2) internal operations; (3) fraud prevention; (4) legal compliance and public purpose; and (5) first-party marketing. In response to the comments received, the Commission revises its approach to focus on the context of the consumer's interaction with a company, as discussed below.

a. General Approach to "Commonly Accepted" Practices

While generally supporting the concept that choice is unnecessary for certain practices, a variety of commenters addressed the issue of whether the list of "commonly accepted" practices was too broad or too narrow.[170] A number of industry commenters expressed concern that the list of practice categories was too narrow and rigid. These commenters stated that, by enumerating a list of specific practices, the proposed framework created a bright-line standard that freezes in place current practices and potentially could harm innovation and restrict the development of new business models.[171] In addition, the commenters asserted that notions of what is "commonly accepted" can change over time with the development of new ways to collect or use data. They also stated that line-drawing in this context could stigmatize business practices that fall outside of the "commonly accepted" category and place companies that engage in them at a competitive disadvantage. To resolve these concerns, commenters called on the Commission to provide guidance on how future practices relate to the "commonly accepted" category.[172] Similarly, one commenter suggested that the practices identified in the preliminary staff report should serve as illustrative guidelines rather than an exhaustive and final list.[173]

Commenters also supported adding additional practices or clarifying that the "commonly accepted" category includes certain practices. Some industry commenters suggested, for example, expanding the concept of fraud prevention to include preventing security attacks, "phishing,"[174] and spamming or to protect intellectual property.[175] Other recommendations included adding analytical data derived from devices that are not tied to individuals, such as smart grid data used for energy conservation and geospatial data used for mapping, surveying or providing emergency services.[176] With respect to online behavioral advertising in particular, some trade associations recommended clarifying that the "commonly accepted" category of practices includes the use of IP addresses and third-party cookie data when used for purposes such as "frequency capping," "attribution measurement," and similar inventory or delivery measurements and to prevent click fraud.[177]

More generally, some commenters discussed the "repurposing" of existing consumer data to develop new products or services. For example, one company supported expanding the "internal operations" category to include the practice of product and service improvement.[178] One commenter recommended treating any uses of data that consumers would "reasonably expect under the circumstances" as commonly accepted.[179] Another noted that, whether a new use of consumer data should be considered commonly accepted would depend upon a variety of factors, including the extent to which the new use is consistent with previously defined uses.[180]

In contrast to the calls for expanding the "commonly accepted" practice categories to cover various practices, a number of consumer and privacy organizations advocated for a more restrictive approach to determining the practices that do not require consumer choice. Although agreeing that choice is not necessary for product and service fulfillment, one commenter stated that most of the other practices enumerated in the proposed framework – including internal operations, fraud prevention, and legal compliance and public purpose – were vague and required additional description. The commenter called on the Commission to define these terms as narrowly as possible so that they would not become loopholes used to undermine consumer privacy.[181]

One privacy advocate expressed reservations about the breadth of the "internal operations" category of practices – specifically, the extent to which it could include product improvement and website analytics. This commenter stated that, if viewed broadly, product improvement could justify, for example, a mobile mapping application collecting precise, daily geolocation data about its customers and then retaining the data long after providing the service for which the data was necessary. Similarly, this commenter noted that companies potentially could use analytics programs to create very detailed consumer profiles to which many consumers might object, without offering them any choice. This commenter recommended that the Commission revise the proposed framework's internal operations category to make it consistent with the "operational purpose" language contained in H.R. 611 from the 112th Congress, which would include, among other things, "basic business functions such as accounting, inventory and supply chain management, quality assurance, and internal auditing."[182]

The Commission believes that for some practices, the benefits of providing choice are reduced – either because consent can be inferred or because public policy makes choice unnecessary. However, the Commission also appreciates the concerns that the preliminary staff report's definition of "commonly accepted practices" may have been both under-inclusive and over-inclusive. To the extent the proposed framework was interpreted to establish an inflexible list of specific practices, it risked undermining companies' incentives to innovate and develop new products and services to consumers, including innovative methods for reducing data collection while providing valued services. On the other hand, companies could read the definition so broadly that virtually any practice could be considered "commonly accepted."

The standard should be sufficiently flexible to allow for innovation and new business models but also should cabin the types of practices that do not require consumer choice. To strike that balance, the Commission refines the standard to focus on the *context of the interaction* between a business and the consumer. This new "context of the interaction" standard is similar to the concept suggested by some commenters that the need for choice should depend on reasonable consumer expectations,[183] but is intended to provide businesses with more concrete guidance. Rather than relying solely upon the inherently subjective test of consumer expectations, the revised standard focuses on more objective factors related to the consumer 's relationship with a business. Specifically, whether a practice requires choice turns on the extent to which the practice is consistent with the context of the transaction or the consumer's existing relationship with the business, or is required or specifically authorized by law.[184]

The purchase of an automobile from a dealership illustrates how this standard could apply. In connection with the sale of the car, the dealership collects personal information about the consumer and his purchase. Three months later, the dealership uses the consumer's address to send him a coupon for a free oil change. Similarly, two years after the purchase, the dealership might send the consumer notice of an upcoming sale on the type of tires that came with the car or information about the new models of the car. In this transaction the data collection and subsequent use is consistent with the context of the transaction and the consumer's relationship with the car dealership. Conversely, if the dealership sells the consumer's personal information to a third-party data broker that appends it to other data in a consumer profile to sell to marketers, the practice would not be consistent with the car purchase transaction or the consumer's relationship with the dealership.

Although the Commission has revised the standard for evaluating when choice is necessary, it continues to believe that the practices highlighted in the preliminary staff report – fulfilment, fraud prevention, internal operations, legal compliance and public purpose, and most first-party marketing[185] – provide illustrative guidance regarding the types of practices that would meet the revised standard and thus would not typically require consumer choice. Further, drawing upon the recommendations of several commenters,[186] the Commission agrees that the fraud prevention category would generally cover practices designed to prevent security attacks or phishing; internal operations would encompass frequency capping and similar advertising inventory metrics; and legal compliance and public purpose would cover intellectual property protection or using location data for emergency services.[187] It should be noted, however, that even within these categories there may be practices that are inconsistent with the context of the interaction standard and thus warrant consumer choice. For instance, there may be contexts in which the "repurposing" of data to improve existing products or services would exceed the internal operations concept. Thus, where a product improvement involves additional sharing of consumer data with third parties, it would no longer be an "internal operation" consistent with the context of the consumer's interaction with a company. On the other hand, product improvements such as a website redesign or a safety improvement would be the type of "internal operation" that is generally consistent with the context of the interaction.[188]

b. First-Party Marketing Generally Does Not Require Choice, but Certain Practices Raise Special Concerns

The preliminary staff report's questions regarding first-party marketing generated a large number of comments. As discussed, the Commission has revised the standard for determining whether a practice requires consumer choice but believes that most first-party marketing practices are consistent with the consumer 's relationship with the business and thus do not necessitate consumer choice. Nevertheless, as a number of the commenters discussed, there are certain practices that raise special concerns and therefore merit additional analysis and clarification.

(i) Companies Must Provide Consumers With A Choice Whether To Be Tracked Across Other Parties' Websites.

Commenters raised questions about companies and other services that have first-party relationships with consumers, but may have access to behavioral activity data that extends beyond the context of that first-party relationship. For example, in response to the question in the preliminary staff report regarding the use of deep packet inspection ("DPI"),[189] a number of commenters cited the ability of ISPs to use DPI to monitor and track consumers' movements across the Internet and use the data for marketing.[190] There appeared to be general consensus among the commenters that, based on the potential scope of the tracking, an ISP's use of DPI for marketing purposes is distinct from other forms of marketing practices by companies that have a first-party relationship with consumers, and thus at a minimum requires consumer choice.[191]

Similarly, commenters cited the use of "social plugins" – such as the Facebook "Like" button – that allow social media services to track consumers across every website that has installed the plugin.[192] The commenter stated that, as with DPI, consumers would not expect social media sites to track their visits to other websites or that the profiles created from such tracking could be used for marketing.

The Commission agrees that where a company that has a first-party relationship with a consumer for delivery of a specific service but also tracks the consumer's activities across other parties' websites, such tracking is unlikely to be consistent with the context of the consumer's first-party relationship with the entity. Accordingly, under the final framework, such entities should not be exempt from having to provide consumers with choices. This is true whether the entity tracks consumers through the use of DPI, social plug-ins, http cookies, web beacons, or some other type of technology.[193]

As an example of how this standard can apply, consider a company with multiple lines of business, including a search engine and an ad network. A consumer has a "first-party relationship" with the company when using the search engine. While it may be consistent with this first-party relationship for the company to offer contextual ads on the search engine site, it would be inconsistent with the first-party search engine relationship for the company to use its third-party ad network to invisibly track the consumer across the Internet.

To use another example, many online retailers engage in the practice of "retargeting," in which the retailer delivers an ad to a consumer on a separate website based on the consumer's previous activity on the retailer's website.[194] Because the ad is tailored to the consumer's activity on the retailer's website, it could be argued that "retargeting" is a first-party marketing practice that does not merit consumer choice. However, because it involves tracking the consumer from the retailer's website to a separate site on which the retailer is a third party and communicating with the consumer in this new context, the Commission believes that the practice of retargeting is inconsistent with the context of consumer's first-party interaction with the retailer. Thus, where an entity has a first-party relationship with a consumer on its own website, and it engages in third-party tracking of the consumer across other websites the entity should provide meaningful choice to the consumer.

(ii) Affiliates Are Third Parties Unless The Affiliate Relationship Is Clear to Consumers.

Several trade organizations stated that first-party marketing should include the practice of data sharing among all of a particular entity's corporate affiliates and subsidiaries.[195] In contrast, a number of commenters – including individual companies and consumer advocates – took a more limited approach that would treat affiliate sharing as a first-party practice only if the affiliated companies share a trademark, are commonly-branded, or the affiliated relationship is otherwise reasonably clear to consumers.[196] One consumer advocate also suggested restricting data sharing to commonly-branded affiliates in the same line of business so that the data would be used in a manner that is consistent with the purpose for which the first party collected it.[197]

The Commission maintains the view that affiliates are third parties, and a consumer choice mechanism is necessary unless the affiliate relationship is clear to consumers. Common branding is one way of making the affiliate relationship clear to consumers. By contrast, where an affiliate relationship is hidden – such as between an online publisher that provides content to consumers through its website and an ad network that invisibly tracks consumers' activities on the site – marketing from the affiliate would not be consistent with a transaction on, or the consumer's relationship with, that website. In this scenario consumers should receive a choice about whether to allow the ad network to collect data about their activities on the publisher's site.

(iii) Cross-Channel Marketing Is Generally Consistent with the Context of a Consumer's Interaction with a Company.

A variety of commenters also discussed the issue of whether the framework should require choice for cross-channel marketing, *e.g.*, where a consumer makes an in-store purchase and receives a coupon – not at the register, but in the mail or through a text message. These commenters stated that the framework should not require choice when a first party markets to consumers through different channels, such as the Internet, email, mobile apps, texts, or in the offline context.[198] In support of this conclusion, one commenter stated that restricting communications from a first party to the initial means of contact would impose costs on business without any consumer benefits.[199]

The Commission agrees that the first-party marketing concept should include the practice of contacting consumers across different channels. Regardless of the particular means of contact, receipt of a message from a company with which a consumer has interacted directly is likely to be consistent with the consumer's relationship with that company.[200] At the same time, as noted above, if an offline or online retailer tracks a customer's activities on a third-party website, this is unlikely to be consistent with the customer's relationship with the retailer; thus, choice should be required.

(iv) Companies Should Implement Measures to Improve The Transparency of Data Enhancement.

A large number of commenters discussed whether the practice of data enhancement, by which a company appends data obtained from third-party sources to information it collects directly from consumers, should require choice. Some of these commenters specifically objected to allowing companies to enhance data without providing consumers choice about the practice.[201]

For example, one academic organization characterized data enhancement without consumer choice as "trick[ing]" consumers into participating in their own profiling for the benefit of companies.[202] As companies develop new means for collecting data about individuals, this commenter stated, consumers should have more tools to control data collection, not fewer.[203]

Similarly, a consumer organization explained that consumers may not anticipate that the companies with which they have a relationship can obtain additional data about them from other sources, such as social networking sites, and use the data for marketing.[204] This commenter concluded that requiring companies to provide choice will necessitate better explanations of the practice, which will lead to improved consumer understanding.

Other stakeholders also raised concerns about data enhancement absent consumer choice. One company focused on the practice of enhancing online cookie data or IP addresses with offline identity data and stated that such enhancement should be subject to consumer choice.[205] In addition, a data protection authority stated that consumers are likely to expect choice where the outcome of data enhancement could negatively affect the consumer or where the sources of data used for enhancement would be unexpected to the consumer.[206]

Alternatively, a number of industry commenters opposed requiring consumer choice for data enhancement in connection with first-party marketing. These commenters described data enhancement as a routine and longstanding practice that allows businesses to better understand and serve their consumers.[207] Commenters enumerated a variety of benefits from the availability and use of third-party data, including: development of new or more relevant products and services; ensuring the accuracy of databases; reducing barriers to small firms seeking to enter markets; helping marketers identify the best places to locate retail stores; and reducing irrelevant marketing communications.[208]

One commenter noted that requiring content publishers such as newspapers to offer consumer choice before buying information from non-consumer-facing data brokers would impose logistical and financial challenges that would interfere with publishers' ability to provide relevant content or sell the advertising to support it.[209] Other commenters claimed that, where the data used for enhancement comes from third-party sources, it was likely subject to choice at the point of collection from the consumer and therefore providing additional choice is unnecessary.[210] Taking a similar approach, one company noted that the third-party source of the data should be responsible for complying with the framework when it shares data, and the recipient should be responsible for any subsequent sharing of the enhanced data.[211]

The issue of whether a first-party marketer should provide choice for data enhancement is particularly challenging because the practice involves two separate and distinct types of consumer data collection. One involves the consumer-to-business transfer of data – for instance, where an online retailer collects information directly from the consumer by tracking the products the consumer purchased in the store or looked at while visiting the retailer's website. The other involves a business-to-business transfer of data – such as where retailer purchases consumer data from a non-consumer-facing data broker.

As to the first type of data collection, for the reasons discussed above, if the first party does not share information with third parties or track consumers across third-party websites, the practice would be consistent with the context of the consumer's interaction with the company.[212] Therefore, the framework would not call for a consumer choice mechanism. In contrast, because the second type of data collection involves the transfer of data from one business to another and does not directly involve the consumer (and therefore is typically unknown to the consumer), it is unlikely to be consistent with a transaction or relationship between the consumer and the first party. The Commission nevertheless recognizes that it would be impractical to require the first-party marketer to offer a choice mechanism when it appends data from third-party sources to the data it collects directly from its consumers. As discussed in the comments, such a requirement would impose costs and logistical problems that could preclude the range of benefits that data enhancement facilitates. Instead, full implementation of the framework's other components should address the privacy concerns that commenters raised about data enhancement.

First, companies should incorporate privacy by design concepts, including limiting the amount of data they collect from consumers and third parties alike to accomplish a specific business purpose, reducing the amount of time they retain such data, and adopting reasonable security measures. The framework also calls for consumer choice where a company shares with a third party the data it collects from a consumer.

Thus, consumers will have the ability to control the flow of their data to third parties who might sell the data to others for enhancement. In addition, companies should improve the transparency of their practices by disclosing that they engage in data enhancement and educating consumers about the practice, identifying the third-party sources of the data, and providing a link or other contact information so the consumer can contact the third-party source directly.

Finally, to further protect consumer privacy, the Commission recommends that first parties that obtain marketing data for enhancement should take steps to encourage their third-party data broker sources to increase their own transparency, including by participating in a centralized data broker website, discussed further below, where consumers could learn more information about data brokers and exercise choices.[213] The first parties may also consider contractually requiring their data broker sources to take these steps.

Data Enhancement Case Study:
Facial Recognition Software

Facial recognition technology[1] enables the identification of an individual based on his or her distinct facial characteristics. While this technology has been used in experiments for over thirty years, until recently it remained costly and limited under real world conditions.[2] However, steady improvements in the technology combined with increased computing power have shifted this technology out of the realm of science fiction and into the marketplace. As costs have decreased and accuracy improved, facial recognition software has been incorporated into a variety of commercial products. Today it can be found in online social networks and photo management software, where it is used to facilitate photo-organizing,[3] and in mobile apps where it is used to enhance gaming.[4]

This surge in the deployment of facial recognition technology will likely boost the desire of companies to use data enhancement by offering yet another means to compile and link information about an individual gathered through disparate transactions and contexts. For instance, social networks such as Facebook and LinkedIn, as well as websites like Yelp and Amazon, all encourage users to upload profile photos and make these photos publicly available. As a result, vast amounts of facial data, often linked with real names and geographic locations, have been made publicly available. A recent paper from researchers at Carnegie Mellon University illustrated how they were able to combine readily available facial recognition software with data mining algorithms and statistical re-identification techniques to determine in many cases an individual's name, location, interests, and even the first five digits of the individual's Social Security number, starting with only the individual's picture.[5]

Companies could easily replicate these results. Today, retailers use facial *detection* software in digital signs to analyze the age and gender of viewers and deliver targeted advertisements.[6] Facial detection does not uniquely identify an individual. Instead, it detects human faces and determines gender and approximate age range. In the future, digital signs and kiosks placed in supermarkets, transit stations, and college campuses could capture images of viewers and, through the use of facial *recognition* software, match those faces to online identities, and return advertisements based on the websites specific individuals have visited or the publicly available information contained in their social media profiles.

Retailers could also implement loyalty programs, ask users to associate a photo with the account, then use the combined data to link the consumer to other online accounts or their in-store actions. This would enable the retailer to glean information about the consumer's purchase habits, interests, and even movements,[7] which could be used to offer discounts on particular products or otherwise market to the consumer.

The ability of facial recognition technology to identify consumers based solely on a photograph, create linkages between the offline and online world, and compile highly detailed dossiers of information, makes it especially important for companies using this technology to implement privacy by design concepts and robust choice and transparency policies.

Such practices should include reducing the amount of time consumer information is retained, adopting reasonable security measures, and disclosing to consumers that the facial data they supply may be used to link them to information from third parties or publicly available sources.

For example, if a digital sign uses data enhancement to deliver targeted advertisements to viewers, it should immediately delete the data after the consumer has walked away. Likewise, if a kiosk is used to invite shoppers to register for a store loyalty program, the shopper should be informed that the photo taken by the kiosk camera and associated with the account may be combined with other data to market discounts and offers to the shopper. If a company received the data from other sources, it should disclose the sources to the consumer.

Notes

1 The Commission held a facial recognition workshop on December 8, 2011. *See* FTC Workshop, *Face Facts: A Forum on Facial Recognition Technology* (Dec. 8, 2011), http://www.ftc.gov/bcp/workshops/ facefacts/.

2 *See* Alessandro Acquisti *et al.*, *Faces of Facebook: Privacy in the Age of Augmented Reality*, http://www.heinz.cmu. edu/~acquisti/face-recognition-study-FAQ/.

3 *See* Justin Mitchell, *Making Photo Tagging Easier*, THE FACEBOOK BLOG (June 30, 2011, 5:16 PM), https://blog. facebook.com/blog.php?post=467145887130; Matt Hickey, *Picasa Refresh Brings Facial Recognition*, TECHCRUNCH (Sept. 2, 2008), http://techcrunch.com/2008/09/02/picasa-refresh-brings-facial-recognition/.

4 *See* Tomio Geron, *Viewdle Launches 'Third Eye' Augmented Reality Game*, FORBES, June 22, 2011, *available at* http:// www.forbes.com/sites/tomiogeron/2011/06/ 22/viewdle-lauches-third-eye-augmented-reality-game/.

5 *See* Alessandro Acquisti *et al.*, *Faces of Facebook: Privacy in the Age of Augmented Reality*, http://www.heinz.cmu. edu/~acquisti/face-recognition-study-FAQ/.

6 *See* Shan Li & David Sarno, *Advertisers Start Using Facial Recognition to Tailor Pitches*, L.A. TIMES, Aug. 21, 2011, *available at* http://articles.latimes.com/2011/ aug/21/business/la-fi-facial-recognition-20110821.

7 For instance, many consumers use services such as Foursquare which allow them to use their mobile phone to "check in" at a restaurant to find friends who are nearby. *See* Foursquare, About Foursquare, https://foursquare. com/about.

(v) Companies Should Generally Give Consumers a Choice Before Collecting Sensitive Data for First-Party Marketing.

Commenters addressed whether companies that collect sensitive data[214] for their own marketing should offer consumer choice. A number of privacy and consumer organizations asserted that even where a business collects data in a first-party setting, any marketing based on sensitive data should require the consumer's affirmative express consent.[215] These commenters stated that the use of sensitive data for marketing could cause embarrassment for consumers or lead to various types of discriminatory conduct, including denial of benefits or being charged higher prices. One such commenter also noted that heightened choice for sensitive data is consistent with the FTC staff's Self-Regulatory Principles for Online Behavioral Advertising ("2009 OBA Report").[216]

Rather than always requiring consent, an industry trade association pushed for a more flexible approach to the use of sensitive data in first-party marketing.[217] This commenter stated that the choice analysis should depend upon the particular context and circumstances in which the data is used. The commenter noted that, for example, with respect to sensitive location data, where a consumer uses a wireless service to find nearby restaurants and receive discounts, the consumer implicitly understands his location data will be used and consent can be inferred.

The Commission agrees with the commenters who stated that affirmative express consent is appropriate when a company uses sensitive data for any marketing, whether first- or third-party. Although, as a general rule, most first-party marketing presents fewer privacy concerns, the calculus changes when the data is sensitive. Indeed, when health or children's information is involved, for example, the likelihood that data misuse could lead to embarrassment, discrimination, or other harms is increased. This risk exists regardless of whether the entity collecting and using the data is a first party or a third party that is unknown to the consumer. In light of the heightened privacy risks associated with sensitive data, first parties should provide a consumer choice mechanism at the time of data collection.[218]

At the same time, the Commission believes this requirement of affirmative express consent for first-party marketing using sensitive data should be limited. Certainly, where a company's business model is *designed to target* consumers based on sensitive data – including data about children, financial and health information, Social Security numbers, and certain geolocation data – the company should seek affirmative express consent before collecting the data from those consumers.[219] On the other hand, the risks to consumers may not justify the potential burdens on general audience businesses that *incidentally collect* and use sensitive information. For example, the Commission has previously noted that online retailers and services such as Amazon.com and Netflix need not provide choice when making product recommendations based on prior purchases. Thus, if Amazon.com were to recommend a book related to health or financial issues based on a prior purchase on the site, it need not provide choice. However, if a health website is designed to target people with particular medical conditions, that site should seek affirmative express consent when marketing to consumers.

Final Principle: Companies do not need to provide choice before collecting and using consumer data for practices that are consistent with the context of the transaction or the company's relationship with the consumer, or are required or specifically authorized by law.

2. For Practices Inconsistent with the Context of Their Interaction with Consumers, Companies Should Give Consumers Choices

Proposed Principle: For practices requiring choice, companies should offer the choice at a time and in a context in which the consumer is making a decision about his or her data.

For those practices for which choice is contemplated, the proposed framework called on companies to provide choice at a time and in a context in which the consumer is making a decision about his or her data. In response, commenters discussed a number of issues, including the methods for providing just in time choice, when "take-it-or-leave-it" choice may be appropriate, how to respond to the call for a Do Not Track mechanism that would allow consumers to control online tracking, and the contexts in which affirmative express consent is necessary.

The Commission adopts the proposed framework's formulation that choice should be provided at a time and in a context in which the consumer is making a decision about his or her data. The Commission also adds new language addressing when a company should seek a consumer's affirmative express consent.

a. Companies Should Provide Choices at a Time and in a Context in Which the Consumer Is Making a Decision About His or Her Data

The call for companies to provide a "just in time" choice generated numerous comments. Several consumer organizations as well as industry commenters stressed the importance of offering consumer choice at the time the consumer provides – and the company collects or uses – the data at issue and pointed to examples of existing mechanisms for providing effective choice.[220] One commenter stated that in order to make choice mechanisms meaningful to consumers, companies should incorporate them as a feature of a product or service rather than as a legal disclosure.[221] Using its vendor recommendation service as an example, this commenter suggested incorporating a user's sharing preferences into the sign-up process instead of setting such preferences as a default that users can later adjust and personalize. Another commenter stated that choice options should occur in a "time-appropriate manner" that takes into account the "functional and aesthetic context" of the product or service.[222]

Others raised concerns about the practicality of providing choice prior to the collection or use of data in different contexts.[223] For instance, a number of commenters discussed the offline retail context and noted that cashiers are typically unqualified to communicate privacy information or to discuss data collection and use practices with customers.[224] One commenter further discussed the logistical problems with providing such information at the point of sale, citing consumer concerns about ease of transaction and in-store wait times.[225] Other commenters described the impracticality of offering and obtaining advance consent in an offline mail context, such as a magazine subscription card or catalogue request that a consumer mails to a fulfillment center.[226] In the online context, one commenter expressed concern that "pop-up" choice mechanisms complicate or clutter the user experience, which could lead to choice "fatigue."[227] Another commenter noted that where data collection occurs automatically, such as in the case of online behavioral advertising, obtaining consent before collection could be impractical.[228]

One theme that a majority of the commenters addressing this issue articulated is the need for flexibility so that companies can tailor the choice options to specific business models and contexts.[229] Rather than a rigid reliance on advance consent, commenters stated that companies should be able to provide choice before collection, close to the time of collection, or a time that is convenient to the consumer.[230] The precise method should depend upon context, the sensitivity of the data at issue, and other factors.[231] Citing its own best practices guidance, one trade organization recommended that the Commission focus not on the precise mechanism for offering choice, but on whether the consent is informed and based on sufficient notice.[232]

The Commission appreciates the concerns that commenters raised about the timing of providing choices. Indeed, the proposed framework was not intended to set forth a "one size fits all" model for designing consumer choice mechanisms. Staff instead called on companies to offer clear and concise choice mechanisms that are easy to use and are delivered at a time and in a context that is relevant to the consumer's decision about whether to allow the data collection or use. Precisely how companies in different industries achieve these goals may differ depending on such considerations as the nature or context of the consumer's interaction with a company or the type or sensitivity of the data at issue.

In most cases, providing choice before or at the time of collection will be necessary to gain consumers' attention and ensure that the choice presented is meaningful and relevant. If a consumer is submitting his or her data online, the consumer choice could be offered, for example, directly adjacent to where the consumer is entering his or her data. In other contexts, the choice might be offered immediately upon signing up for a service, as in the case of a social networking website.

In some contexts, however, it may be more practical to communicate choices at a later point. For example, in the case of an offline retailer, the choice might be offered close to the time of a sale, but in a manner that will not unduly interfere with the transaction. This could include communicating the choice mechanism through a sales receipt or on a prominent poster at the location where the transaction takes place. In such a case, there is likely to be a delay between when the data collection takes place and when the consumer is able to contact the company in order to exercise any choice options. Accordingly, the company should wait for a disclosed period of time before engaging in the practices for which choice is being offered.[233] The Commission also encourages companies to examine the effectiveness of such choice mechanisms periodically to determine whether they are sufficiently prominent, effective, and easy to use.

Industry is well positioned to design and develop choice mechanisms that are practical for particular business models or contexts, and that also advance the fundamental goal of giving consumers the ability to make informed and meaningful decisions about their privacy. The Commission calls on industry to use the same type of creativity industry relies on to develop effective marketing campaigns and user interfaces for consumer choice mechanisms. One example of such a creative approach is the online behavioral advertising industry's development of a standardized icon and text that is embedded in targeted advertisements. The icon and text are intended to communicate that the advertising may rely on data collected about consumers. They also serve as a choice mechanism to allow the consumer to exercise control over the delivery of such ads.[234] Even though in most cases, cookie placement has already occurred, the in-ad disclosure provides a logical "teachable moment" for the consumer who is making a decision about his or her data.[235]

b. Take-it-or-Leave-it Choice for Important Products or Services Raises Concerns When Consumers Have Few Alternatives

Several commenters addressed whether it is appropriate for a company to make a consumer's use of its product or service contingent upon the consumer's acceptance of the company's data practices. Two industry commenters suggested that "take-it-or-leave-it" or "walk away" choice is common in many business models, such as retail and software licensing, and companies have a right to limit their business to those who are willing to accept their policies.[236] Another commenter stated that preventing companies from offering takeit-

or-leave-it choice might be unconstitutional under the First Amendment.[237] Other commenters, however, characterized walk away choice as generally inappropriate.[238] Some argued that the privacy framework should prevent companies from denying consumers access to goods or services, including website content, where consumers choose to limit the collection or use of their data.[239]

Most of the commenters that addressed this issue took a position somewhere in between.[240] In determining whether take-it-or-leave-it choice is appropriate, these commenters focused on three main factors. First, they noted that there must be adequate competition, so that the consumer has alternative sources to obtain the product or service in question.[241] Second, they stated that the transaction must not involve an essential product or service.[242] Third, commenters stated that the company offering take-it-orleave-it choice must clearly and conspicuously disclose the terms of the transaction so that the consumer is able to understand the value exchange. For example, a company could clearly state that in exchange for receiving a service at "no cost," it collects certain information about your activity and sells it to third parties.[243] Expanding upon this point, commenters stressed that to ensure consumer understanding of the nature of the take-it-or-leave-it bargain, the disclosure must be prominent and not buried within a privacy policy.[244]

The Commission agrees that a "take it or leave it" approach is problematic from a privacy perspective, in markets for important services where consumers have few options.[245] For such products or services, businesses should not offer consumers a "take it or leave it" choice when collecting consumers' information in a manner inconsistent with the context of the interaction between the business and the consumer. Take, for example, the purchase of an important product that has few substitutes, such as a patented medical device. If a company offered a limited warranty for the device only in exchange for the consumer's agreeing to disclose his or her income, religion, and other highly-personal information, the consumer would not have been offered a meaningful choice and a take-it-or-leave approach would be inappropriate.

Another example is the provision of broadband Internet access. As consumers shift more aspects of their daily lives to the Internet – shopping, interacting through social media, accessing news, entertainment, and information, and obtaining government services – broadband has become a critical service for many American consumers. When consumers have few options for broadband service, the take-it-or-leave-it approach becomes one-sided in favor of the service provider. In these situations, the service provider should not condition the provision of broadband on the customer's agreeing to, for example, allow the service provider to track all of the customer's online activity for marketing purposes. Consumers' privacy interests ought not to be put at risk in such one-sided transactions.

With respect to less important products and services in markets with sufficient alternatives, take-it-orleave-it choice can be acceptable, provided that the terms of the exchange are transparent and fairly disclosed – *e.g.*, "we provide you with free content in exchange for collecting information about the websites you visit and using it to market products to you." Under the proper circumstances, such choice options may result in lower prices or other consumer benefits, as companies develop new and competing ways of monetizing their business models.

c. Businesses Should Provide a Do Not Track Mechanism to Give Consumers Control over the Collection of Their Web Surfing Data

Like the preliminary staff report, this report advocates the continued implementation of a universal, one-stop choice mechanism for online behavioral tracking, often referred to as Do Not Track. Such a mechanism should give consumers the ability to control the tracking of their online activities.

Many commenters discussed the progress made by industry in developing such a choice mechanism in response to the recommendations of the preliminary staff report and the 2009 OBA Report, and expressed support for these self-regulatory initiatives.[246] These initiatives include the work of the online advertising industry over the last two years to simplify disclosures and improve consumer choice mechanisms; efforts by the major browsers to offer new choice mechanisms; and a project of a technical standards body to standardize opt outs for online tracking.[247] A number of commenters, however, expressed concerns that existing mechanisms are still insufficient. Commenters raised questions about the effectiveness and comprehensiveness of existing mechanisms for exercising choice and the legal enforceability of such mechanisms.[248] Due to these concerns, some commenters advocated for legislation mandating a Do Not Track mechanism.[249]

The Commission commends recent industry efforts to improve consumer control over behavioral tracking and looks forward to final implementation. As industry explores technical options and implements self-regulatory programs, and Congress examines Do Not Track, the Commission continues to believe that in order to be effective, any Do Not Track system should include five key principles. First, a Do Not Track system should be implemented universally to cover all parties that would track consumers. Second, the choice mechanism should be easy to find, easy to understand, and easy to use. Third, any choices offered should be persistent and should not be overridden if, for example, consumers clear their cookies or update their browsers. Fourth, a Do Not Track system should be comprehensive, effective, and enforceable. It should opt consumers out of behavioral tracking through any means and not permit technical loopholes.[250] Finally, an effective Do Not Track system should go beyond simply opting consumers out of receiving targeted advertisements; it should opt them out of collection of behavioral data for all purposes other than those that would be consistent with the context of the interaction (*e.g.*, preventing click-fraud or collecting de-identified data for analytics purposes).[251]

Early on the companies that make web browsers stepped up to the challenge to give consumers choice about how they are tracked online, sometimes known as the "browser header" approach. The browser header is transmitted to all types of entities, including advertisers, analytics companies, and researchers, that track consumers online. Just after the FTC's call for Do Not Track, Microsoft developed a system to let users of Internet Explorer prevent tracking by different companies and sites.[252] Mozilla introduced a Do Not Track privacy control for its Firefox browser that an impressive number of consumers have adopted.[253]

Apple subsequently included a similar Do Not Track control in Safari.[254] Google has taken a slightly different approach – providing consumers with a tool that persistently opts them out of most behavioral advertising.[255]

In another important effort, the online advertising industry, led by the DAA, has implemented a behavioral advertising opt-out program. The DAA's accomplishments are notable: it has developed a notice and choice mechanism through a standard icon in ads and on publisher sites; deployed the icon broadly, with over 900 billion impressions served each month; obtained commitments to follow the self-regulatory principles from advertisers, ad networks, and publishers that represent close to 90 percent of the online behavioral advertising market; and established an enforcement mechanism designed to ensure compliance with the principles.[256] More recently, the DAA addressed one of the long-standing criticisms of its approach – how to limit secondary use of collected data so that the consumer opt out extends beyond simply blocking targeted ads to the collection of information for other purposes. The DAA has released new principles that include limitations on the collection of tracking data and prohibitions on the use or transfer of the data for employment, credit, insurance, or health care eligibility purposes.[257] Just as important, the DAA recently moved to address some persistence and usability criticisms of its icon-based opt out by committing to honor the tracking choices consumers make through their browser settings.[258]

At the same time, the W3C Internet standards-setting body has gathered a broad range of stakeholders to create an international, industry-wide standard for Do Not Track. The group includes a wide variety of stakeholders, including DAA members; other U.S. companies; international companies; industry groups; and public-interest groups. The W3C group has done admirable work to flesh out the details required to make a Do Not Track system practical in both desktop and mobile settings. The group has issued two public working drafts of its standards. Some important details remain to be filled in, and the Commission encourages all of the stakeholders to work within the W3C group to resolve these issues.

While more work remains to be done on Do Not Track, the Commission believes that the developments to date are significant and provide an effective path forward. The advertising industry, through the DAA, has committed to deploy browser-based technologies for consumer control over online tracking, alongside its ubiquitous icon program. The W3C process, thanks in part to the ongoing participation of DAA member companies, has made substantial progress toward specifying a consensus consumer choice system for tracking that is practical and technically feasible.[259] The Commission anticipates continued progress in this area as the DAA members and other key stakeholders continue discussions within the W3C process to work to reach consensus on a Do Not Track system in the coming months.

d. Large Platform Providers That Can Comprehensively Collect Data Across the Internet Present Special Concerns

As discussed above, even if a company has a first-party relationship with a consumer in one setting, this does not imply that the company can track the consumer for purposes inconsistent with the context of the interaction across the Internet, without providing choice. This principle applies fully to large platform providers such as ISPs, operating systems, and browsers, who have very broad access to a user's online activities.

For example, the preliminary staff report sought comment on the use of DPI for marketing purposes. Many commenters highlighted the comprehensive nature of DPI.[260] Because of the pervasive tracking that DPI allows, these commenters stated that its use for marketing should require consumers' affirmative express consent.[261] Privacy concerns led one commenter to urge the Commission to oppose DPI and hold workshops and hearings on the issue.[262] Another commenter argued that a lack of significant competition among broadband providers argues in favor of heightened requirements for consumer choice before ISPs can use DPI for marketing purposes.[263]

Two major ISPs emphasized that they do not use DPI for marketing purposes and would not do so without first seeking their customers' affirmative express consent.[264] They cautioned against singling out DPI as a practice that presents unique privacy concerns, arguing that doing so would unfairly favor certain technologies or business models at the expense of others. One commenter also stated that the framework should not favor companies that use other means of tracking consumers.[265] This commenter noted that various technologies – including cookies – allow companies to collect and use information in amounts similar to that made possible through DPI, and the framework's principles should apply consistently based on the type of information collected and how it is used.[266] Rather than isolating a specific technology, commenters urged the Commission to focus on the type of data collected and how it is used.[267]

ISPs serve as a major gateway to the Internet with access to vast amounts of unencrypted data that their customers send or receive over the ISP's network. ISPs are thus in a position to develop highly detailed and comprehensive profiles of their customers – and to do so in a manner that may be completely invisible. In addition, it may be difficult for some consumers to obtain alternative sources of broadband Internet access, and they may be inhibited from switching broadband providers for reasons such as inconvenience or expense. Accordingly, the Commission has strong concerns about the use of DPI for purposes inconsistent with an ISP's interaction with a consumer, without express affirmative consent or more robust protection.[268]

At the same time, the Commission agrees that any privacy framework should be technology neutral. ISPs are just one type of large platform provider that may have access to all or nearly all of a consumer's online activity. Like ISPs, operating systems and browsers may be in a position to track all, or virtually all, of a consumer's online activity to create highly detailed profiles.[269] Consumers, moreover, might have limited ability to block or control such tracking except by changing their operating system or browser.[270] Thus, comprehensive tracking by any such large platform provider may raise serious privacy concerns.

The Commission also recognizes that the use of cookies and social widgets to track consumers across unrelated websites may create similar privacy issues.[271] However, while companies such as Google and Facebook are expanding their reach rapidly, they currently are not so widespread that they could track a consumer 's every movement across the Internet.[272] Accordingly, although tracking by these entities warrants consumer choice, the Commission does not believe that such tracking currently raises the same level of privacy concerns as those entities that can comprehensively track all or virtually of a consumer's online activity.

These are complex and rapidly evolving areas, and more work should be done to learn about the practices of all large platform providers, their technical capabilities with respect to consumer data, and their current and expected uses of such data. Accordingly, Commission staff will host a workshop in the second half of 2012 to explore the privacy issues raised by the collection and use of consumer information by a broad range of large platform providers such as ISPs, operating systems, browsers, search engines, and social media platforms as well as how competition issues may bear on appropriate privacy protection.[273]

e. Practices Requiring Affirmative Express Consent

Numerous commenters focused on whether certain data collection and use practices warrant a heightened level of consent – *i.e.*, affirmative express consent.[274] These practices include (1) making material retroactive changes to a company's privacy representations; and (2) collection of sensitive data. These comments and the Commission's analysis are discussed here.

(i) Companies Should Obtain Affirmative Express Consent Before Making Material Retroactive Changes To Privacy Representations.

The preliminary staff report reaffirmed the Commission's bedrock principle that companies should provide prominent disclosures and obtain affirmative express consent before using data in a manner materially different than claimed at the time of collection.[275]

Although many commenters supported the affirmative express consent standard for material retroactive changes,[276] some companies called for an opt-out approach for material retroactive changes, particularly for changes that provide benefits to consumers.[277] One example cited was the development of Netflix's personalized video recommendation feature using information that Netflix originally collected in order to send consumers the videos they requested.[278] Other companies sought to scale the affirmative consent requirement according to the sensitivity of the data and whether the data is personally identifiable.[279] Many commenters sought clarification on when a change is material – for example, whether a change in data retention periods would be a material change requiring heightened consent.[280] One company posited that the affirmative express consent standard would encourage vague disclosures at the outset to avoid the requirement for obtaining such consent.[281]

The Commission reaffirms its commitment to requiring companies to give prominent disclosures and to obtain express affirmative consent for material retroactive changes. Indeed, the Commission recently confirmed this approach in its settlements with Google and Facebook. The settlement agreements mandate that the companies give their users clear and prominent notice and obtain affirmative express consent prior to making certain material retroactive changes to their privacy practices.[282]

In response to the request for clarification on what constitutes a material change, the Commission notes that, at a minimum, sharing consumer information with third parties after committing at the time of collection not to share the data would constitute a material change. There may be other circumstances in which a change would be material, which would have to be determined on a case-by-case basis, analyzing the context of the consumer's interaction with the business.

The Commission further notes that commenters' concerns that the affirmative express consent requirement would encourage vague disclosures at the outset should be addressed by other elements of the framework. For example, other elements of the framework call on companies to improve and standardize their privacy statements so that consumers can easily glean and compare information about various companies' data practices. The framework also calls on companies to give consumers specific information and choice at a time and in a context that is meaningful to consumers. These elements, taken together, are intended to result in disclosures that are specific enough to be meaningful to consumers.

The preliminary staff report posed a question about the appropriate level of consent for prospective changes to companies' data collection and use. One commenter cited the rollout of Twitter's new user interface – "new Twitter" – as a positive example of a set of prospective changes about which consumers received ample and adequate notice and ability to exercise choice.[283] When "new Twitter" was introduced, consumers were given the opportunity to switch to or try out the new interface, or to keep their traditional Twitter profile. The Commission supports innovative efforts such as these to provide consumers with meaningful choices when a company proposes to change its privacy practices on a prospective basis.

(ii) Companies Should Obtain Consumers' Affirmative Express Consent Before Collecting Sensitive Data.

A variety of commenters discussed how to delineate which types of data should be considered sensitive. These comments reflect a general consensus that information about children, financial and health information, Social Security numbers, and precise, individualized geolocation data is sensitive and merits heightened consent methods.[284] In addition, some commenters suggested that information related to race, religious beliefs, ethnicity, or sexual orientation, as well as biometric and genetic data, constitute sensitive data.[285] One commenter also characterized as sensitive information about consumers' online communications or reading and viewing habits.[286] Other commenters, however, noted the inherent subjectivity of the question and one raised concerns about the effects on market research if the definition of sensitive data is construed too broadly.[287]

Several commenters focused on the collection and use of information from teens, an audience that may be particularly vulnerable. A diverse coalition of consumer advocates and others supported heightened protections for teens between the ages of 13 and 17.[288] These commenters noted that while teens are heavy Internet users, they often fail to comprehend the long-term consequences of sharing their personal data. In order to better protect this audience, the commenters suggested, for example, limiting the amount of data that websites aimed at teens can collect or restricting the ability of teens to share their data widely through social media services. Conversely, a number of industry representatives and privacy advocates objected to the establishment of different rules for teens.[289] These commenters cited the practical difficulties of age verification and the potential that content providers will simply elect to bar teen audiences.[290] Rather than requiring different choice mechanisms for this group, one company encouraged the FTC to explore educational efforts to address issues that are unique to teens.[291] Given the general consensus regarding information about children, financial and health information, Social Security numbers, and precise geolocation data, the Commission agrees that these categories of information are sensitive. Accordingly, before collecting such data, companies should first obtain affirmative express consent from consumers. As explained above, the Commission also believes that companies should follow this practice irrespective of whether they use the sensitive data for first-party marketing or share it with third parties.[292]

The Commission is cognizant, however, that whether a particular piece of data is sensitive may lie in the "eye of the beholder" and may depend upon a number of subjective considerations. In order to minimize the potential of collecting any data – whether generally recognized as sensitive or not – in ways that consumers do not want, companies should implement *all* of the framework's components. In particular, a consumer's ability to access – and in appropriate cases to correct or delete – data will allow the consumer to protect herself when she believes the data is sensitive but others may disagree. With respect to whether information about teens is sensitive, despite the difficulties of age verification and other concerns cited in the comments, the Commission agrees that companies that target teens should consider additional protections. Although affirmative express consent may not be necessary in every advertising campaign directed to teens, other protections may be appropriate. For example, all companies should consider shorter retention periods for teens' data. In addition, the Commission believes that social networking sites should consider implementing more privacy-protective default settings for teens. While some teens may circumvent these protections, they can function as an effective "speed bump" for this audience and, at the same time, provide an opportunity to better educate teens about the consequences of sharing their personal information. The Commission also supports access and deletion rights for teens, as discussed below.[293]

> **Final Principle:** For practices requiring choice, companies should offer the choice at a time and in a context in which the consumer is making a decision about his or her data. Companies should obtain affirmative express consent before (1) using consumer data in a materially different manner than claimed when the data was collected; or (2) collecting sensitive data for certain purposes.

D. Transparency

> **Baseline Principle:** Companies should increase the transparency of their data practices.

Citing consumers' lack of awareness of how, and for what purposes, companies collect, use, and share data, the preliminary staff report called on companies to improve the transparency of their data practices. Commission staff outlined a number of measures to achieve this goal. One key proposal, discussed in the previous section, is to present choices to consumers in a prominent, relevant, and easily accessible place at a time and in a context when it matters to them. In addition, Commission staff called on industry to make privacy statements clearer, shorter, and more standardized; give consumers reasonable access to their data; and undertake consumer education efforts to improve consumers' understanding of how companies collect, use, and share their data. Commenters offered proposals for how to achieve greater transparency and sought clarification on how they should implement these elements of the framework. Although the Commission adopts the proposed framework's transparency principle without change, it clarifies the application of the framework in response to these comments, as discussed below.

1. Privacy Notices

> **Proposed Principle:** Privacy notices should be clearer, shorter, and more standardized to enable better comprehension and comparison of privacy practices.

The preliminary staff report highlighted the consensus among roundtable participants that most privacy policies are generally ineffective for informing consumers about a company's data practices because they are too long, are difficult to comprehend, and lack uniformity.[294] While acknowledging privacy policies' current deficiencies, many roundtable participants agreed that the policies still have value – they provide an important accountability function by educating consumer advocates, regulators, the media, and other interested parties about the companies' data practices.[295] Accordingly, Commission staff called on companies to provide clear and concise descriptions of their data collection and use practices. Staff further called on companies to standardize the format and the terminology used in privacy statements so that consumers can compare the data practices of different companies and exercise choices based on privacy concerns, thereby encouraging companies to compete on privacy.

Despite the consensus from the roundtables that privacy statements are not effective at communicating a company's data collection and use practices to consumers, one commenter disagreed that privacy notices need to be improved.[296] Another commenter pointed out that providing more granular information about data collection and use practices could actually increase consumer confusion by overloading the consumer with information.[297] Other industry commenters highlighted the work they have undertaken since the preliminary staff report to improve their own privacy statements.[298]

Many consumer groups supported staff's call to standardize the format and terminology used in privacy statements so that consumers could more easily compare the practices of different companies.[299] Some commenters suggested a "nutrition label" approach for standardizing the format of privacy policies and cited research underway in this area.[300] Another suggested the "form builder" approach used for GLBA Short Notices to standardize the format of privacy notices outside the financial context.[301] One consumer group called for standardization of specific terms like "affiliate" and "anonymize" so that companies' descriptions of their data practices are more meaningful.[302] A wide range of commenters suggested that different industry sectors come together to develop standard privacy notices.[303] Other commenters opposed the idea of mandated standardized notices, arguing that the Commission should require only that privacy statements be clear and in plain language. These commenters stated that privacy statements need to take into account differences among business models and industry sectors.[304]

Privacy statements should account for variations in business models across different industry sectors, and prescribing a rigid format for use across all sectors is not appropriate. Nevertheless, the Commission believes that privacy statements should contain some standardized elements, such as format and terminology, to allow consumers to compare the privacy practices of different companies and to encourage companies to compete on privacy. Accordingly, Commission calls on industry sectors to come together to develop standard formats and terminology for privacy statements applicable to their particular industries. The Department of Commerce will convene multi-stakeholder groups to work on privacy issues; this could be a useful venue in which industry sectors could begin the exercise of developing more standardized, streamlined privacy policies.

Machine-readable policies,[305] icons, and other alternative forms of providing notice also show promise as tools to give consumers the ability to compare privacy practices among different companies.[306] In response to the preliminary staff report's question on machine-readable policies, commenters agreed that such policies could improve transparency.[307] One commenter proposed combining the use of machine-readable policies with icons and standardized policy statements (*e.g.*, "we collect but do not share consumer data with third parties") to simplify privacy decision-making for consumers.[308] Other commenters described how icons work or might work in different business contexts. One browser company described efforts underway to develop icons that might be used to convey information, such as whether a consumer's data is sold or may be subject to secondary uses, in a variety of business contexts.[309] Representatives from online behavioral advertising industry groups also described their steps in developing and implementing an icon to communicate that online behavioral advertising may be taking place.[310]

Commenters also discussed the particular challenges associated with providing notice in the mobile context, noting the value of icons, summaries, FAQs, and videos.[311] Indeed, some work already has been done in this area to increase the transparency of data practices. For example, the advocacy organization Common Sense Media reviews and rates mobile apps based on a variety of factors including privacy[312] and a platform provider uses an icon to signal to consumers when a mobile application is using location information.[313] In addition, CTIA – a wireless industry trade group – in conjunction with the Entertainment Software Rating Board, recently announced plans to release a new rating system for mobile apps.[314] This rating system, which is based on the video game industry's model, will use icons to indicate whether specific apps are appropriate for "all ages," "teen," or only "adult" audiences. The icons will also detail whether the app shares consumers' personal information. Noting the complexity of the mobile ecosystem, which includes device manufacturers, operating system providers, mobile application developers, and wireless carriers, some commenters called for public workshops to bring together different stakeholders to develop a uniform approach to icons and other methods of providing notice.[315] Also, as noted above, the Mobile Marketing Association has released its Mobile Application Privacy Policy.[316]

The Commission appreciates the complexities of the mobile environment, given the multitude of different entities that want to collect and use consumer data and the small space available for disclosures on mobile screens. These factors increase the urgency for the companies providing mobile services to come together and develop standard notices, icons, and other means that the range of businesses can use to communicate with consumers in a consistent and clear way.

To address this issue, the Commission notes that it is currently engaged in a project to update its existing business guidance about online advertising disclosures.[317] In conjunction with this project, Commission staff will host a workshop later this year.[318] One of the topics to be addressed is mobile privacy disclosures: How can these disclosures be short, effective, and accessible to consumers on small screens? The Commission hopes that the discussions at the workshop will spur further industry self-regulation in this area.

> **Final Principle:** Privacy notices should be clearer, shorter, and more standardized to enable better comprehension and comparison of privacy practices.

2. Access

> **Proposed Principle:** Companies should provide reasonable access to the consumer data they maintain; the extent of access should be proportionate to the sensitivity of the data and the nature of its use.

There was broad agreement among a range of commenters that consumers should have some form of access to their data. Many of these commenters called for flexibility, however, and requested that access rights be tiered according to the sensitivity and intended use of the data at issue.[319] One commenter argued that access rights should be limited to sensitive data, such as financial account information, because a broader access right would be too costly for offline retailers.[320] Some companies and industry representatives supported providing consumers full access to data that is used to deny benefits; several commenters affirmed the significance of the FCRA in providing access to information used for critical decisionmaking. For other less sensitive data, such as marketing data, they supported giving consumers a general notice describing the types of data they collect and the ability to suppress use of the data for future marketing.[321]

One commenter raised concerns about granting access and correction rights to data files used to prevent fraudulent activity, noting that such rights would create risks of fraud and identity theft. This commenter also stated that companies would need to add sensitive identifying information to their marketing databases in order to authenticate a consumer's request for information, and that the integration of multiple databases would raise additional privacy and security risks.[322]

A number of commenters raised issues about the costs associated with providing access. One company suggested that access rights be flexible, taking into account the company's existing data infrastructure.[323] Others argued that access be granted only to consumer information that is "reasonably accessible in the course of business"[324] and one commenter said that companies should be able to charge for providing access where there are costs associated with retrieving and presenting data.[325]

Commenters also asserted that companies should tell consumers the entities with which their data has been shared.[326] Citing California's "Shine the Light" law, one commenter stated that companies should not only identify the third parties with which they share consumer data but should also disclose how the third parties use the data for marketing.[327] Another commenter pointed out that many marketers do not maintain records about data sold to other companies on an individual basis. Thus, marketers have the ability to identify the companies to which they have sold consumer data in general, but not the third parties with which they may have shared the information about any individual consumer.[328]

Some comments reflect support for requiring companies to identify for consumers the sources of data collected about them so that consumers can correct erroneous data at the source, if appropriate.[329] One commenter noted that the DMA self-regulatory guidelines currently require that a marketer identify the sources of data maintained about consumers.[330]

The Commission agrees with the commenters who stated that consumer access should be proportional to the sensitivity and the intended use of the data at issue. Indeed, the comments generally support treating access in accordance with three categories that reflect different levels of data sensitivity: (1) entities that maintain data for marketing purposes; (2) entities subject to the FCRA; and (3) entities that may maintain data for other, non-marketing purposes that fall outside of the FCRA.

At one side of the spectrum are companies that maintain data for marketing purposes. For data used solely for marketing purposes, the Commission agrees with the commenters who stated that the costs of providing individualized access and correction rights would likely outweigh the benefits. The Commission continues to support the idea of businesses providing consumers with access to a list of the categories of consumer data they hold, and the ability to suppress the use of such data for marketing. This approach will provide consumers with an important transparency tool without imposing significant new costs for businesses.[331]

The Commission does, however, encourage companies that maintain consumer data for marketing purposes to provide more individualized access when feasible. One example of an innovation in this area is the advertising preference managers that companies such as Google and Yahoo! have implemented. Yahoo!, for example, offers consumers, through its Ad Interest Manager, the ability to access the specific interest categories that Yahoo! associates with individual consumers and allows them to suppress marketing based on some or all of these categories. Using this service, an elementary school teacher who conducted online research for pet food during the time she owned a dog, but continues to receive advertisements for dog food, could remove herself from the "Consumer Packaged Goods > Pets and Animals > Food and Supplies" category while still opting to remain part of the "Life Stages > Education > K to 12" category.[332] The Commission supports efforts by companies to provide consumers with these types of granular choices to give them greater control over the marketing materials and solicitations they receive.

At the other end of the spectrum are companies that assemble and evaluate consumer information for use by creditors, employers, insurance companies, landlords, and other entities involved in eligibility decisions affecting consumers. The preliminary staff report cited the FCRA as an important tool that provides consumers with the right to access their own data that has been used to make such decisions, and if it is erroneous, to correct it. Several commenters echoed this view.[333]

The FCRA recognizes the sensitivity of the data that consumer reporting agencies maintain and the ways in which various entities use it to evaluate whether a consumer is able to participate in so many activities central to modern life; therefore, it provides consumers with access and correction rights for information contained in consumer reports. Pursuant to the FCRA, consumer reporting agencies are required to disclose to consumers, upon request, all items in the consumer's file, no matter how or where they are stored, as well as the entities with which the consumer reporting agency shared the information in a consumer's report. When consumers identify information in their report that is incomplete or inaccurate, and report it to a consumer reporting agency, the agency must investigate and correct or delete such information in certain circumstances.

As more and more consumer data becomes available from a variety of sources, companies are increasingly finding new opportunities to compile, package, and sell that information. In some instances, companies could be compiling and selling this data to those who are making decisions about a consumer's eligibility for credit, insurance, employment, and the like. To the extent companies are assembling data and marketing or selling it for such purposes, they are subject to the FCRA. For example, companies that compile social media information and provide it to employers for use in making hiring decisions are consumer reporting agencies and thus required to provide consumers with access and correction rights under the FCRA.[334] These companies would also be required to inform employers about their FCRA obligation to provide adverse action notices when, for example, employment is denied.

Even if a company is not compiling and sharing data for the specific purpose of making employment, credit, or insurance eligibility decisions, if the company has reason to believe the data will be used for such purposes, it would still be covered by the FCRA. For example, recently, the Commission issued warning letters to the developers of mobile apps that compiled public record information on individuals and created apps for the purposes of learning information about friends, co-workers, neighbors, or potential suitors.[335] The Commission noted that if these apps marketed their services for employment purposes or otherwise had reason to believe that they were being used for employment purposes, the FCRA requirements would apply.

Finally, some businesses may maintain and use consumer data for purposes that do not fall neatly within either the FCRA or marketing categories discussed above. These businesses may encompass a diverse range of industry sectors. They may include businesses selling fraud prevention or risk management services, in order to verify the identities of customers. They may also include general search engines, media publications, or social networking sites. They may include debt collectors trying to collect a debt. They may also include companies collecting data about how likely a consumer is to take his or her medication, for use by health care providers in developing treatment plans.[336]

For these entities, the Commission supports the sliding scale approach, which several commenters endorsed,[337] with the consumer's ability to access his or her own data scaled to the use and sensitivity of the data. At a minimum, these entities should offer consumers access to (1) the types of information the companies maintain about them;[338] and (2) the sources of such information.[339] The Commission believes that requiring companies to identify data sources would help consumers to correct erroneous information at the source. In appropriate circumstances the Commission urges companies to provide the names of the third parties with whom consumer information is shared.

In instances where data is more sensitive or may affect benefits, more individualized notice, access, and correction rights may be warranted. For example, if a company denies services to a consumer because it could not verify the consumer's identity, it may be appropriate for the company to disclose the name of the identity verification service used. This will allow the consumer to contact the data source, which can then provide the consumer with access to the underlying information, as well as any appropriate remedies, such as the ability to correct the information.[340] To ensure that the consumer knows that she has been denied a benefit based on her own data, as a best practice the company should notify the consumer of the denial and the information on which the denial was based.

Verifying the identity of users who seek access to their own information is an important consideration and should be approached from a risk management perspective, focusing on the likelihood of and potential harm from misidentification. Indeed, in the example of identity verification services described above, one would not want a criminal to be able to "correct" his or her own truthful data, and it would be appropriate to require somewhat more stringent safeguards and proof of identity before allowing access and correction. Certainly, consumer reporting agencies have developed procedures allowing them to verify the identity of requesting consumers using the multiple pieces of information they have about consumers to match information provided by the requesting consumer. Companies engaged in providing data for making eligibility determinations should develop best practices for authenticating consumers for access purposes.

On the other hand, the significantly reduced risks associated with providing the wrong person's information contained in a marketing database that contains no sensitive information may justify less stringent authentication procedures.[341] As with other issues discussed in this Report, reasonableness should be the touchstone: the degree of authentication employed should be tied to the sensitivity of the information maintained and how such information is used.

a. Special Access Mechanism for Data Brokers

Data brokers are companies that collect information, including personal information about consumers, from a wide variety of sources for the purpose of reselling such information to their customers for various purposes, including verifying an individual's identity, differentiating records, marketing products, and preventing financial fraud. Several commenters noted the lack of transparency about the practices of these entities, which often have a wealth of information about consumers but never interact directly with them.[342] Consumers are often unaware of the existence of these entities, as well as the purposes for which they collect and use data.[343] One commenter noted that data brokers may sell data to employers, background screeners, and law enforcement, among others, without the consumer's knowledge.[344] The Commission has monitored data brokers since the 1990s, hosting workshops, drafting reports, and testifying before Congress about the privacy implications of data brokers' practices.[345] Following a Commission workshop, the data broker industry created the Individual References Services Group (IRSG), a self-regulatory organization for certain data brokers.[346] Although industry ultimately terminated this organization, a series of public breaches – including one involving ChoicePoint – led to renewed scrutiny of the practices of data brokers.[347] And, indeed, there have been few broad-based efforts to implement self-regulation in this area in the recent past.

The access rights discussed above will help to improve the transparency of companies' data practices generally, whether or not they have a direct consumer interface. Because most data brokers are invisible to consumers, however, the Commission makes two additional recommendations as to these entities.

First, since 2009, the Commission has supported legislation giving access rights to consumers for information held by data brokers. During the 111th Congress, the House approved a bill that included provisions to establish a procedure for consumers to access information held by data brokers.[348] To improve the transparency of this industry's practices, the Commission has testified in support of the goals of this legislation[349] and continues to support legislation in this area.[350]

Second, the Commission recommends that the data broker industry explore the idea of creating a centralized website where data brokers that compile and sell data for marketing could identify themselves to consumers and describe how they collect consumer data and disclose the types of companies to which they sell the information. Additionally, data brokers could use the website to explain the access rights and other choices they offer consumers, and could offer links to their own sites where consumers could exercise such options.[351] This website will improve transparency and give consumers control over the data practices of companies that maintain and share data about them for marketing purposes. It can also provide consumer-facing entities such as retailers a means for ensuring that the information brokers from which they purchase "enhancement" information have instituted appropriate transparency and control mechanisms. Indeed, the consumer-facing entities could provide consumers with a link to the centralized mechanism, after having made sure that the data brokers from which they buy data participate in such a system. The Commission will discuss with relevant industry members how this mechanism could be developed and implemented voluntarily, in order to increase the transparency of their data practices and give consumers tools to opt out.[352]

b. Access to Teen Data

One commenter proposed that teens be given regular access to whether and how their data has been shared because of their particular vulnerability to ubiquitous marketing messages and heavy use of social media and mobile devices.[353] Others noted that teens in particular may not appreciate the persistence and future effects of data that they post about themselves online and thus need a "right to be forgotten." In its comment, the French Data Protection authority advocated the "right to be forgotten," which would allow consumers to withdraw data posted online about themselves at any point, for all users, but noted in particular the need to have control over information posted in one's youth.[354] In the United States, legislation has been introduced that would give teens an eraser button, which would allow them to erase certain material on social networking sites.[355]

The Commission generally supports exploration of the idea of an "eraser button," through which people can delete content that they post online. Many companies already offer this type of feature,[356] which is consistent with the principles of data access and suppression. Such an "eraser button" could be particularly useful for teens who might not appreciate the long-term consequences of their data sharing. Teens tend to be more impulsive than adults[357] and, as a result, may voluntarily disclose more information online than they should, leaving them vulnerable to identity theft or adversely affecting potential employment or college admissions opportunities. In supporting an eraser button concept, the Commission notes that such a feature would have to be carefully crafted in order to avoid implicating First Amendment concerns.[358] It would also need to be technically feasible and proportional to the nature, sensitivity, and amount of data collected.

Final Principle: Companies should provide reasonable access to the consumer data they maintain; the extent of access should be proportionate to the sensitivity of the data and the nature of its use.

3. Consumer Education

Proposed Principle: All stakeholders should expand their efforts to educate consumers about commercial data privacy practices.

In its preliminary report, FTC staff called for all stakeholders to accelerate their efforts to raise consumer awareness about data practices and to provide additional transparency tools to consumers. Staff pointed out that consumers need more education about the privacy implications of various data practices so that they can make informed decisions about the trade-offs involved. Staff posed questions about how the range of interested stakeholders – companies, industry associations, consumer groups, and government – can do a better job of informing consumers about privacy. Many commenters expressed general support for the notion that consumer education is a vital component of improving privacy protections for consumers.[359] One commenter suggested that businesses use their creative talents to make privacy more accessible for consumers, and as support, pointed to its own privacy game.[360] The game teaches players about privacy by inviting them to tour a virtual small town in which the buildings represent different parts of the commenter's privacy policy.

Over the last few years, a number of other companies and industry and consumer groups have stepped up their efforts to educate consumers about privacy and their privacy choices.[361]

The Commission encourages more such efforts, with an eye toward developing clear and accessible messages that consumers will see and understand.

A range of commenters suggested that the FTC explicitly endorse or sponsor various private sector-led consumer education efforts.[362] The Commission certainly supports private sector education efforts, and encourages private sector entities to freely use the FTC's extensive consumer and business education materials, under their own branding.

For example, the FTC encourages businesses to use information from its OnGuardOnline.gov website, which aims to help people be safe, secure and responsible online. The OnGuardOnline.gov campaign is a partnership of 15 federal agencies. The site includes articles, videos, games and tutorials to teach home users, small businesses or corporate employees about privacy-related topics like using Wi-Fi networks, peer-to-peer file sharing, mobile apps, and online tracking. The OnGuard Online Blog provides the latest cybersecurity news and practical tips from the FTC and other federal agencies. The FTC publishes this blog regularly and encourages companies to copy and disseminate it. Additionally, the FTC has continued its own consumer education efforts in the privacy area. Over the last year, the Commission released consumer education materials on a variety of topics including: using Wi-Fi hot spots; managing browser and "Flash" cookies; understanding mobile privacy; and protecting against child identity theft.[363]

> **Final Principle:** All stakeholders should expand their efforts to educate consumers about commercial data privacy practices.

CONCLUSION

The final privacy framework set forth in this Report reflects the extensive record developed through the Commission's privacy roundtables as well as the over 450 public comments received in response to the proposed framework issued in December of 2010. The FTC recommends that Congress consider baseline privacy legislation while industry implements the final privacy framework through individual company initiatives and through strong and enforceable self-regulatory initiatives. As discussed throughout the report, there are a number of specific areas where policy makers have a role in assisting with the implementation of the self-regulatory principles that make up the privacy framework. Areas where the FTC will be active over the course of the next year include the following.

- **Do Not Track:** As discussed above, industry has made significant progress in implementing Do Not Track. The browser vendors have developed tools that consumers can use to signal that they do not want to be tracked; the DAA has developed its own icon-based tool and has committed to honor the browser tools; and the W3C has made substantial progress in creating an international standard for Do Not Track. However, the work is not done. The Commission will work with these groups to complete implementation of an easy-to use, persistent, and effective Do Not Track system.
- **Mobile:** The Commission calls on companies providing mobile services to work toward improved privacy protections, including the development of short,

meaningful disclosures. To this end, FTC staff has initiated a project to update its business guidance about online advertising disclosures.[364] As part of this project, staff will host a workshop on May 30, 2012 and will address, among other issues, mobile privacy disclosures and how these disclosures can be short, effective, and accessible to consumers on small screens. The Commission hopes that the workshop will spur further industry self-regulation in this area.

- **Data Brokers:** To address the invisibility of, and consumers' lack of control over, data brokers' collection and use of consumer information, the Commission supports targeted legislation – similar to that contained in several of the data security bills introduced in the 112th Congress – that would provide consumers with access to information about them held by a data broker.[365] To further increase transparency, the Commission calls on data brokers that compile data for marketing purposes to explore creating a centralized website where data brokers could (1) identify themselves to consumers and describe how they collect and use consumer data and (2) detail the access rights and other choices they provide with respect to the consumer data they maintain.
- **Large Platform Providers:** To the extent that large platforms, such as Internet Service Providers, operating systems, browsers, and social media, seek to comprehensively track consumers' online activities, it raises heightened privacy concerns. To further explore privacy and other issues related to this type of comprehensive tracking, FTC staff intends to host a public workshop in the second half of 2012.
- **Promoting enforceable self-regulatory codes:** The Department of Commerce, with the support of key industry stakeholders, is undertaking a project to facilitate the development of sector-specific codes of conduct. FTC staff will participate in that project. To the extent that strong privacy codes are developed, the Commission will view adherence to such codes favorably in connection with its law enforcement work. The Commission will also continue to enforce the FTC Act to take action against companies that engage in unfair or deceptive practices, including the failure to abide by self-regulatory programs they join.

In all other areas, the Commission calls on individual companies, trade associations, and self-regulatory bodies to adopt the principles contained in the privacy framework, to the extent they have not already done so. For its part, the FTC will focus its policy efforts on the five areas identified above, vigorously enforce existing laws, work with industry on self-regulation, and continue to target its education efforts on building awareness of existing data collection and use practices and the tools to control them.

APPENDIX A. FTC PRIVACY MILESTONES

1970	Fair Credit Reporting Act enacted
1972	First Fair Credit Reporting Act (FCRA) case: In the Matter of Credit Bureau of Lorain
1975	FTC sues tax preparer for improperly using customers' information to market its loans: FTC v. Beneficial Corporation
1970s	FTC brings 15 additional enforcement actions against credit bureaus and report users
1983	First FCRA case against a nationwide credit bureau: FTC v. TransUnion

1985	FCRA sweep against users of consumer reports
1990	Commission staff issues comprehensive commentary on the FCRA
1991	FTC sues TRW for FCRA violations: FTC v. TRW
1992	FCRA sweep against employers using credit reports
1995	FTC sues Equifax for FCRA violations: In the Matter of Equifax Credit Information Services
1996	First major revision of the Fair Credit Reporting Act
	FTC sponsors workshop: Consumer Privacy on the Global Information Infrastructure
1997	First spam case: FTC v. Nia Cano
	FTC hosts traveling workshops to discuss revisions of FCRA
	FTC sponsors workshop: Consumer Information Privacy
	FTC issues Individual Reference Services: A Federal Trade Commission Report to Congress
1998	FTC issues Privacy Online: A Federal Trade Commission Report to Congress
1999	First case involving children's privacy: In the Matter of Liberty Financial
	First consumer privacy case: In the Matter of GeoCities
	FTC issues Self-Regulation and Privacy Online: A Federal Trade Commission Report to Congress
	FTC sponsors workshop: Online Profiling
	FTC launches ID Theft website: consumer.gov/idtheft and ID Theft Online Complaint Form
	FTC's 877-ID-THEFT consumer helpline established
2000	Children's Online Privacy Protection Rule (COPPA) goes into effect
	Gramm-Leach-Bliley Financial Privacy Rule goes into effect
	Three nationwide consumer reporting agencies pay $2.5 million in civil penalties for FCRA violations: US v. Equifax Credit Information Services, US v. TransUnion, and US v. Experian Information Solutions
	First COPPA case: FTC v. Toysmart.com
	FTC issues Online Profiling: A Federal Trade Commission Report to Congress
	FTC issues Privacy Online: Fair Information Practices in the Electronic Marketplace: A Federal Trade Commission Report to Congress
	FTC sponsors workshop: The Mobile Wireless Web, Data Services and Beyond: Emerging Technologies and Consumer Issues
	FTC publishes ID Theft booklet for victims: When Bad Things Happen to Your Good Name
2001	COPPA Safe Harbor Program begins
	First civil penalty cases under COPPA: US v. Looksmart, US v. Monarch Services, US v. Bigmailbox
	FTC sponsors workshops: The Information Marketplace: Merging and Exchanging Consumer Data; Gramm-Leach-Bliley Educational Program on Financial Privacy; and Get Noticed: Effective Financial Privacy Notices: An Interagency Workshop
	TCpublishes ID Theft Affidavit
2002	First data security case: In the Matter of Eli Lilly & Company
	FTC settles data security charges related to Microsoft's Passport service: In the Matter of Microsoft
	FTC sponsors workshop: Consumer Information Security Workshop
	FTC issues report on Public Workshop: The Mobile Wireless Web, Data Services and Beyond: Emerging Technologies and Consumer Issues
	FTC launches 10-minute educational ID Theft video
	FTC distributes over 1 million ID Theft booklets for victims

(Continued)

2003	Fair and Accurate Credit Transactions Act (FACTA) passed
	National Do Not Call Registry goes into effect
	Gramm-Leach-Bliley Safeguards Rule goes into effect
	FTC sues companies for sharing students' survey data with commercial marketers: In the Matter of Education Research Center of America and Student Marketing Group
	Guess settles FTC data security charges: In the Matter of Guess?
	FTC issues Technologies for Protecting Personal Information: A Staff Workshop Report
	FTC sponsors workshops: Technologies for Protecting Personal Information; Spam Forum; and Costs and Benefits Related To the Collection and Use of Consumer Information
2004	CAN-SPAM Rule goes into effect
	CAN-SPAM Adult Labeling Rule goes into effect
	Free Annual Credit Report Rule goes into effect
	First spyware case: FTC v. Seismic Entertainment
	FTC charges company with exposing consumers' purchases: In the Matter of MTS (dba Tower Records)
	FTC charges company with renting consumer information it had pledged to keep private: In the Matter of Gateway Learning FTC Privacy Milestones continued
	FTC issues The CAN-SPAM Act of 2003: National Do Not Email Registry: A Federal Trade Commission Report to Congress
	FTC sponsors workshops: Monitoring Software on Your PC: Spyware, Adware and Other Software; Radio Frequency IDentification: Applications and Implications for Consumers; and Peer-to-Peer File-Sharing Technology: Consumer Protection and Competition Issues
	FTC publishes The CAN-SPAM Act: A Compliance Guide for Business
2005	FACTA Disposal Rule goes into effect
	FACTA Pre-Screen Opt Out Rule goes into effect
	National Do Not Call Registry tops 100 million phone numbers
	First Do Not Call enforcement action: FTC v. National Consumer Council
	First Do Not Call civil penalty action: US v. Braglia Marketing
	Highest civil penalty in a Do Not Call case: US v. DirecTV ($5.3 million)
	First enforcement actions under Gramm-Leach-Bliley Safeguards Rule: In the Matter of Sunbelt Lending and In the Matter of Nationwide Mortgage Group
	First unfairness allegation in a data security case: In the Matter of BJ's Wholesale Club
	FTC issues RFID: Radio Frequency IDentification: Applications and Implications for Consumers: A Workshop Report From the Staff of the Federal Trade Commission
	FTC issues Spyware Workshop: Monitoring Software On Your Personal Computer: Spyware, Adware, and Other Software: Report of the Federal Trade Commission Staff
	FTC launches online safety website: OnGuardOnline.gov
2006	FACTA Rule Limiting Marketing Solicitations from Affiliates goes into effect
	Highest civil penalty in a consumer protection case: US v. ChoicePoint ($10 million civil penalty for violations of FCRA as well as $5 million redress for victims)
	First adware case: In the Matter of Zango
	Highest civil penalty to date in a COPPA case: US v. Xanga ($1 million)
	FTC settles charges against a payment processor that had experienced the largest breach of financial data to date: In the Matter of CardSystems Solutions
	FTC issues Peer-to-Peer File-Sharing Technology: Consumer Protection and Competition Issues: A Federal Trade Commission Staff Workshop Report
	FTC sponsors workshop: Protecting Consumers in the Next Tech-Ade

	FTC launches national educational campaign on identity theft and publishes Deter, Detect, Defend: Avoid ID Theft brochure
2007	First Disposal Rule case: US v. American United Mortgage Company
	Adult-oriented online social networking operation settles FTC charges; unwitting consumers pelted with sexually graphic pop-ups: FTC v. Various (dba AdultFriendFinder)
	FTC issues Spam Summit: The Next Generation of Threats and Solutions: A Staff Report by the Federal Trade Commission's Division of Marketing Practices
	FTC issues Implementing the Children's Online Privacy Protection Act: A Federal Trade Commission Report to Congress
	FTC co-chairs President's Identity Theft Task Force (with DOJ) and issues Strategic Plan
	FTC sponsors workshops: Security in Numbers: SSNs and ID Theft; Ehavioral Advertising: Tracking, Targeting, and Technology; and Spam Summit: The Next Generation of Threats and Solutions
	FTC publishes Protecting Personal Information: A Guide for Business and launches interactive tutorial
2008	Highest civil penalty in a CAN-SPAM case: US v. ValueClick ($2.9 million)
	FTC settles charges against data broker Lexis Nexis and retailer TJX related to the compromise of hundreds of thousands of consumers' information: In the Matter of Reed Elsevier and Seisent and In the Matter of TJX Companies
	FTC issues Protecting Consumers in the Next Tech-ade: A Report by the Staff of the Federal Trade Commission
	FTC issues Security In Numbers: Social Security Numbers and Identity Theft – A Federal Trade Commission Report Providing Recommendations On Social Security Number Use In the Private Sector
	President's Identity Theft Task Force Report released
	FTC sponsors workshops: Protecting Personal Information: Best Practices for Business (Chicago, Dallas, and Los Angeles); Pay on the Go: Consumers and Contactless Payment, Transatlantic RFID Workshop on Consumer Privacy and Data Security; and Beyond Voice: Mapping the Mobile Marketplace
	U.S. Postal Service sends FTC ID Theft prevention brochure to every household in the country
2009	Robocall Rule goes into effect
	Health Breach Notification Rule goes into effect
	First case alleging failure to protect employee information: In the Matter of CVS Caremark
	First cases alleging six companies violated the EU-US Safe Harbor Agreement: In the Matter of World Innovators, In the Matter of ExpatEdge Partners, In the Matter of Onyx Graphics, In the Matter of Directors Desk, In the Matter of Progressive Gaitways, and In the Matter of Collectify
	FTC issues Self-Regulatory Principles For Online Behavioral Advertising: Tracking, Targeting, and Technology
	FTC sponsors workshops: Exploring Privacy: A Roundtable Series; Protecting Personal Information: Best Practices for Business (New York); and Securing Personal Data in the Global Economy
	FTC publishes Net Cetera: Chatting with Kids About Being Online
2010	FTC jointly publishes Model Privacy Form under the Gramm-Leach-Bliley Act
	National Do Not Call Registry tops 200 million phone numbers
	First data security case involving social media: In the Matter of Twitter
	First case shutting down a rogue ISP: FTC v. Pricewert
	First data security case against an online seal provider: FTC v. ControlScan

(Continued)

	Highest judgment in a spyware case: FTC v. Innovative Marketing ($163 million)
	Largest FTC-state coordinated settlement on privacy: FTC v. Lifelock
	FTC conducts sweep against companies for exposure of employee and/or customer data on peerto-peer (P2P) file-sharing networks
	FTC releases Preliminary FTC Staff Report Protecting Consumer Privacy in an Era of Rapid Change: A Proposed Framework for Businesses and Policymakers
	FTC sponsors COPPA Rule Review Roundtable
	FTC publishes Peer-to-Peer File Sharing: A Guide for Businesses; Medical Identity Theft: How to Minimize Your Risk; and Copier Data Security: A Guide for Businesses
	FTC distributes 6+ million printed copies of Deter, Detect, Defend: Avoid ID Theft brochures and 5+million printed copies of Net Cetera: Chatting with Kids About Being Online
2011	FTC seeks comment on proposed changes to COPPA rule
	First case alleging substantive Safe Harbor violation and imposing privacy assessment program and audit requirements: In the Matter of Google
	First case against an online advertising network for offering deceptive privacy controls: In the Matter of Chitika
	First COPPA case against a mobile application developer: US v. W3 Innovations
	First case alleging unfairness based on default privacy settings: FTC v. Frostwire
	Largest FTC privacy case to date: In the Matter of Facebook
	FTC releases report 40 Years of Experience with the Fair Credit Reporting Act
	FTC co-hosts Stolen Futures: A Forum on Child ID Theft
	FTC hosts Face Facts: A Forum on Facial Recognition Workshop
	FTC publishes Tips for Using Public Wireless Networks
	FTC publishes Facts from the FTC: What You Should Know About Mobile Apps
	FTC publishes Online Safety for Teens and Tweens
2012	FTC releases report Using FACTA Remedies: An FTC Staff Report on a Survey of Identity Theft Victims
	FTC releases report Mobile Apps for Kids: Current Privacy Disclosures Are Disappointing
	FTC announces workshop: Paper, Plastic... or Mobile? An FTC Workshop on Mobile Payments
	FTC announces workshop to Explore Disclosures in Online and Mobile Media
	FTC publishes Blog Post: FCRA & Mobile Apps: A Word of Warning

Appendix B. Personal Data Ecosystem

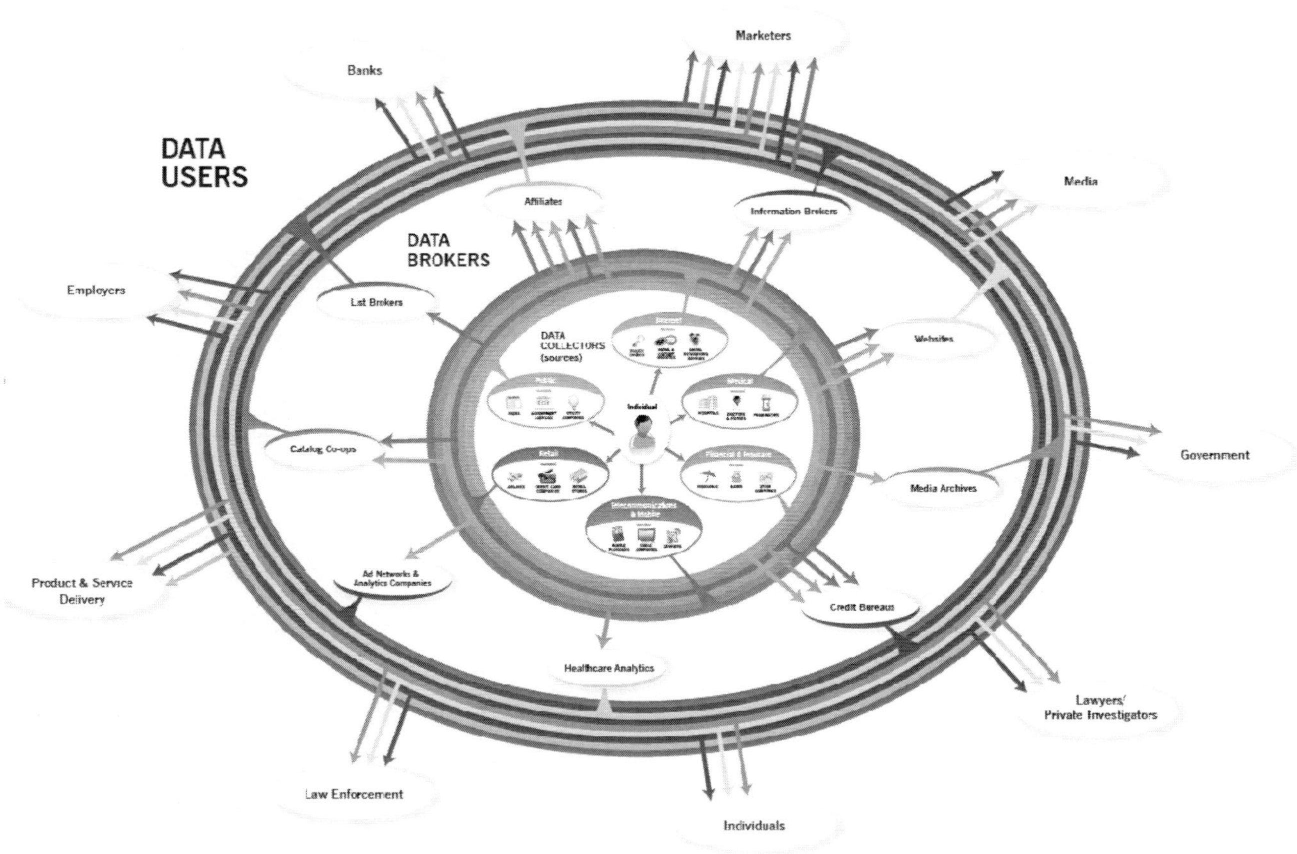

DATA USES:

Examples of uses of consumer information in personally identifiable or aggregated form:

- Financial services, such as for banking or investment accounts
- Credit granting, such as for credit or debit cards; mortgage, automobile or specialty loans; automobile rentals; or telephone services
- Insurance granting, such as for health, automobile or life
- Retail coupons and special offers
- Catalog and magazine solicitations
- Web and mobile services, including content, e-mail, search, and social networking
- Product and service delivery, such as streaming video, package delivery, or a cable signal
- Attorneys, such as for case investigations
- Journalism, such as for fact checking
- Marketing, whether electronically, through direct mail, or by telephone
- Data brokers for aggregation and resale to companies and/or consumers
- Background investigations by employers or landlords
- Locating missing or lost persons, beneficiaries, or witnesses
- Law enforcement
- Research (e.g., health, financial, and online search data) by academic institutions, government agencies, and commercial companies
- Fraud detection and prevention
- Government benefits and services, such as licensing

Appendix C. Dissenting Statement of Commissioner J. Thomas Rosch

Dissenting Statement of Commissioner J. Thomas Rosch
Protecting Consumer Privacy in an Era of Rapid Change: Recommendations for Businesses and Policymakers
March 26, 2012

Introduction

I agree in several respects with what the "final" Privacy Report says. Specifically, although I disagree that the consumer has traditionally ever been given any "choice" about information collection practices (other than to "take-it-or-leave-it" after reviewing a firm's privacy notice), I agree that consumers ought to be given a broader range of choices if for no other reason than to customize their privacy protection. However, I still worry about the constitutionality of banning take-it-or-leave-it choice (in circumstances where the consumer has few alternatives); as a practical matter, that prohibition may chill information collection, and thus impact innovation, regardless whether one's privacy policy is deceptive or not.[1]

I also applaud the Report's recommendation that Congress enact "targeted" legislation giving consumers "access" to correct misinformation about them held by a data broker.[2] I also support the Report's recommendation that Congress implement federal legislation that would require entities to maintain reasonable security and to notify consumers in the event of certain security breaches.[3]

Finally, I concur with the Report insofar as it recommends that information brokers who compile data for marketing purposes must disclose to consumers how they collect and use consumer data.[4] I have long felt that we had no business counseling Congress or other agencies about privacy concerns without that information. Although I have suggested that compulsory process be used to obtain such information (because I am convinced that is the only way to ensure that our information is complete and accurate),[5] a voluntary centralized website is arguably a step in the right direction.

Privacy Framework

My disagreement with the "final" Privacy Report is fourfold. First, the Report is rooted in its insistence that the "unfair" prong, rather than the "deceptive" prong, of the Commission's Section 5 consumer protection statute, should govern information gathering practices (including "tracking"). "Unfairness" is an elastic and elusive concept. What is "unfair" is in the eye of the beholder. For example, most consumer advocacy groups consider behavioral tracking to be unfair, whether or not the information being tracked is personally identifiable ("PII") and regardless of the circumstances under which an entity does the tracking. But, as I have said, consumer surveys are inconclusive, and individual consumers by and large do not "opt out" from tracking when given the chance to do so.[6] Not surprisingly, large enterprises in highly concentrated industries, which may be tempted to raise the privacy bar so high that it will disadvantage rivals, also support adopting more stringent privacy principles.[7]

The "final" Privacy Report (incorporating the preliminary staff report) repeatedly sides with consumer organizations and large enterprises. It proceeds on the premise that behavioral tracking is "unfair."[8] Thus, the Report expressly recommends that "reputational harm" be considered a type of harm that the Commission should redress.[9] The Report also expressly says that privacy be the default setting for commercial data practices.[10] Indeed, the Report says that the "traditional distinction between PII and nonPII has blurred,"[11] and it recommends "shifting the burdens away from consumers and placing obligations on businesses."[12] To the extent the Report seeks consistency with international privacy standards,[13] I would urge caution. We should always carefully consider whether each individual policy choice regarding privacy is appropriate for this country in all contexts.

That is not how the Commission itself has traditionally proceeded. To the contrary, the Commission represented in its 1980, and 1982, Statements to Congress that, absent deception, it will not generally enforce Section 5 against alleged intangible harm.[14] In other contexts, the Commission has tried, through its advocacy, to convince others that our policy judgments are sensible and ought to be adopted. And, as I stated in connection with the recent *Intel* complaint, in the competition context, one of the principal virtues of applying Section 5 was that that provision was "self-limiting," and I advocated that Section 5 be applied on a stand-alone basis only to a firm with monopoly or near-monopoly power.[15] Indeed, as I have remarked, absent such a limiting principle, privacy may be used as a weapon by firms having monopoly or near-monopoly power.[16]

There does not appear to be any such limiting principle applicable to many of the recommendations of the Report. If implemented as written, many of the Report's recommendations would instead apply to almost all firms and to most information collection practices. It would install "Big Brother" as the watchdog over these practices not only in the online world but in the offline world.[17] That is not only paternalistic, but it goes well beyond what the Commission said in the early 1980s that it would do, and well beyond what Congress has permitted the Commission to do under Section 5(n).[18] I would instead stand by what we have said and challenge information collection practices, including behavioral tracking, only when these practices are deceptive, "unfair" within the strictures of Section 5(n) and our commitments to Congress, or employed by a firm with market power and therefore challengeable on a stand-alone basis under Section 5's prohibition of unfair methods of competition.

Second, the current self-regulation and browser mechanisms for implementing Do Not Track solutions may have advanced since the issuance of the preliminary staff Report.[19] But, as the final Report concedes, they are far from perfect,[20] and they may never be, despite efforts to create a standard through the World Wide Web Consortium ("W3C") for the browser mechanism.[21]

More specifically, as I have said before, the major browser firms' interest in developing Do Not Track mechanisms begs the question of whether and to what extent those major browser firms will act strategically and opportunistically (to use privacy to protect their own entrenched interests).[22]

In addition, the recent announcement by the Digital Advertising Alliance (DAA) that it will honor the tracking choices consumers make through their browsers raises more questions than answers for me. The Report is not clear, and I am concerned, about the extent to which this latest initiative will displace the standard-setting effort that has recently been undertaken by the W3C. Furthermore, it is not clear that all the interested players in the Do Not Track arena – whether it be the DAA, the browser firms, the W3C, or consumer advocacy groups – will be able to come to agreement about what "Do Not Track" even means.[23] It may be that the firms professing an interest in self-regulation are really talking about a "Do Not Target" mechanism, which would only prevent a firm from serving targeted ads, rather than a "Do Not Track" mechanism, which would prevent the collection of consumer data altogether. For example, the DAA's Self-Regulatory Principles for Multi-Site Data do not apply to data collected for "market research" or "product development."[24] For their part, the major consumer advocacy groups may not be interested in a true "Do Not Track" mechanism either. They may only be interested in a mechanism that prevents data brokers from compiling consumer profiles instead of a comprehensive solution. It is hard to see how the W3C can adopt a standard unless and until there is an agreement about what the standard is supposed to prevent.[25]

It is also not clear whether or to what extent the lessons of the Carnegie Mellon Study respecting the lack of consumer understanding of how to access and use Do Not Track will be heeded.[26] Similarly, it is not clear whether and to what extent Commissioner Brill's concern that consumers' choices, whether it be "Do Not Collect" or merely "Do Not Target," will be honored.[27]

Along the same lines, it is also not clear whether and to what extent a "partial" Do Not Track solution (offering nuanced choice) will be offered or whether it is "all or nothing." Indeed, it is not clear whether consumers can or will be given complete and accurate information about the pros and the cons of subscribing to Do Not Track before they choose it. I find this last question especially vexing in light of a recent study that indicated 84% of users polled prefer targeted advertising in exchange for free online content.[28]

Third, I am concerned that "opt-in" will necessarily be selected as the *de facto* method of consumer choice for a wide swath of entities that have a first-party relationship with consumers but who can potentially track consumers' activities across unrelated websites, under circumstances where it is unlikely, because of the "context" (which is undefined) for such tracking to be "consistent" (which is undefined) with that first-party relationship:[29] 1) companies with multiple lines of business that allow data collection in different contexts (such as Google);[30] 2) "social networks," (such as Facebook and Twitter), which could potentially use "cookies," "plug-ins," applications, or other mechanisms to track a consumer's activities across the Internet;[31] and 3) "retargeters," (such as Amazon or Pacers), which include a retailer who delivers an ad on a third-party website based on the consumer's previous activity on the retailer's website.[32]

These entities might have to give consumers "opt-in" choice now or in the future: 1) regardless whether the entity's privacy policy and notices adequately describe the information collection practices at issue; 2) regardless of the sensitivity of the information being collected; 3) regardless whether the consumer cares whether "tracking" is actually occurring; 4) regardless of the entity's market position (whether the entity can use privacy strategically – *i.e.*, an opt-in requirement – in order to cripple or eliminate a rival); and 5) conversely, regardless whether the entity can compete effectively or innovate, as a practical matter, if it must offer "opt in" choice.[33]

Fourth, I question the Report's apparent mandate that ISPs, with respect to uses of deep packet inspection, be required to use opt-in choice.[34] This is not to say there is no basis for requiring ISPs to use opt-in choice without requiring opt-in choice for other large platform providers. But that kind of "discrimination" cannot be justified, as the Report says, because ISPs have "are in a position to develop highly detailed and comprehensive profiles of their customers."[35] So does any large platform provider who makes available a browser or operating system to consumers.[36]

Nor can that "discrimination" be justified on the ground that ISPs may potentially use that data to "track" customer behavior in a fashion that is contrary to consumer expectations. There is no reliable data establishing that most ISPs presently do so. Indeed, with a business model based on subscription revenue, ISPs arguably lack the same incentives as do other platform providers whose business model is based on attracting advertising and advertising revenue: ISPs assert that they track data only to perform operational and security functions; whereas other platform providers that have business models based on advertising revenue track data in order to maximize their advertising revenue.

What really distinguishes ISPs from most other "large platform providers" is that their markets can be highly concentrated.[37] Moreover, even when an ISP operates in a less concentrated market, switching costs can be, or can be perceived as being, high.[38] As I said in connection with the *Intel* complaint, a monopolist or near monopolist may have obligations which others do not have.[39]

The only similarly situated platform provider may be Google, which, because of its alleged monopoly power in the search advertising market, has similar power. For any of these "large platform providers," however, affirmative express consent should be required only when the provider *actually* wants to use the data in this fashion, not just when it *has the potential* to do so.[40]

Conclusion

Although the Chairman testified recently before the House Appropriations Subcommittee chaired by Congresswoman Emerson that the recommendations of the final Report are supposed to be nothing more than "best practices,"[41] I am concerned that the language of the Report indicates otherwise, and broadly hints at the prospect of enforcement.[42] The Report also acknowledges that it is intended to serve as a template for legislative recommendations.[43] Moreover, to the extent that the Report's "best practices" mirror the Administration's privacy "Bill of Rights," the President has specifically asked either that the "Bill of Rights" be adopted by the Congress or that they be distilled into "enforceable codes of conduct."[44]

As I testified before the same subcommittee, this is a "tautology;" either these practices are to be adopted voluntarily by the firms involved or else there is a federal requirement that they be adopted, in which case there can be no pretense that they are "voluntary."[45] It makes no difference whether the federal requirement is in the form of enforceable codes of conduct or in the form of an act of Congress.

Indeed, it is arguable that neither is needed if these firms feel obliged to comply with the "best practices" or face the wrath of "the Commission" or its staff.

End Notes

[1] FTC, Protecting Consumer Privacy in an Era of Rapid Change, A Proposed Framework for Businesses and Policymakers, Preliminary FTC Staff Report (Dec. 2010), available at http://www.ftc.gov/os/2010/12/101201privacyreport.pdf.

[2] Privacy by Design is an approach that Ann Cavoukian, Ph.D., Information and Privacy Commissioner, Ontario, Canada, has advocated. See Information and Privacy Commissioner, Ontario, Canada, Privacy by Design, http://privacybydesign.ca/.

[3] The first roundtable took place on December 7, 2009, the second roundtable on January 28, 2010, and the third roundtable on March 17, 2010. See FTC, Exploring Privacy – A Roundtable Series, http://www.ftc.gov/bcp/workshops/privacyroundtables/index.shtml.

[4] See, e.g., 1st Roundtable, Remarks of Fred Cate, Indiana University Maurer School of Law, at 280-81; 1st Roundtable, Remarks of Lorrie Cranor, Carnegie Mellon University, at 129; see also Written Comment of Fred Cate, 2nd Roundtable, Consumer Protection in the Age of the 'Information Economy,' cmt. #544506-00057, at 343-79.

[5] See, e.g., 1st Roundtable, Remarks of Marc Rotenberg, Electronic Privacy Information Center, at 301; 1st Roundtable, Remarks of Leslie Harris, Center for Democracy & Technology, at 36-38; 1st Roundtable, Remarks of Susan Grant, Consumer Federation of America, at 38-39.

[6] See, e.g., 3rd Roundtable, Remarks of Kathryn Montgomery, American University School of Communication, at 200-01; 2nd Roundtable, Remarks of Kevin Bankston, Electronic Frontier Foundation, at 277.

[7] See Press Release, Department of Commerce, Commerce Secretary Gary Locke Discusses Privacy and Innovation with Leading Internet Stakeholders (May 7, 2010), available at http://www.commerce.gov/news/press-releases/2010/05/07/ commerce-secretary-gary-locke-discusses-privacy-and-innovation-leadin.

[8] See Department of Commerce Internet Policy Task Force, Commercial Data Privacy and Innovation in the Internet Economy: A Dynamic Policy Framework (Dec. 16, 2010), available at http://www.ntia.doc.gov/files/ntia/publications/iptf_privacy_ greenpaper_ 12162010.pdf.

[9] White House, Consumer Data Privacy in a Networked World: A Framework for Protecting Privacy and Promoting Innovation in the Global Digital Economy (Feb. 2012), available at http://www.whitehouse.gov/sites/default/files/privacy-final.pdf. The FIPPs as articulated in the Administration paper are: Transparency, Individual Control, Respect for Context, Security, Access, Accuracy, Focused Collection, and Accountability.

[10] See National Telecommunications and Information Administration, Request for Public Comment, Multistakeholder Process to Develop Consumer Data Privacy Codes of Conduct, 77 Fed. Reg. 13098 (Mar. 5, 2012).

[11] See Do-Not-Track Online Act of 2011, S. 913, 112th Congress (2011); Do Not Track Me Online Act, H.R. 654, 112th Congress (2011).

[12] See Press Release, Microsoft, Providing Windows Customers with More Choice and Control of Their Privacy Online with Internet Explorer 9 (Dec. 7, 2010), available at http://www.microsoft.com/presspass/features/2010/dec10/12-07ie9privacyqa. mspx; Mozilla Firefox 4 Beta, Now Including "Do Not Track" Capabilities, MOzIIIA BIOG (Feb. 8, 2011), http://blog.mozilla. com/blog/2011/02/08/mozilla-firefox-4-beta-now-including-do-not-track-capabilities/; Nick Wingfield, Apple Adds Do-NotTrack Tool to New Browser, WAII ST. J., Apr. 13, 2011, available at http://online.wsj.com/article/ SB1000142405274870355 1304576261272308358858.html. Google recently announced that it will also offer this capability in the next version of its browser. Gregg Kaizer, FAQ: What Google's Do Not Track Move Means, COMPUTERWORID (Feb. 24, 2012), available at http:// www.computerworld.com/s/article/9224583/ FAQ_What_Google_s_ Do_Not_Track_move_means.

[13] See Mozilla, Do Not Track FAQs, http://dnt.mozilla.org.

[14] See Press Release, Interactive Advertising Bureau, Major Marketing/Media Trade Groups Launch Program to Give Consumers Enhanced Control Over Collection and Use of Web Viewing Data for Online Behavioral Advertising (Oct. 4, 2010), available at http://www.iab.net/about_the_iab/recent_press_releases/press_ release_archive/press_release/pr-100410.

[15] The W3C is an international standard-setting body that works "to lead the World Wide Web to its full potential by developing protocols and guidelines that ensure the long-term growth of the Web." See W3C Mission, http://www.w3.org/ Consortium/mission.html.

[16] See Commercial Privacy Bill of Rights Act of 2011, S. 799, 112th Congress (2011); Building Effective Strategies To Promote Responsibility Accountability Choice Transparency Innovation Consumer Expectations and

Safeguards Act, H.R. 611, 112th Congress (2011); Consumer Privacy Protection Act of 2011, H.R. 1528, 112th Congress (2011).

[17] Children's Online Privacy Protection Act of 1998, 15 U.S.C. §§ 6501-6506.

[18] See Do Not Track Kids Act of 2011, H.R. 1895, 112th Congress (2011). In September 2011, the Commission issued a Notice of Proposed Rulemaking, proposing changes to the COPPA Rule to address changes in technology. See FTC Children's Online Privacy Protection Rule, 76 Fed. Reg. 59804 (proposed Sep. 27, 2011), available at http://www.ftc.gov/ os/2011/09/110915coppa.pdf.

[19] See Personal Data Privacy and Security Act of 2011, S. 1151, 112th Congress (2011); Data Security and Breach Notification Act of 2011, S. 1207, 112th Congress (2011); Data Breach Notification Act of 2011, S.1408, 112th Congress (2011); Data Security Act of 2011, S.1434, 112th Congress (2011); Personal Data Protection and Breach Accountability Act of 2011, S. 1535, 112th Congress (2011); Data Accountability and Trust Act, H.R. 1707, 112th Congress (2011); Data Accountability and Trust Act of 2011, H.R. 1841, 112th Congress (2011); Secure and Fortify Electronic Data Act, H.R. 2577, 112th Congress (2011).

[20] See In the Matter of Upromise, Inc., FTC File No. 102 3116 (Jan. 18, 2012) (proposed consent order), available at http://www. ftc.gov/os/caselist/1023116/index.shtm; In the Matter of ACRAnet, Inc., FTC Docket No. C-4331 (Aug. 17, 2011) (consent order), available at http://www.ftc.gov/os/caselist/0923088/index.shtm; In the Matter of SettlementOne Credit Corp., FTC Docket No. C-4330 (Aug. 17, 2011) (consent order), available at http://www.ftc.gov/os/caselist/0823208/index.shtm; In the Matter of Ceridian Corp., FTC Docket No. C-4325 (June 8, 2011) (consent order), available at http://www.ftc.gov/os/ caselist/1023160/index.shtm; In the Matter of Lookout Servs., Inc., FTC Docket No. C-4326 (June 15, 2011) (consent order), available at http://www.ftc.gov/os/ caselist/1023076/index.shtm; In the Matter of Twitter, Inc., FTC Docket No. C-4316 (Mar. 2, 2011) (consent order), available at http://www.ftc.gov/os/caselist/0923093/index.shtm; In the Matter of Fajilan & Assocs., Inc., FTC Docket No. C-4332 (Aug. 17, 2011) (consent order), available at http://www.ftc.gov/os/caselist/0923089/index. shtm.

[21] See In the Matter of Google, Inc., FTC Docket No. C-4336 (Oct. 13, 2011) (consent order), available at http://www.ftc.gov/ os/caselist/1023136/index.shtm (requiring company to implement privacy program subject to independent third-party audit); In the Matter of Facebook, Inc., FTC File No. 092 3184 (Nov. 29, 2011) (proposed consent order), available at http://www. ftc.gov/os/caselist/0923184/index.shtm (requiring company to implement privacy program subject to independent third-party audit); In the Matter of Chitika, Inc., FTC Docket No. C-4324 (June 7, 2011) (consent order), available at http:// www.ftc.gov/os/caselist/1023087/index.shtm (requiring company's behavioral advertising opt out to last for five years); In the Matter of ScanScout, Inc., FTC Docket No. C-4344 (Dec. 14, 2011) (consent order), available at http://www.ftc.gov/os/ caselist/1023185/index.shtm (requiring company to improve disclosure of its data collection practices and offer consumers a user-friendly opt out mechanism).

[22] Fair Credit Reporting Act, 15 U.S.C. § 1681 et seq.; COPPA Rule, 16 C.F.R. Part 312; see also, e.g., United States v. W3 Innovations, LLC, No. CV-11-03958 (N.D. Cal. Sept. 8, 2011) (COPPA consent decree); United States v. Teletrack, Inc., No. 1 11-CV-2060 (N.D. Ga. filed June 24, 2011) (FCRA consent decree); United States v. Playdom, Inc., No. SACV-11-00724- AG (ANx) (C.D. Cal. May 24, 2011) (COPPA consent decree).

[23] See Press Release, FTC Extends Deadline for Comments on Proposed Amendments to the Children's Online Privacy Protection Rule Until December 23 (Nov. 18, 2011), available at http://www.ftc.gov/opa/2011/11/ coppa.shtm.

[24] See FCC Workshop, Helping Consumers Harness the Potential of Location-Based Services (June 28, 2011), available at http:// www.fcc.gov/events/location-based-services-forum.

[25] See The Office of the National Coordinator for Health Information Technology, Personal Health Record (PHR) Model Privacy Notice, http://healthit.hhs.gov/portal/server.pt/ community/healthit_hhs_gov__draft_phr_ model_notice/1176.

[26] See HHS Workshop, Mobile Devices Roundtable: Safeguarding Health Information, available at http://healthit.hhs.gov/portal/ server.pt/community/healthit_hhs_gov__ mobile_devices_ roundtable/3815.

[27] See Advanced Sign-In Security For Your Google Account, GOOGlE OFFIcIAl BlOG (Feb. 10, 2011, 11:30 AM), http:// googleblog.blogspot.com/2011/02/advanced-sign-in-security-for-your.html#!/2011/02/advanced-sign-in-security-for-your. html; Andrew Song, Introducing Login Approvals, FAcEBOOK BlOG (May 12, 2011, 9:58 AM), http://www.facebook.com/ note.php?note_id=10150172618258920.

[28] See HTTPS Everywhere, ElEcTRONIc FRONTIER FOUNDATION, https://www.eff.org/ https-everywhere.

[29] See Press Release, Mobile Marketing Association, Mobile Marketing Association Releases Final Privacy Policy Guidelines for Mobile Apps (Jan. 25, 2012), available at http://mmaglobal.com/news/mobile-marketing-association -releases-final-privacypolicy-guidelines-mobile-apps.

[30] See Comment of TRUSTe, cmt. #00450, at 3; Comment of Berlin Commissioner for Data Protection & Freedom of Information, cmt. #00484, at 1.

[31] See Comment of Patient Privacy Rights, cmt. #00470, at 2.

[32] See Comment of Technology Policy Institute, cmt. #00301, at 5-8; Comment of Experian, cmt. #00398, at 9-11; Comment of Global Privacy Alliance, cmt. #00367, at 6-7.

[33] See Comment of Facebook, Inc., cmt. #00413, at 1-2, 7-8; Comment of Google, Inc., cmt. #00417, at 4; Comment of Global Privacy Alliance, cmt. #00367, at 16.

[34] One former FTC Chairman, in analyzing a spyware case, emphasized that consumers should have control over what is on their computers. Chairman Majoras issued the following statement in connection with the Commission's settlement against Sony BMG resolving claims about the company's installation of invasive tracking software: "Consumers' computers belong to them, and companies must adequately disclose unexpected limitations on the customary use of their products so consumers can make informed decisions regarding whether to purchase and install that content." Press Release, FTC, Sony BMG Settles FTC Charges (Jan. 30, 2007), available at http://www.ftc.gov/opa/ 2007/01/sony.shtm; see also Walt Mossberg, Despite Others' Claims, Tracking Cookies Fit My Spyware Definition, ALLTHINGSD (July 14, 2005, 12:01 AM), http://allthingsd. com/20050714/tracking-cookies/ ("Suppose you bought a TV set that included a component to track what you watched, and then reported that data back to a company that used or sold it for advertising purposes. Only nobody told you the tracking technology was there or asked your permission to use it. You would likely be outraged at this violation of privacy. Yet that kind of Big Brother intrusion goes on everyday on the Internet . . . [with tracking cookies].").

[35] See In re Google Inc., FTC Docket No. C-4336 (Oct. 13, 2011) (consent order), available at http://www.ftc.gov/os/caselist/10 23136/110330googlebuzzcompt.pdf.

[36] See In re Facebook, Inc., FTC File No. 092 3184 (Nov. 29, 2011) (proposed consent order), available at http://www.ftc.gov/os/ caselist/0923184/111129facebookagree.pdf.

[37] Although the complaint against Google alleged that the company used deceptive tactics and violated its own privacy promises when it launched Google Buzz, even in the absence of such misrepresentations, revealing previously-private consumer data could cause consumer harm. See Press Release, FTC, FTC Charges Deceptive Privacy Practices in Google's Rollout of its Buzz Social Network (Mar. 30, 2011), available at http://www.ftc.gov/opa/2011/03/google.shtm (noting that in response to the Buzz launch, Google received thousands of complaints from consumers who were concerned about public disclosure of their email contacts which included, in some cases, ex-spouses, patients, students, employers, or competitors).

[38] See, e.g., Statement of John M. Montgomery, GroupM Interaction, The State of Online Consumer Privacy: Hearing Before the S. Comm. on Commerce, Sci., and Transp., 112th Cong. (Mar. 16, 2011), available at http://www.iab.net/media/file/ DC1DOCS1-432016-v1-John_Montgomery_-_Written_Testimony.pdf ("We at GroupM strongly believe in protecting consumer privacy. It is not only the right thing to do, but it is also good for business."); Statement of Alan Davidson, Director of Public Policy, Google Inc., Protecting Mobile Privacy: Your Smartphones, Tablets, Cell Phones and Your Privacy: Hearing Before the S. Subcomm. on Privacy, Tech., and the Law, 112th Cong. (May 10, 2011), available at http://www. judiciary.senate.gov/pdf/11-5-10%20Davidson%20Testimony.pdf ("Protecting privacy and security is essential for Internet commerce.").

[39] See RESEARCH: Consumers Feel Better About Brands That Give Them Transparency and Control Over Ads, EVIDON BlOG (Nov. 10, 2010), http://blog.evidon.com/tag/better-advertising ("when advertisers empower consumers with information and control over the ads they receive, a majority feels more positive toward those brands, and 36% even become more likely to purchase from those brands").

[40] See Comment of Google Inc., cmt. #00417, at 4.

[41] See Comment of Intuit, Inc., cmt. #00348, at 6-8 ("The more transparent (meaning open, simple and clear) the company is, the more customer trust increases. . . .").

[42] See DuckDuckGo, Privacy Policy, https://duckduckgo.com/privacy.html.

[43] See Frank X. Shaw, Gone Google? Got Concerns? We Have Alternatives, THE OFFIcIAl MIcROSOFT BlOG (Feb. 1, 2012, 2:00 AM), http://blogs.technet.com/b/microsoft_blog/ archive/2012/02/01/gone-google-got-concerns-we-have-alternatives.aspx.

[44] See infra at Section IV.C.1.a.

[45] See Comment of AT&T Inc., cmt. #00420, at 12-13; Comment of IBM, cmt. #00433, at 2; see also Comment of General Electric, cmt. #00392, at 3 (encouraging international harmonization).

[46] White House, Consumer Data Privacy in a Networked World: A Framework for Protecting Privacy and Promoting Innovation in the Global Digital Economy, ii, Foreword (Feb. 2012), available at http://www.whitehouse.gov/sites/default/files/privacy-final. pdf.

[47] The nine principles in the APEC Privacy Framework are preventing harm, notice, collection limitations, uses of personal information, choice, integrity of personal information, security safeguards, access and correction, accountability. Businesses have developed a code of conduct based on these nine principles and will obtain third-party certification of their compliance. A network of privacy enforcement authorities from participating APEC economies, such as the FTC, will be able to take enforcement actions against companies that violate their commitments under the code of conduct. See Press Release, FTC, FTC Welcomes a New Privacy System for the Movement of Consumer Data Between the United States and Other Economies in the Asia-Pacific Region (Nov. 14, 2011), available at http://www.ftc.gov/opa/2011/11/apec.shtm).

[48] See Organization for Economic Co-operation and Development, The Evolving Privacy Landscape: 30 Years after the OECD Privacy Guidelines (Apr. 2011), available at http://www.oecd.org/dataoecd/22/25/47683378.pdf.

[49] European Commission, Proposal for a REGULATION OF THE EUROPEAN PARLIAMENT AND OF THE COUNCIL on the protection of individuals with regard to the processing of personal data and on the free movement of such data (General Data Protection Regulation) (Jan. 25, 2012), available at http://ec.europa.eu/justice/data-protection/document/ review2012/ com_2012_11_en.pdf.

[50] See, e.g., Comment of eBay, cmt. #00374, at 2; Comment of Intel Corp., cmt. #00246, at 3-7; Comment of Microsoft Corp., cmt. #00395, at 4; Comment of Intuit, Inc., cmt. #00348, at 13-14; Comment of Center for Democracy & Technology, cmt. #00469, at 1, 7; Comment of Gregory Byrd, cmt. #00144, at 1; Comment of Ellen Klinefelter, cmt. #00095, at 1.

[51] See Comment of Microsoft Corp., cmt. #00395, at 4.

[52] See Comment of Intel Corp., cmt. #00246, at 3.

[53] See Comment of Intuit, Inc., cmt. #00348, at 13.

[54] See Comment of Electronic Privacy Information Center, cmt. #00386, at 2; Comment of World Privacy Forum, cmt. #00376, at 2-3, 8-17.

[55] See Comment of World Privacy Forum, cmt. #00376, at 2-3, 8-17.

[56] See Comment of Consumer Data Industry Ass'n, cmt. #00363, at 4-5; Comment of American Catalog Mailers Ass'n, cmt. #00424, at 3; Comment of Facebook, Inc., cmt. #00413, at 13-14; Comment of Google Inc., cmt. #00417, at 8; Comment of Verizon, cmt. #00428, at 2-3, 6-7, 14-17; Comment of Mortgage Bankers Ass'n, cmt. #00308, at 2; Comment of National Cable & Telecommunications Ass'n, cmt. #00432, at 3, 5, 7-13; Comment of CTIA – The Wireless Ass'n, cmt. #00375, at 15.

[57] See Comment of National Cable & Telecommunications Ass'n, cmt. #00432, at 32-37; Comment of USTelecom, cmt. #00411, at 5-7; Comment of Verizon, cmt. #00428, at 4-6; Comment of Direct Marketing Ass'n, Inc., cmt. #00449, at 5-6.

[58] See Comment of Consumer Data Industry Ass'n, cmt. #00363, at 4-6; see also Comment of CTIA - The Wireless Ass'n, cmt. #00375, at 8-11; Comment of Direct Marketing Ass'n, Inc., cmt. #00449, at 13.

[59] FTC Staff, Mobile Apps for Kids: Current Privacy Disclosures are Disappointing (Feb. 2012), available at http://www.ftc.gov/ os/2012/02/120216mobile_apps_kids.pdf; FPF Finds Nearly Three-Quarters of Most Downloaded Mobile Apps Lack a Privacy Policy, FUTURE OF PRIVACY FORUM, http://www.futureofprivacy.org/2011/05/12/fpf-finds-nearly-three-quarters-of-mostdownloaded-mobile-apps-lack-a-privacy-policy/.

[60] See Comment of Center for Democracy & Technology, cmt. #00469, at 2-3; Comment of World Privacy Forum, cmt. #00376, at 2-3. Discussed more fully infra at Section IV.D.2.a.

[61] See Grant Gross, Lawmakers Question Sony, Epsilon on Data Breaches, PC WoRLD (June 2, 2011 3:40 PM), available at http:// www.pcworld.com/businesscenter/article/ 229258/lawmakers_question_sony_epsilon_on_data_breaches.html; Dwight Silverman, App Privacy: Who's Uploading Your Contact List?, HoUSToN CHRoNIcLE (Feb. 15, 2012 8:10 AM), http://blog. chron.com/techblog/2012/02/app-privacy-whos-uploading-your-contact-list/; Dan Graziano, Like iOS apps, Android Apps Can Secretly Access Photos Thanks to Loophole, BGR (Mar. 1, 2012 3:45 PM), http://www.bgr.com/2012/03/01/like-ios-appsandroid-apps-can-also-secretly-access-photos-thanks-to-security-hole/.

[62] CEO Apologizes After Path Social App Uploads Contact Lists, KMOV.coM (Feb. 9, 2012 11:11AM), http://www.kmov.com/ news/consumer/CEO-apologizes-after-Path-uploads-contact-lists--139015729.html; Daisuke Wakabayashi, A Contrite Sony Vows Tighter Security, WALL ST. J. May 1, 2011, available at http://online.wsj.com/article/SB1000142 4052748704436004576 296302384608280.html.

[63] Kevin Parrish, OnStar Changes its Mind About Tracking Vehicles, ToM'S GUIDE (Sept. 29, 2011 7:30 AM), http://www. tomsguide.com/us/OnStar-General-motors-Linda-Marshall-GPS-Terms-and-conditions,news-12677.html.

[64] Surveys of consumer attitudes towards privacy conducted in the past year are illuminating. For example, a USA Today/Gallup poll indicated that a majority of the Facebook members or Google users surveyed were "very" or "somewhat concerned" about their privacy while using these services. Lymari Morales, Google and Facebook Users Skew Young, Affluent, and Educated, GALLUP (Feb. 17, 2011), available at http://www.gallup.com/poll/146159/ facebook-google-users-skew-young-affluenteducated.aspx.

[65] The Commission has long supported federal laws requiring companies to implement reasonable security measures and to notify consumers in the event of certain security breaches. See, e.g., Prepared Statement of the FTC, Data Security: Hearing Before the H. Comm. on Energy and Commerce, Subcomm. on Commerce, Manufacturing, and Trade, 112th Cong. (June 15, 2011), available at http://www.ftc.gov/os/testimony/ 110615datasecurityhouse.pdf; Prepared Statement of the FTC, Protecting Social Security Numbers From Identity Theft: Hearing Before the Before the H. Comm. on Ways and Means, Subcomm. on Social Security, 112th Cong. (April 13, 2011), available at http://www.ftc.gov/os/testimony/110411ssn-idtheft.pdf; FTC, Security in Numbers, SSNs and ID Theft (Dec. 2008), available at http://www.ftc.gov/os/2008/12/P075414 ssnreport.pdf; President's Identity Theft Task Force, Identity Theft Task Force Report (Sept. 2008), available at http://www.idtheft.gov/reports/ IDTReport2008.pdf.

[66] Former FTC Chairman Casper "Cap" Weinberger recognized the value of civil penalties as a deterrent to unlawful conduct. See Hearings on H.R. 14931 and Related Bills before the Subcomm. on Commerce and Finance of the H. Comm. on Interstate and Foreign Commerce, 91st Cong. 53, 54 (1970) (statement of FTC Chairman Caspar Weinberger); Hearings on S. 2246, S. 3092, and S. 3201 Before the Consumer Subcomm. of the S. Comm. on Commerce, 91st Cong. 9 (1970) (Letter from FTC Chairman Caspar W. Weinberger) (forwarding copy of House testimony).

[67] With this report, the Commission is not seeking to impose civil penalties for privacy violations under the FTC Act. Rather, in the event Congress enacts privacy legislation, the Commission believes that such legislation would be more effective if the FTC were authorized to obtain civil penalties for violations.

[68] See Press Release, FTC, FTC Seeks Input to Revising its Guidance to Businesses About Disclosures in Online Advertising (May 26, 2011), available at http://www.ftc.gov/ opa/2011/05/dotcom.shtm.

[69] See Data Accountability and Trust Act, H.R. 1707, 112th Congress (2011); Data Accountability and Trust Act of 2011, H.R. 1841, 112th Congress (2011); Data Security and Breach Notification Act of 2011, S. 1207, 112th Congress (2011).

[70] See Comment of eBay, Inc., cmt. #00374, at 3; Comment of Microsoft Corp., cmt. #00395, at 4.

[71] Id.

[72] See BEST PRACTICES ACT, H.R. 5777, 111th Congress (2010); Staff Discussion Draft, H.R. __, 111th Congress (2010), available at http://www.nciss.org/legislation/Boucher Stearnsprivacydiscussiondraft.pdf.

[73] Comment of the Center for Democracy & Technology, cmt. #00469, at 1.

[74] See Comment of the Electronic Frontier Foundation, cmt. #00400, at 1; Comment of the Consumer Federation of America, cmt. #00358, at 2.

[75] See infra at Sections IV.C.1.b.(v) and IV.C.2.e.(ii), for a discussion of what constitutes sensitive data.

[76] See Comment of the Confidentiality Coalition c/o the Healthcare Leadership Council, cmt. #00349, at 1-4; Comment of Experian, cmt. #00398, at 8-10; Comment of IMS Health, cmt. #00380, at 2-3; Comment of Medco Health Solutions, Inc., cmt. #00393, at 3; Comment of SIFMA, cmt. #00265, at 2-3.

[77] Comment of The Markle Foundation, cmt. #00456, at 3-10.

[78] Any baseline privacy law Congress may enact would likely consider the best way to take into account obligations under existing statutes.

[79] There may be entities that operate within covered sectors but that nevertheless fall outside of a specific law's scope. For instance, a number of entities that collect health information are not subject to HIPAA. These entities include providers of personal health records – online portfolios that consumers can use to store and keep track of their medical information. In 2009, Congress passed the HITECH Act, which required HHS, in consultation with the FTC, to develop legislative recommendations on privacy and security requirements that should apply to these providers of personal health records and related entities. Health Information Technology ("HITECH") Provisions of American Recovery and Reinvestment Act of 2009, Title XIII, Subtitle D (Pub. L. 111-5, 123 Stat. 115, codified in relevant part at 42 U.S.C. §§ 17937 and 17954). FTC staff is consulting with HHS on this project.

[80] See Comment of the Center for Democracy & Technology, cmt. #00469, at 2; Comment of the Computer & Communications Industry Ass'n, cmt. #00434, at 14; Comment of Consumers Union, cmt. #00362, at 4-5; Comment of the Department of Veterans Affairs, cmt. #00479, at 3; Comment of Experian, cmt. #00398, at 1; Comment of Google Inc., cmt. #00417, at 7; Comment of Microsoft Corp., cmt. #00395, at 4.

[81] See Comment of the Department of Veterans Affairs, cmt. #00479, at 3 n.7; Comment of the Computer & Communications Industry Ass'n, cmt. #00434, at 14; Comment of Consumers Union, cmt. #00362, at 1.

[82] See Comment of the Department of Veterans Affairs, cmt. #00479, at 3 n.7; Comment of the Computer & Communications Industry Ass'n, cmt. #00434, at 14.

[83] Comment of Center for Democracy & Technology, cmt. #00469, at 2.

[84] Comment of Center for Democracy & Technology, cmt. #00469, at 2-3.

[85] Comment of the Financial Services Forum, cmt. #00381, at 8-9.

[86] Comment of National Retail Federation, cmt. #00419, at 6 (urging FTC to limit privacy framework to online collection of consumer data because applying it to offline collection would be onerous for businesses and consumers).

[87] See Comment of the Center for Democracy & Technology, cmt. #00469, at 3; Comment of Consumers Union, cmt. #00362, at 4-5. In addition, in their comments both AT&T and Mozilla recognized that the distinction between PII and non-PII is blurring. Comment of AT&T Inc., cmt. #00420, at 13; Comment of Mozilla, cmt. #00480, at 6.

[88] Comment of Center for Democracy & Technology, cmt. #00469, at 3 (citing Edward C. Baig, Internet Users Say, Don't Track Me, USA TODAY, Dec. 14, 2010, available at http://www.usatoday.com/money/advertising/2010-12-14-donottrackpoll14_ ST_N.htm); Scott Cleland, Americans Want Online Privacy – Per New Zogby Poll, THE PRECURSOR BLOG (June 8, 2010), http://www.precursorblog.com/content/americans-want-online-privacy-new-zogby-poll); Comment of Consumers Union, cmt. #00362, at 4 (discussing the potential for discriminatory pricing (citing Annie Lowery, How Online Retailers Stay a Step Ahead of Comparison Shoppers, WASH. POST, Dec. 12, 2010, available at http://www.washingtonpost.com/wp-dyn/content/article/2010/12/11/AR2010121102435.html)).

[89] For a brief discussion of such incidents, see FTC, Protecting Consumer Privacy in an Era of Rapid Change, A Proposed Framework for Businesses and Policymakers, Preliminary FTC Staff Report, at 38 (Dec. 2010), available at http://www.ftc.gov/ os/2010/12/101201 privacyreport.pdf.

[90] Comment of Electronic Frontier Foundation, cmt. #00400, at 4 (citing Julia Angwin & Steve Stecklow, 'Scrapers' Dig Deep for Data on Web, WaLL ST. J., Oct. 12, 2010, available at http://online.wsj.com/article/SB 10001424052748703358504575544381288117888.html); Sorrell v. IMS Health Inc., 131 S. Ct. 2653 (2011).

[91] Comment of Mozilla, cmt. #00480, at 4-5; Comment of Google Inc., cmt. #00417, at 8.

[92] The term "browser fingerprints" refers to the specific combination of characteristics – such as system fonts, software, and installed plugins – that are typically made available by a consumer's browser to any website visited. These characteristics can be used to uniquely identify computers, cell phones, or other devices. Browser fingerprinting does not rely on cookies. See Erik Larkin, Browser Fingerprinting Can ID You Without Cookies, PCWorLD, Jan. 29, 2010, available at http://www.pcworld. com/article/188161/browser_fingerprinting_can_id_you_without_cookies.html.

[93] Comment of Mozilla, cmt. #00480, at 4-5 (citing FTC, Protecting Consumer Privacy in an Era of Rapid Change: A Proposed Framework for Businesses and Policymakers, Preliminary FTC Staff Report, at 36-37 (Dec. 2010), available at http://www.ftc. gov/os/2010/12/101201privacyreport.pdf).

[94] Comment of Google Inc., cmt. #00417, at 8.

[95] Comment of Google Inc., cmt. #00417, at 8.

[96] Comment of Direct Marketing Ass'n, Inc., cmt. #00449, at 13-14; Comment of National Cable & Telecommunications Ass'n, cmt. #00432, at 13-17.

97 See Comment of AT&T Inc., cmt. #00420, at 13-15; Comment of Center for Democracy & Technology (Feb. 18, 2011), cmt. #00469, at 3-4; Comment of CTIA - The Wireless Ass'n, cmt. #00375, at 3-4; Comment of Consumers Union, cmt. #00362, at 4-5; Comment of Electronic Frontier Foundation, cmt. #00400, at 1-4; Comment of Google Inc., cmt. #00417, at 7-8; Comment of Mozilla, cmt. #00480, at 4-6; Comment of Phorm Inc., cmt. #00353, at 3-4.

[98] Comment of AT&T Inc., cmt. #00420, at 13; Comment of CTIA - The Wireless Ass'n, cmt. #00375 at 3-4; Comment of Google Inc., cmt. #00417, at 8; Comment of Phorm Inc., cmt. #00353, at 4.

[99] Comment of GS1, cmt. #00439, at 2.

[100] Comment of AT&T Inc., cmt. #00420, at 13-14; Comment of CTIA - The Wireless Ass'n, cmt. #00375, at 4; Comment of Experian, cmt. #00398, at 11; Comment of National Cable & Telecommunications Ass'n, cmt. #00432, at 16.

[101] Comment of United States Council for International Business, cmt. #00366, at 1; Comment of Phorm Inc., cmt. #00353, at 3.

[102] Comment of Retail Industry Leaders Ass'n, cmt. #00352, at 4; Comment of Yahoo! Inc., cmt. #00444, at 3-4; Comment of GS1, cmt. #00439, at 3.

[103] Comment of AT&T Inc., cmt. #00420, at 13.

[104] Comment of Intel Corp., cmt. #00246, at 9.

[105] Comment of Intel Corp., cmt. #00246, at 9.

[106] FTC, Protecting Consumer Privacy in an Era of Rapid Change: A Proposed Framework for Businesses and Policymakers, Preliminary FTC Staff Report, 35-38 (Dec. 2010), available at http://www.ftc.gov/os/2010/12/101201privacyreport.pdf; Comment of Center for Democracy & Technology, cmt. #00469, at 3; Comment of Statz, Inc., cmt. #00377, at 11-12. See supra note 89.

[107] See FTC, FTC Staff Report: Self-Regulatory Principles for Online Behavioral Advertising, 21-24, 43-45 (Feb. 2009), available at http://www.ftc.gov/os/2009/02/P0085400 behavadreport.pdf; Paul M. Schwartz & Daniel J. Solove, The PII Problem: Privacy and a New Concept of Personally Identifiable Information, 86 N.Y.U. L. Rev. 1814, 1836-1848 (2011).

[108] The Commission's approach in data security cases is a flexible one. Where a company has offered assurances to consumers that it has implemented reasonable security measures, the Commission assesses the reasonableness based, among other things, on the sensitivity of the information collected, the measures the company has implemented to protect such information, and whether the company has taken action to address and prevent well-known and easily addressable security vulnerabilities.

[109] See, e.g., Cynthia Dwork, A Firm Foundation for Private Data Analysis, 54 COMM. OF THE ACM 86-95 (2011), available at http://research.microsoft.com/pubs/116123/ dwork_cacm.pdf, and references cited therein.

[110] See In the Matter of Superior Mortg. Corp., FTC Docket No. C-4153 (Dec. 14, 2005), available at, http://www.ftc.gov/os/ caselist/0523136/0523136.shtm (alleging a violation of the GLB Safeguards Rule for, among other things, a failure to ensure that service providers were providing appropriate security for customer information and addressing known security risks in a timely manner).

[111] Letter from Maneesha Mithal, Assoc. Dir., Div. of Privacy & Identity Prot., FTC, to Reed Freeman, Morrison & Foerster LLP, Counsel for Netflix, 2 (Mar. 12, 2010), available at http://www.ftc.gov/os/closings/100312 netflixletter.pdf (closing letter).

[112] Id.

[113] To the extent that a company maintains and uses both data that is identifiable and data that it has taken steps to de-identify as outlined here, the company should silo the data separately.

[114] A company that violates its policy against re-identifying data could be subject to liability under the FTC Act or other laws.

[115] Comment of Office of the Information and Privacy Commissioner of Ontario, cmt. #00239, at 2-3; Comment of Intel Corp., cmt. #00246, at 12-13; Comment of CNIL, cmt. #00298, at 2-3.

[116] Comment of CNIL, cmt. #00298, at 2; Comment of the Information Commissioner's Office of the UK, cmt. #00249, at 2; Comment of World Privacy Forum, cmt. #00369, at 7; Comment of Intel Corp., cmt. #00246, at 4; see also Organisation for Economic Co-operation & Development, OECD Guidelines on the Protection of Privacy and Transborder Flows of Personal Data (Sept. 1980), available at http://www.oecd.org/document/ 18/0,3343,en_2649_34255_1815186_1_1_1_1,00&&enUSS_01DBC.html (these principles include purpose specification, individual participation, accountability, and principles to govern cross-border data transfers). Another commenter called for baseline legislation based on the Fair Information Practice Principles and the principles outlined in the 1974 Privacy Act. Comment of Electronic Privacy Information Center, cmt. #00386, at 17-20.

[117] Comment of CNIL, cmt. #00298, at 3.

[118] The concept of the "right to be forgotten," and its importance to young consumers, is discussed in more detail below in the Transparency Section, infra at Section IV.D.2.b.

[119] Comment of Consumers Union, cmt. #00362, at 1-2, 5-9, 18-19.

[120] See In the Matter of Facebook, Inc., FTC File No. 092 3184 (Nov. 29, 2011) (proposed consent order), available at http:// www.ftc.gov/os/caselist/0923184/index.shtm (requiring Facebook to make inaccessible within thirty days data that a user deletes); see also Do Not Track Kids Act of 2011, H.R. 1895, 112th Cong. (2011).

[121] In the Matter of Upromise, Inc., FTC File No. 102 3116 (Jan. 18, 2012) (proposed consent order), available at http://www. ftc.gov/os/caselist/1023116/index.shtm; In the Matter of ACRAnet, Inc., FTC Docket No. C-4331(Aug. 17, 2011) (consent order), available at http://ftc.gov/os/caselist/0923088/index.shtm; In the Matter of Fajilan & Assocs., Inc., FTC Docket No. C-4332 (Aug. 17, 2011) (consent order), available at http://ftc.gov/os/ caselist/0923089/index.shtm; In the Matter of SettlementOne Credit Corp., FTC Docket No. C-4330 (Aug. 17, 2011) (consent order), available at http://ftc.gov/os/ caselist/0823208/index.shtm; In the Matter of Lookout Servs., Inc., FTC Docket No. C-4326 (June 15, 2011) (consent order), available at http://www.ftc.gov/os/caselist/ 102376/index.shtm; In the Matter of Ceridian Corp., FTC Docket No. C-4325 (June 8, 2011) (consent order), available at http://www.ftc.gov/os/caselist/1023160/index.shtm; In the Matter of Twitter, Inc., FTC Docket No. C-4316 (Mar. 11, 2011) (consent order), available at http://www.ftc.gov/os/caselist/0923093/index.shtm.

[122] See, e.g., Federal Financial Institutions Examination Council ("FFIEC"), Information Society IT Examination Handbook (July 2006), available at http://ithandbook.ffiec.gov/it-booklets/information-security.aspx; Letter from Richard Spillenkothen, Dir., Div. of Banking Supervision & Regulation, Bd. of Governors of the Fed. Reserve Sys., SRO1-11: Identity Theft and Pretext Calling (Apr. 26, 2011), available at http://www.federal reserve.gov/boarddocs/srletters/2001/sr0111.htm (guidance on pretexting and identity theft); Securities & Exchange Commission, CF Disclosure Guidance: Topic No. 2, on Cybersecurity (Oct. 13, 2011), available at http://www.sec.gov/divisions/ corpfin/guidance/cfguidance-topic2.htm; U.S. Small Business Administration, Information Security Guidance, http://www.sba.gov/content/information-security; National Institute of Standards & Technology, Computer Security Division, Computer Security Resource Center, available at http://csrc.nist. gov/groups/SMA/sbc/index.html; HHS, Health Information Privacy, available at http://www.hhs.gov/ocr/privacy/hipaa/ understanding/coveredentities/ index.html (guidance and educational materials for entities required to comply with the HIPPA Privacy and Security Rules); Centers from Medicare and Medicaid Services, Educational Materials, available at http:// www.cms.gov/EducationMaterials/ (educational materials for HIPPA compliance).

[123] FTC, OnGuard Online, http://onguardonline.gov/.

[124] See FTC, Protecting Personal Information: A Guide for Business (Nov. 2011), available at http://business.ftc.gov/documents/ bus69-protecting-personal-information-guide-business; see generally FTC, Bureau of Consumer Protection Business Center, Data Security Guidance, available at http://business.ftc.gov/privacy-and-security/data-security.

[125] See PCI Security Standards Council, PCI SSC Data Security Standards Overview, available at https://www. pcisecuritystandards.org/security_standards/; SANS Institute, Information Security Policy Templates, available at http://www. sans.org/security-resources/policies/; BITS, Financial Services Roundtable BITS Publications, available at http://www.bits.org/ publications/index.php; see also, e.g., Better Business Bureau, Security and Privacy – Made Simpler: Manageable Guidelines to help You Protect Your Customers' Security & Privacy from Identity Theft & Fraud, available at http://www.bbb.org/us/storage/16/ documents/Security PrivacyMadeSimpler.pdf; National Cyber Security Alliance, For Business, http://www.staysafeonline.org/ for-business (guidance for small and midsize businesses); Direct Marketing Association, Information Security: Safeguarding Personal Data in Your Care (May 2005), available at http://www.the-dma.org/privacy/InfoSec Data.pdf; Messaging Anti-Abuse Working Group & Anti-Phishing Working Group, Anti-Phishing Best Practices for ISPs and Mailbox Providers (July 2006), available at http://www.antiphishing.org/ reports/bestpracticesforisps.pdf.

[126] Comment of Google Inc., cmt. #00417, at 2-3.

[127] Comment of Mozilla, cmt. #00480, at 7.

[128] See Chloe Albanesius, Twitter Adds Always-On Encryption, PC MAGAZINE, Feb. 12, 2012, http://www.pcmag.com/ article2/0,2817,2400252,00.asp.

[129] See, e.g., Comment of Intel Corp., cmt. #00246, at 4-5, 7, 40-41; Comment of Electronic Frontier Foundation, cmt. #00400, at 4-6; Comment of Center for Democracy & Technology, cmt. #00469, at 4-5; Comment of Electronic Privacy Information Center, cmt. #00386, at 18.

[130] See, e.g., Comment of Facebook, Inc., cmt. #00413, at 2, 7-8, 18; Comment of Google Inc., cmt. #00417, at 4; Comment of Direct Marketing Ass'n, Inc., cmt. #00449, at 14-15; Comment of Intuit, Inc., cmt. #00348, at 5, 9; Comment of TRUSTe, cmt. #00450, at 9.

[131] Comment of Facebook, Inc., cmt. #00413, at 7-8.

[132] See Comment of SAS, cmt. #00415, at 51; Comment of Yahoo! Inc., cmt. #00444, at 5.

[133] Comment of Yahoo! Inc., cmt. #00444, at 5.

[134] This approach mirrors the revised standard for determining whether a particular data practice warrants consumer choice (see infra at section IV.C.1.a.) and is consistent with a number of commenters' calls for considering the context in which a particular practice takes place. See, e.g., Comment of CTIA - The Wireless Ass'n, cmt. #00375, at 2-4; Comment of Consumer Data Industry Ass'n, cmt. #00363, at 5; Comment of TRUSTe, cmt. #00450, at 3.

[135] See White House, Consumer Data Privacy in a Networked World: A Framework for Protecting Privacy and Promoting Innovation in the Global Digital Economy, 15-19, (Feb. 2012), available at http://www.whitehouse.gov/sites/default/files/privacy-final.pdf. For a further discussion of this point, see infra at Section IV.C.1.a.

[136] See Jay Cline, GMAC: Navigating EU Approval for Advanced Biomterics, INsIDE PRIVACY BLOG (Oct. 15, 2010), https://www. privacyassociation.org/publications/ 2010_10_20_gmac_navigating_eu_approval_for_ advanced_biometrics (explaining GMAC's adoption of palm print technology); cf. Kashmir Hill, Why 'Privacy by Design' is the New Corporate Hotness, FORBEs, July 28, 2011, available at http://www.forbes.com/sites/kashmirhill/2011/07/28/why-privacy-by-design-is-the-new-corporatehotness/.

[137] See Comment of CTIA - The Wireless Ass'n, cmt. #00375, at 2-4, 14; Comment of American Catalog Mailers Ass'n, cmt. #000424, at 5; Comment of IBM, cmt. #00433, at 4; Comment of Intuit, Inc., cmt. #00348, at 9.

[138] Comment of Verizon, cmt. #00428, at 10-11.

[139] See, e.g., Comment of CTIA - The Wireless Ass'n, cmt. #00375, at 14.

[140] Comment of Yahoo! Inc., cmt. #00444, at 6; see also Comment of American Catalog Mailers Ass'n, cmt. #00424, at 3-4.

[141] Comment of Consumer Federation of America, cmt. #00358, at 4 (citing Legislative Primer: Online Behavioral Tracking and Targeting Concerns and Solutions from the Perspective of the Center for Digital Democracy and U.S. PIRG, Consumer Federation of America, Consumers Union, Consumer Watchdog, Electronic Frontier Foundation, Privacy Lives, Privacy Rights Clearinghouse, Privacy Times, U.S. Public Interest Research group, The World Privacy Forum (Sept. 2009), available at http://www.consumerfed. org/elements/www.consumer fed.org/file/OnlinePrivacyLegPrimerSEPT09.pdf).

[142] Comment of Center for Democracy & Technology, cmt. #00469, at 6 ("Flexible approaches to data retention should not, however, give carte blanche to companies to maintain consumer data after it has outlived its reasonable usefulness.").

[143] In the alternative, companies may consider taking steps to de-identify the data they maintain, as discussed above.

[144] See Comment of Consumers Union, cmt. #00362, at 8.

[145] See infra at Section IV.D.2.b.

[146] See Comment of Experian, cmt. #00398, at 2.

[147] See Comment of SIFMA, cmt. #00265, at 4.

[148] Comment of Phorm Inc., cmt. #00353, at 4.

[149] Comment of Experian, cmt. #00398, at 11 (arguing against enhanced standards for accuracy, access, and correction for marketing data); see also Comment of Yahoo! Inc., cmt. #00444, at 6-7.

[150] Id.

[151] Cf. Comment of Yahoo! Inc., cmt. #00444, at 7 (arguing that it would be costly, time consuming, and contrary to privacy objectives to verify the accuracy of user registration information such as gender, age or hometown).

[152] See infra at Section IV.D.2. The Commission notes that some privacy-enhancing technologies operate by introducing deliberate "noise" into data. The data accuracy principle is not intended to rule out the appropriate use of these methods, provided that the entity using them notifies any recipients of the data that it is inaccurate.

[153] See, e.g., Comment of The Centre for Information Policy Leadership at Hunton & Williams LLP, cmt. #00360, at 2-3; Comment of Intel Corp., cmt. #00246, at 6; Comment of Office of the Information & Privacy Commissioner of Ontario, cmt. #00239, at 3.

[154] Comment of GS1, cmt. #00439, at 3; Comment of Office of the Information & Privacy Commissioner of Ontario, cmt. #00239, at 6.

[155] Comment of Office of the Information & Privacy Commissioner of Ontario, cmt. #00239, at 7.

[156] Comment of Intel Corp., cmt. #00246, at 6; Comment of United States Council for International Business, cmt. #00366, at 2; Comment of Consumer Federation of America, cmt. #00358, at 3.

[157] Comment of Intel Corp., cmt. #00246, at 6.

[158] Comment of Zynga Inc., cmt. #00459, at 2.

[159] Of course, the privacy programs required by these orders may not be appropriate for all types and sizes of companies that collect and use consumer data.

[160] In the Matter of Google Inc., FTC Docket No. C-4336 (Oct. 13, 2011) (consent order), available at http://www.ftc.gov/os/ caselist/index.shtm.

[161] Comment of Electronic Frontier Foundation, cmt. #00400, at 5.

[162] Comment of Business Software Alliance, cmt. #00389, at 7-9.

[163] Comment of The Centre for Information Policy Leadership at Hunton & Williams LLP, cmt. #00360, at 3; Comment of the Information Commissioner's Office of the UK, cmt. #00249, at 2; Comment of CTIA - The Wireless Ass'n, cmt. #00375, at 14.

[164] Comment of Yahoo! Inc., cmt. #00444, at 7.

[165] Comment of Direct Marketing Ass'n, Inc., cmt. #00449, at 16; Comment of Interactive Advertising Bureau, cmt. #00388, at 8-9.

[166] Several commenters expressed support for consumer choice generally. See, e.g., Comment of Center for Democracy & Technology, cmt. #00469, at 11-12; Comment of Consumer Federation of America, cmt. #00358, at 6-12. One governmental agency, for instance, expressly supported a general rule requiring consumer consent for the collection and any use of their information with only limited exceptions. Comment of Department of Veteran Affairs, cmt. #00479, at 5. Another commenter, supporting consumer choice, emphasized the importance of offering opportunities for choice beyond a consumer's initial transaction. Comment of Catalog Choice, cmt. #00473, at 10-18.

[167] Comment of Center for Democracy & Technology, cmt. #00469, at 8-11; Comment of Consumer Federation of America, cmt. #00358, at 6-10.

[168] Comment of Computer and Communications Industry Ass'n, cmt. #00434, at 16; Comment of BlueKai, cmt. #00397, at 3-4; Comment of Retail Industry Leaders Ass'n, cmt. #00352, at 5-7; U.S. Chamber of Commerce, cmt. #00452, at 5; Comment of National Cable & Telecommunications Ass'n, cmt. #00432, at 23-24; Comment of Yahoo! Inc., cmt. #00444, at 9-10.

[169] Comment of Phorm Inc., cmt. #00353, at 5; Comment of Verizon, cmt. #00428, at 11-13.

[170] Comment of AT&T Inc., cmt. #00420, at 18-22; Comment of Center for Democracy & Technology, cmt. #00469, at 8-11; Comment of Consumers Union, cmt. #00362, at 9-12; Comment of Consumer Federation of America, cmt. #00358, at 6-10; Comment of National Cable & Telecommunications Ass'n, cmt. #00432, at 23-25.

[171] Comment of Computer and Communications Industry Ass'n, cmt. #00434, at 16; Comment of BlueKai, cmt. #00397, at 4; Comment of Retail Industry Leaders Ass'n, cmt. #00352, at 6-7; Comment of Yahoo! Inc., cmt. #00444, at 9-12; Comment of National Cable & Telecommunications Ass'n, cmt. #00432, at 23-24.

[172] Comment of eBay, cmt. #00374, at 6-7; Comment of Phorm Inc., cmt. #00353, at 5.

[173] See Comment of AT&T Inc., cmt. #00420, at 18.

[174] Phishing uses deceptive spam that appears to be coming from legitimate, well-known sources to trick consumers into divulging sensitive or personal information, such as credit card numbers, other financial data, or passwords.

[175] See Comment of Microsoft Corp., cmt. #00395, at 8 (security attacks, phishing schemes, and spamming); Comment of Business Software Alliance, cmt. #00389, at 5-6 (security access controls and user and employee authentication, cybercrime and fraud prevention and detection, protecting and enforcing intellectual property and trade secrets).

[176] See Comment of IBM, cmt. #00433, at 5 (energy conservation); Comment of Management Ass'n for Private Programming Surveyors, cmt. #00205, at 2-3 (mapping, surveying or providing emergency services).

[177] See Comment of Online Publishers Ass'n, cmt. #00315, at 5 (frequency capping, click fraud); Comment of Interactive Advertising Bureau, cmt. #00388, at 9 (attribution measurement).

[178] See Comment of AT&T Inc., cmt. #00420, at 18-19.

[179] See Comment of Microsoft Corp., cmt. #00395, at 8.

[180] See Comment of Future of Privacy Forum, cmt. #00341, at 5.

[181] See Comment of Consumer Federation of America, cmt. #00358, at 6.

[182] See Comment of Center for Democracy & Technology, cmt. #00469, at 8-9 (citing BEST PRACTICES Act, H.R. 611, 112th Congress § 2(5)(iii) (2011).

[183] See Comment of Microsoft Corp., cmt. #00395, at 8; Comment of National Cable & Telecommunications Ass'n, cmt. #00432, at 23-26; Comment of Pharmaceutical Research & Manufacturers of America, cmt. #00477, at 13.

[184] As noted above, focusing on the context of the interaction is consistent with the Respect for Context principle in the Consumer Privacy Bill of Rights proposed by the White House. See White House, Consumer Data Privacy in a Networked World: A Framework for Protecting Privacy and Promoting Innovation in the Global Digital

Economy, App. A. (Feb. 2012), available at http://www.whitehouse.gov/sites/default/files/privacy-final.pdf. The Respect for Context principle requires companies to limit their use of consumer data to purposes that are consistent with the company's relationship with the consumer and with the context in which the consumer disclosed the data, unless the company is legally required to do otherwise. If a company will use data for other purposes it must provide a choice at a prominent point, outside of the privacy policy.

[185] See supra at Section IV.C.1.

[186] See supra note 175.

[187] With respect to use of geolocation data for mapping, surveying or similar purposes, if the data cannot reasonably be linked to a specific consumer, computer, or device, a company collecting or using the data would not need to provide a consumer choice mechanism. Similarly, if a company takes reasonable measures to de-identify smart grid data and takes the other steps outlined above, the company would not be obligated to obtain consent before collecting or using the data. See supra Section IV.A.4.

[188] Moreover, even if a given practice does not necessitate consumer choice, the framework's other elements – e.g., data collection limits and disposal requirements, increased transparency – would still apply, thereby preventing a company from exploiting these categories.

[189] Deep packet inspection ("DPI") refers to the ability of ISPs to analyze the information, comprised of data packets, that traverses their networks when consumers use their services.

[190] See Comment of AT&T Inc., cmt. #00420, at 21-22 & n.34; Comment of Berlin Commissioner for Data Protection & Freedom of Information, cmt. #00484, at 2-3; Comment of Computer & Communications Industry Ass'n, cmt. #00434, at 15; Comment of Phorm Inc., cmt. #00353, App. A at 3-4; Comment of U.S. Public Policy Council of the Ass'n for Computing Machinery, cmt. #00431, at 6.

[191] See Comment of Phorm Inc., cmt. #00353, App. A at 3-4; Comment of Center for Democracy & Technology, cmt. #00469, at 14- 15; Comment of AT&T Inc., cmt. #00420, at 21-22 & n.34.

[192] See Comment of Consumer Federation of America, cmt. #00358, at 8 (citing Justin Brookman, Facebook Pressed to Tackle Lingering Privacy Concerns, Center for Democracy & Technology (June 16, 2010), available at https://www.cdt.org/blogs/ justin-brookman/facebook-pressed-tackle-lingering-privacy-concerns); Comment of Berkeley Center for Law & Technology, cmt. #00347, at 8; see also Arnold Roosendaal, Facebook Tracks and Traces Everyone: Like This!, (Nov. 30, 2010), available at http://papers.ssrn.com/so13/papers.cfm?abstract_id=1717563 (detailing how Facebook tracks consumers through the Like button, including non-Facebook members and members who have logged out of their Facebook accounts); Nik Cubrilovic, Logging Out Of Facebook Is Not Enough, NEW WEB ORDER (Sept. 25, 2011), http://nikcub.appspot.com/posts/logging-out-offacebook-is-not-enough.

[193] See infra at Section IV.C.2.d. (discussing special concerns that arise by comprehensive tracking by large platform providers).

[194] For example, a consumer visits an online sporting goods retailer, looks at but does not purchase running shoes, and then visits a different website to read about the local weather forecast. A first party engages in retargeting if it delivers an ad for running shoes to the consumer on the third-party weather site.

[195] See Comment of Direct Marketing Ass'n, Inc., cmt. #00449, at 16; Comment of Interactive Advertising Bureau, cmt. #00388, at 8; Comment of National Cable & Telecommunications Ass'n, cmt. #00432, at 24.

[196] See Comment of Yahoo! Inc., cmt. #00444, at 11; Comment of IBM, cmt. #00433, at 6; Comment of AT&T Inc., cmt. #00420, at 20; Comment of Catalog Choice, cmt. #00473, at 10; Comment of Consumers Union, cmt. #00362, at 10-11.

[197] See Comment of Consumers Union, cmt. #00362, at 10-11.

[198] See Comment of Yahoo! Inc., cmt. #00444, at 10; Comment of IBM, cmt. #00433, at 6; Comment of AT&T Inc., cmt. #00420, at 20; Comment of Catalog Choice, cmt. #00473, at 9-10; Comment of Direct Marketing Ass'n, Inc., cmt. #00449, at 16; Comment of Interactive Advertising Bureau, cmt. #00388, at 8.

[199] See Comment of American Catalog Mailers Ass'n, cmt. #00424, at 7.

[200] Such marketing communications would, of course, still be subject to any existing restrictions, including the CAN-SPAM Act, 15 U.S.C. §§ 7701-7713 (2010).

[201] See Comment of Consumer Federation of America, cmt. #00358, at 10; Comment of Consumers Union, cmt. #00362, at 11.

[202] Comment of Berkeley Center for Law & Technology, cmt. #00347, at 9-10.

[203] Id., at 8-10 (describing Williams-Sonoma's collection of consumers' zip codes in Pineda v. Williams-Sonoma Stores, Inc., 246 P.3d 612 (Cal. 2011)).

[204] Comment of Consumer Federation of America, cmt. #00358, at 10.

[205] See Comment of Phorm Inc., cmt. #00353, at 5.

[206] See Comment of the Information Commissioner's Office of the UK, cmt. #00249, at 3.

[207] See Comment of Newspaper Ass'n of America, cmt. #00383, at 7-8; Comment of National Cable & Telecommunications Ass'n, cmt. #00432, at 24-26; Comment of Experian, cmt. #00398, at 5-6; Comment of Magazine Publishers of America, cmt. #00332, at 4; Consumer Data Industry Ass'n, cmt. #00363, at 2-3.

[208] Comment of Experian, cmt. #00398, at 6; see Comment of Newspaper Ass'n of America, cmt. #00383, at 6-8.

[209] Comment of Newspaper Ass'n of America, cmt. #00383, at 7-8.

[210] Comment of Experian, cmt. #00398, at 9 (citing the Direct Marketing Association's Guidelines for Ethical Business Practice); Comment of Magazine Publishers of America, cmt. #00332, at 5-6.

[211] Comment of Microsoft Corp., cmt. #00395, at 8.

[212] See supra Section IV.C.1.b.(i).

[213] The concept of such a website is discussed, infra, Section IV.D.2.a.

[214] The Commission defines as sensitive, at a minimum, data about children, financial and health information, Social Security numbers, and certain geolocation data, as discussed below. See infra Section IV.C.2.e.(ii).

[215] Comment of Center for Democracy & Technology, cmt. #00469, at 10; Comment of Consumer Federation of America, cmt. #00358, at 8-9; Comment of Consumers Union, cmt. #00362, at 12-13.

[216] See Comment of Center for Democracy & Technology, cmt. #00469 at 10 (citing FTC, FTC Staff Report: Self-Regulatory Principles for Online Behavioral Advertising, 43-44 (2009), http://www.ftc.gov/os/2009/02/P085400behavadreport.pdf).

[217] Comment of CTIA – The Wireless Ass'n, cmt. #00375, at 4-6.

[218] Additional discussion regarding the necessary level of consent for the collection or use of sensitive data, as well as other practices that raise special privacy considerations, is set forth below. See infra Section IV.C.2.e.(ii).

[219] These categories of sensitive data are discussed further below. See infra Section IV.C.2.e.(ii).

[220] See Comment of Consumer Federation of America, cmt. #00358, at 10; Comment of Center for Democracy & Technology, cmt. #00469, at 23-24; Comment of AT&T Inc., cmt. #00420, at 22-23; Comment of Phorm Inc., cmt. #00353, at 9-10.

[221] Comment of AT&T Inc., cmt. #00420, at 22-23.

[222] Comment of Center for Democracy & Technology, cmt. #00469, at 11.

[223] See Comment of Microsoft Corp., cmt. #00395, at 8-10, 14; Comment of SIFMA, cmt. #00265, at 5-6; Comment of Retail Industry Leaders Ass'n, cmt. #00352, at 8-10.

[224] Comment of Retail Industry Leaders Ass'n, cmt. #00352, at 8; Comment of Experian, cmt. #00398, at 9.

[225] Comment of Retail Industry Leaders Ass'n, cmt. #00352, at 8.

[226] See Comment of Magazine Publishers of America, cmt. #00332, at 4 (noting that the "blow-in cards" in magazines often used to solicit new subscriptions have very limited space, and including lengthy disclosures on these cards could render them unreadable); Comment of American Catalogue Mailers Ass'n, cmt. #00424, at 7.

[227] See Comment of Retail Industry Leaders Ass'n, cmt. #00352 at 7; see also Comment of Experian, cmt. #00398, at 9 (noting that the proposed changes in notice and choice procedures would be inconvenient for consumers and would damage the consumer experience).

[228] Comment of Retail Industry Leaders Ass'n, cmt. #00352, at 8.

[229] Comment of Microsoft Corp., cmt. #00395, at 2; Comment of AT&T Inc., cmt. #00420 at 3, 7; Comment of Consumers Union, cmt. #00362, at 5, 11-12; Comment of Consumer Federation of America, cmt. #00358, at 10.

[230] Comment of Retail Industry Leaders Ass'n, cmt. #00352, at 9.

[231] Comment of Facebook, Inc., cmt. #00413, at 10; Comment of Retail Industry Leaders Ass'n, cmt. #00352, at 9; see also Comment of Experian, cmt. #00398, at 9 (generally disputing the need for "just-in-time" notice, but acknowledging that it might be justified for the transfer to non-affiliated third parties of sensitive information for marketing purposes).

[232] See Comment of CTIA - The Wireless Ass'n, cmt. #00375, at 10 (describing the form of consent outlined in the CTIA's "Best Practices and Guidelines for Location-Based Services").

[233] The FTC recognizes that incorporating this delay period may require companies to make programming changes to their systems. As noted above, in the discussion of legacy data systems, see supra at Section IV.B.2., these changes may take time to implement.

[234] As noted in Section IV.C.2.c., industry continues to consider ways to make the icon and opt out mechanism more usable and visible for consumers.

[235] But see Comment of Center for Digital Democracy and U.S. PIRG, cmt. #00338, at 29 (criticizing visibility of the icon to consumers).

[236] Comment of Performance Marketing Ass'n, cmt. #00414, at 6; Comment of Business Software Alliance, cmt. #00389, at 11-12.

[237] Comment of Tech Freedom, cmt. #00451, at 17.

[238] Comment of Consumer Federation of America, cmt. #00358, at 11; Comment of ePrio, Inc., cmt. #00267, at 4-5.

[239] Comment of Consumer Federation of America, cmt. #00358, at 11; see also Comment of Consumers Union, cmt. #00362, at 12 (urging that consumers who choose to restrict sharing of their PII with unknown third parties should not be punished for that choice).

[240] See, e.g., Comment of Center for Democracy & Technology, cmt. #00469, at 13 (stating that it has no objection to take-itor-leave-it approaches, provided there is competition and the transaction does not involve essential services); Comment of Microsoft Corp., cmt. #00395, at 10 (stating that take-it-or-leave-it choice is appropriate provided the "deal" is made clear to the consumer); Comment of the Information Commissioner's Office of the UK, cmt. #00249, at 4 (stating that take-it-or-leave-it choice would be inappropriate where the consumer has no real alternative but to use the service); Comment of Reed Elsevier, Inc., cmt. #00430, at 11 (stating that while acceptable for the websites of private industry, websites that provide a public service and may be the single source of certain information, such as outsourced government agency websites, should not condition their use on take-it-or-leave-it terms).

[241] Comment of Center for Democracy & Technology, cmt. #00469, at 13; Comment of the Information Commissioner's Office of the UK, cmt. #00249, at 4.

[242] Comment of Center for Democracy & Technology, cmt. #00469, at 13; Comment of Reed Elsevier, Inc., cmt. #00430, at 11.

[243] Comment of Microsoft Corp., cmt. #00395, at 10; see also Comment of Center for Democracy & Technology, cmt. #00469, at 13 (stating that the terms of the bargain should be clearly and conspicuously disclosed).

[244] Comment of TRUSTe, cmt. #00450, at 11; see also Comment of Center for Democracy & Technology, cmt. #00469, at 13 (stating that terms should be "transparent and fairly presented").

[245] This Report is not intended to reflect Commission guidance regarding Section 5's prohibition on unfair methods of competition.

[246] See, e.g., Comment of American Ass'n of Advertising Agencies et. al, cmt. #00410, at 3 (describing the universal choice mechanisms used in the coalition's Self-Regulatory Principles for Online Behavioral Advertising Program); Comment of BlueKai, cmt. #00397, at 3 (describing its development of the NAI Opt-Out Protector for Firefox); Comment of Computer & Communications Industry Ass'n, cmt. #00434, at 17 (describing both company-specific and industry-wide opt-out mechanisms currently in use); Comment of Direct Marketing Ass'n, Inc., cmt. #00449, at 3 (stating that the Self-Regulatory Principles for Online Behavioral Advertising Program addresses the concerns that motivate calls for a "Do-Not-Track" mechanism); Comment of Facebook, Inc., cmt. #00413, at 13 (describing behavioral advertising opt-out mechanisms developed by both browser makers and the advertising industry); Comment of Future of Privacy Forum, cmt. #00341, at 2-4 (describing the development of a browser-based Do-Not-Track header and arguing that the combined efforts of browser companies, ad networks, consumers, and government are likely to result in superior choice mechanisms); Comment of Google, Inc., cmt. #00417, at 5 (describing its Ad Preferences Manager and Keep My Opt-Outs tools); Comment of Interactive Advertising Bureau, cmt. #00388, at 5-7 (describing the Self-Regulatory Principles for Online Behavioral Advertising Program); Comment of Microsoft Corp., cmt. #00395, at 11-14 (describing a variety of browser-based and ad network-based choice tools currently available); Comment of U.S. Chamber of Commerce, cmt. #00452, at 5-6 (describing a variety of browser-based and ad network-based choice tools currently available).

[247] See supra at Section II.C.1.

[248] Comment of American Civil Liberties Union, cmt. #00425, at 12; Comment of Center for Digital Democracy and U.S. PIRG, cmt. #00338, at 28; Comment of Consumer Federation of America, cmt. #00358, at 13; Comment of Consumers Union, cmt. #00362, at 14; see also Comment of World Privacy Forum, cmt. #00369, at 3 (noting prior failures of self-regulation in the online advertising industry).

[249] E.g., Comment of Consumers Union, cmt. #00362, at 14; Comment of World Privacy Forum, cmt. #00369, at 3.

[250] For example, consumers may believe they have opted out of tracking if they block third-party cookies on their browsers; yet they may still be tracked through Flash cookies or other mechanisms. The FTC recently brought an action against a company that told consumers they could opt out of tracking by exercising choices through their browsers; however, the company used Flash cookies for such tracking, which consumers could not opt out of through their browsers. In the Matter of ScanScout, Inc., FTC Docket No. C-4344 (Dec. 21, 2011) (consent order), available at http://www.ftc.gov/os/caselist/1023185/111221s canscoutdo.pdf.

[251] Such a mechanism should be different from the Do Not Call program in that it should not require the creation of a "Registry" of unique identifiers, which could itself cause privacy concerns.

[252] Comment of Microsoft Corp., cmt. #00395, at 12.

[253] Comment of Mozilla, cmt. #00480, at 2; Alex Fowler, Do Not Track Adoption in Firefox Mobile is 3x Higher than Desktop, MozILLA PRIVACY BLoG, (Nov. 2, 2011), http://blog.mozilla.com/privacy/2011/11/02/do-not-track-adoption-in-firefoxmobile-is-3x-higher-than-desktop/.

[254] Nick Wingfield, Apple Adds Do-Not-Track Tool to New Browser, WALL ST. J. Apr. 13, 2011, available at http://online.wsj.com/ article/SB1000142405274870355 130457 6261272308358858.html.

[255] Comment of Google Inc., cmt. #00417, at 5.

[256] Peter Kosmala, Yes, Johnny Can Benefit From Transparency & Control, SELF-REGULATORY PROGRAM FOR ONLINE BEHAVIORAL ADVERTISING, http://www.aboutads.info/blog/yes-johnny-can-benefit-transparency-and-control (Nov. 3, 2011); see also Press Release, Digital Advertising Alliance, White House, DOC and FTC Commend DAA's Self-Regulatory Program to Protect Consumers Online Privacy, (Feb. 23, 2012), available at http://www.aboutads.info/resource/download/DAA%20White%20 House%20Event.pdf.

[257] Digital Advertising Alliance, About Self-Regulatory Principles for Multi-Site Data (Nov. 2011), available at http://www. aboutads.info/resource/download/Multi-Site-Data-Principles.pdf.

[258] Press Release, Digital Advertising Alliance, DAA Position on Browser Based Choice Mechanism (Feb. 22, 2012), available at http://www.aboutads.info/resource/ download/ DAA.Commitment.pdf.

[259] A system practical for both businesses and consumers would include, for users who choose to enable Do Not Track, significant controls on the collection and use of tracking data by third parties, with limited exceptions such as security and frequency capping. As noted above, first-party sharing with third parties is not consistent with the context of the interaction and would be subject to choice. Do Not Track is one way for users to express this choice.

[260] Comment of Computer and Communications Industry Ass'n, cmt. #00233, at 15; Comment of Center for Democracy & Technology, cmt. #00469, at 14-15.

[261] See Comment of Center for Democracy & Technology, cmt. #00469, at 14; Comment of Phorm Inc., cmt. #00353, at 5; see also Comment of Computer and Communications Industry Ass'n, cmt. #00233, at 15 (urging that heightened requirements for consumer choice apply for the use of DPI); Comment of Online Trust Alliance, cmt. #00299, at 6 ("The use of DPI and related technologies may also be permissible when consumers have the ability to opt-in and receive appropriate and proportional quantifiable benefits in return.")

[262] Comment of Center for Digital Democracy and U.S. PIRG, cmt. #00338, at 37.

[263] Comment of Computer and Communications Industry Ass'n, cmt. #00233, at 15.

[264] Comment of AT&T Inc., cmt. #00420, at 21; see also Comment of Verizon, cmt. #00428, at 7 n.6. Likewise, a trade association of telecommunications companies represented that ISPs have not been extensively involved in online behavioral advertising. See Comment of National Cable & Telecommunications Ass'n, cmt. #00432, at 33.

[265] See Comment of Verizon, cmt. #00428, at 7.

[266] Id. at 7-8.

[267] See, e.g., Comment of Internet Commerce Coalition, cmt. #00447, at 10; Comment of KINDSIGHT, cmt. #00344, at 7-8 ; Comment of National Cable & Telecommunications Ass'n, cmt. #00432, at 36; Comment of Verizon, cmt. #00428, at 7-8.

[268] This discussion does not apply to ISPs' use of DPI for network management, security, or other purposes consistent with the context of a consumer's interaction with their ISP.

[269] This discussion is not meant to imply that ISPs, operating systems, or browsers are currently building these profiles for marketing purposes.

[270] ISPs, operating systems, and browsers have different access to users' online activity. A residential ISP can access unencrypted traffic from all devices currently located in the home. An operating system or browser, on the other hand, can access all traffic regardless of location and encryption, but only from devices on which the operating system or browser is installed. Desktop users have the ability to change browsers to avoid monitoring, but mobile users have fewer browser options.

[271] A social widget is a button, box, or other possibly interactive display associated with a social network that is embedded into another party's website.

[272] BrightEdge, Social Share Report: Social Adoption Among Top Websites, 3-4 (July 2011), available at http://www.brightedge. com/resfiles/brightedge-report-socialshare-2011-07.pdf (reporting that by mid-2011, the Facebook Like button appeared on almost 11% of top websites' front pages and Google's +1 button appeared on 4.5% of top websites' front pages); see also Justin Osofsky, After f8: Personalized Social Plugins

Now on 100,000+ Sites, FACEBOOK DEVELOPER BLOG (May 11, 2010, 9:15 AM), http://developers.facebook.com/blog/post/382/.

[273] See Comment of Center for Digital Democracy and U.S. PIRG, cmt. #00338, at 37 (recommending FTC hold a workshop to address DPI).

[274] Companies may seek "affirmative express consent" from consumers by presenting them with a clear and prominent disclosure, followed by the ability to opt in to the practice being described. Thus, for example, requiring the consumer to scroll through a ten-page disclosure and click on an "I accept" button would not constitute affirmative express consent.

[275] In the preliminary report, this principle appeared under the heading of "transparency." See, e.g., In the Matter of Gateway Learning Corp., FTC Docket No. C-4120 (Sept. 10, 2004) (consent order) (alleging that Gateway violated the FTC Act by applying material changes to a privacy policy retroactively), available at http://www.ftc.gov/os/caselist/ 0423047/040917 do0423047.pdf; see also FTC, Self-Regulatory Principles for Online Behavioral Advertising (Feb. 2009), available at http://www. ftc.gov/os/2009/02/P085400behavadreport.pdf (noting the requirement that companies obtain affirmative express consent before making material retroactive changes to their privacy policies).

[276] See Comment of Consumers Union, cmt. #00362, at 17; Comment of Future of Privacy Forum, cmt. #00341, at 5; Comment of Privacy Rights Clearinghouse, cmt. #00351, at 21.

[277] See Comment of Facebook, Inc., cmt. #00413, at 11; see also Comment of Retail Industry Leaders Ass'n, cmt. #00352, at 12; Comment of AT&T Inc., cmt. #00420, at 29-30; Comment of National Cable & Telecommunications Ass'n, cmt. #00432, at 30- 31.

[278] Comment of Facebook, Inc., cmt. #00413, at 8.

[279] See Comment of AT&T Inc., cmt. #00420, at 30; Comment of Phorm Inc., cmt. #00353, at 1.

[280] See Comment of Future of Privacy Forum, cmt. #00341, at 4; Comment of Retail Industry Leaders Ass'n, cmt. #00352, at 12; Comment of Microsoft Corp., cmt. #00395, at 17.

[281] Comment of Facebook, Inc., cmt. #00413, at 10.

[282] See In the Matter of Google Inc., FTC Docket No. C-4336 (Oct. 13, 2011) (consent order), available at http://www.ftc.gov/ os/caselist/1023136/111024googlebuzzdo.pdf; In the Matter of Facebook, Inc., FTC File No. 092-3184 (Nov. 29, 2011) (proposed consent order), available at http://www.ftc.gov/os/caselist/0923184/111129facebookagree.pdf.

[283] Comment of Electronic Frontier Foundation, cmt. #00400, at 15.

[284] See, e.g., Comment of Consumer Federation of America, cmt. #00358, at 9; Comment of CNIL, cmt. #00298, at 4; Comment of Massachusetts Office of the Attorney General, cmt. #00429, at 3; Comment of Kindsight, cmt. #00344, at 11; Comment of Experian, cmt. #00398, at 9; Comment of Center for Democracy & Technology, cmt. #00469, at 14; Comment of Office of the Information and Privacy Commissioner of Ontario, cmt. #00239, at 2; see also Comment of TRUSTe, cmt. #00450, at 11 (agreeing that sensitive information should be defined to include information about children, financial and medical information, and precise geolocation information but urging that sensitive information be more broadly defined as "information whose unauthorized disclosure or use can cause financial, physical, or reputational harm"); Comment of Facebook, Inc., cmt. #00413, at 23 (agreeing that sensitive information may warrant enhanced consent, but noting that enhanced consent may not be possible for activities such as the posting of status updates by users where those updates may include sensitive information such as references to an illness or medical condition).

[285] See Comment of Consumer Federation of America, cmt. #00358, at 9; see also Comment of CNIL, cmt. #00298, at 4, Comment of Center for Digital Democracy and U.S. PIRG, cmt. #00338, at 35.

[286] See Comment of Electronic Frontier Foundation, cmt. #00400, at 7.

[287] See Comment of Marketing Research Ass'n, cmt. #00405, at 6-7; Comment of American Trucking Ass'ns, cmt. #00368, at 2-3; Comment of Microsoft Corp., cmt. #00395, at 10.

[288] See Comment of Institute for Public Representation, cmt. #00346, at 4; Comment of Consumers Union, cmt. #00362, at 13.

[289] See Comment of Center for Democracy & Technology, cmt. #00469, at 15; Comment of CTIA – The Wireless Ass'n, cmt. #00375, at 12-13; Comment of Microsoft Corp., cmt. #00395, at 10; see also Comment of Electronic Frontier Foundation, cmt. #00400, at 14 (opposing the creation of special rules giving parents access to data collected about their teenaged children); Comment of PrivacyActivism, cmt. #00407, at 4 (opposing the creation of special rules giving parents access to data collected about their teenaged children).

[290] See Comment of Center for Democracy & Technology, cmt. #00469, at 15; Comment of CTIA – The Wireless Ass'n, cmt. #00375, at 12-13; Comment of Microsoft Corp., cmt. #00395, at 10.

[291] See Comment of Microsoft Corp., cmt. #00395, at 10.

[292] See infra at Section IV.C.1.b.(v).

[293] See infra at Section IV.D.2.b.

[294] Recent research and surveys suggests that many consumers (particularly among lower income brackets and education levels) do not read or understand privacy policies, thus further heightening the need to make them more comprehensible. Notably, in a survey conducted by Zogby International, 93% of adults – and 81% of teens – indicated they would take more time to read terms and conditions for websites if they were shorter and written in clearer language. See Comment of Common Sense Media, cmt. #00457, at 1.

[295] See Comment of AT&T , Inc., cmt. #00420, at 17; Comment of Center for Democracy & Technology, cmt. #00469, at 24.

[296] See Comment of National Cable & Telecommunications Ass'n, cmt. #00432, at 22.

[297] See Comment of United States Council for International Business, cmt. #00366, at 3.

[298] See Comment of Google Inc., cmt. #00417, at 1; Comment of Facebook, Inc., cmt. #00413, at 9; Comment of AT&T Inc., cmt. #00420, at 24.

[299] See Comment of Privacy Rights Clearinghouse, cmt. #00351, at 15-16; Comment of Consumer Federation of America, cmt. #00358, at 16; Comment of Consumer Watchdog, cmt. #00402, at 2.

[300] See Comment of Consumer Watchdog, cmt. #00402, at 2; Comment of Consumer Federation of America, cmt. #00358, at 16; see also Comment of Lorrie Faith Cranor, cmt. #00453, at 2 n.7 (discussing P3P authorizing tools that enable automatic generation of "nutrition label" privacy notices).

[301] See Comment of Privacy Rights Clearinghouse, cmt. #00351, at 16.

[302] See Comment of Electronic Frontier Foundation, cmt. #00400, at 6.

[303] See Comment of General Electric, cmt. #00392, at 2; Comment of the Information Commissioner's Office of the UK, cmt. #00249, at 4; Comment of Consumers Union, cmt. #00362, at 15-16; Comment of Facebook, Inc., cmt. #00413, at 9.

[304] See Comment of AT&T Inc., cmt. #00420, at 25; Comment of eBay, cmt. #00374, at 10; Comment of National Cable & Telecommunications Ass'n, cmt. #00432, at 29; Comment of Retail Industry Leaders Ass'n, cmt. #00352, at 12; Comment of Microsoft Corp., cmt. #00395, at 15.

[305] A machine-readable privacy policy is a statement about a website's privacy practices – such as the collection and use of data – written in a standard computer language (not English text) that software tools such as consumer's web browser can read automatically. For example, when the browser reads a machine-readable policy, the browser can compare the policy to the consumer's browser privacy preferences, and can inform the consumer when these preferences do not match the practices of the website he is visiting. If the consumer decides he does not want to visit websites that sell information to third parties, he might set up a rule that recognizes that policy and blocks such sites or display a warning upon visiting such a site. Machine-readable language will be the subject of an upcoming summit. See White House, National Archives & Records Administration, Informing Consumers Through Smart Disclosures (Mar. 1, 2012), available at http://www.nist.gov/ineap/upload/Summit_ Invitation_to_Agencies_FINAL.pdf (describing upcoming summit).

[306] Likewise, new tools like privacyscore.com may help consumers more readily compare websites' data practices. See Tanzina Vega, A New Tool in Protecting Online Privacy, N.Y. TIMES, Feb. 12, 2012, available at http://mediadecoder.blogs.nytimes. com/2012/02/12/a-new-tool-in-protecting-online-privacy/?scp=2&sq=privacy&st=cse.

[307] Comment of Phorm Inc., cmt. #00353, at 9; Comment of Lorrie Faith Cranor, cmt. #00453, at 6.

[308] Comment of Lorrie Faith Cranor, cmt. #00453, at 6 (explaining how icons combined with standard policies might work: "For example, a type I policy might commit to not collecting sensitive categories of information and not sharing personal data except with a company's agents, while a type II policy might allow collection of sensitive information but still commit to not sharing them, a type III policy might share non-identified information for behavioral advertising, and so on. Companies would choose which policy type to commit to. They could advertise their policy type with an associated standard icon, while also providing a more detailed policy. Users would be able to quickly determine the policy for the companies they interact with.").

[309] Comment of Mozilla, cmt. #00480, at 12.

[310] Comment of American Ass'n of Advertising Agencies, American Advertising Federation, Ass'n of National Advertisers, Direct Marketing Ass'n, Inc., and Interactive Advertising Bureau, cmt. #00410 at 2-3; Comment of Digital Marketing Alliance, cmt. #00449, at 18-24; Comment of Evidon, cmt. #00391, at 3-6; Comment of Internet Advertising Bureau, cmt. #00388, at 4.

[311] Comment of General Electric, cmt. #00392, at 1-2; Comment of CTIA - The Wireless Ass'n, cmt. #00375, at 2-3; Comment of Mozilla, cmt. #00480, at 12.

[312] See Common Sense Media, App Reviews, http://www.commonsensemedia.org/app-reviews.

[313] See Letter from Bruce Sewell, General Counsel & Senior Vice President of Legal and Governmental Affairs, Apple, to Hon. Edward J. Markey, U.S. House of Representatives (May 6, 2011), available at http://robert.accettura.com/wp-content/ uploads/2011/05/apple_ letter_to_ejm_05.06.11.pdf.

[314] See Press Release, CTIA – The Wireless Ass'n, CTIA – The Wireless Ass'n to Announce Mobile Application Rating System with ESRB (Nov. 21, 2011), available at http://www.ctia.org/media/press/body.cfm/prid/2145.

[315] Comment of Consumer Federation of America, cmt. #00358, at 16; Comment of GSMA, cmt. #00336, at 10.

[316] Although this effort is promising, more work remains. The Mobile Marketing Association's guidelines are not mandatory and there is little recourse against companies who elect not to follow them. More generally, there are too few players in the mobile ecosystem who are committed to self-regulatory principles and providing meaningful disclosures and choices.

[317] See Press Release, FTC, FTC Seeks Input to Revising its Guidance to Business About Disclosures in Online Advertising (May 26, 2011), available at http://www.ftc.gov/opa/ 2011/05/dotcom.shtm.

[318] See Press Release, FTC, FTC Will Host Public Workshop to Explore Advertising Disclosures in Online and Mobile Media on May 30, 2012 (Feb. 29, 2012), available at http://www.ftc.gov/opa/2012/02/dotcom.shtm.

[319] Comment of Intuit, Inc., cmt. #00348, at 12; Comment of eBay, cmt. #00374, at 10; Comment of IBM, cmt. #00433, at 3; Comment of Consumers Union, cmt. #00362, at 16.

[320] Comment of Meijer, cmt. #00416, at 7.

[321] Comment of Intel Corp., cmt. #00246, at 8; Comment of The Centre for Information Policy Leadership at Hunton & Williams LLP, cmt. #00360, at 8; Comment of Experian, cmt. #00398, at 11.

[322] Comment of Experian, cmt. #00398, at 10-11.

[323] Comment of AT&T Inc., cmt. #00420, at 28-29.

[324] Comment of CTIA - The Wireless Ass'n, cmt. #00375, at 3; Comment of Yahoo!, Inc., cmt. #00444, at 20; Comment of The Centre for Information Policy Leadership at Hunton & Williams LLP, cmt. #00360, at 5-6.

[325] Comment of U.S. Council for International Business, cmt. #00366, at 3.

[326] Comment of Catalog Choice, cmt. #00473, at 8-9; Comment of the Information Commissioner's Office of the UK, cmt. #00249, at 5.

[327] See Comment of Catalog Choice, cmt. #00473, at 20. Under this law, businesses, upon request, must provide their customers, free of charge and within 30 days: (1) a list of the categories of personal information disclosed by the business to third parties for the third parties' marketing purposes, (2) the names and addresses of all of the third parties that received personal information from the business in the preceding calendar year, (3) and if the nature of the third parties's business cannot reasonably be determined from the third parties' name, examples of the products or services marketed by the third party. Cal. Civ. Code § 1798.83.

[328] Comment of The Centre for Information Policy Leadership at Hunton & Williams, LLP, cmt. #00360, at 7.

[329] Comment of Reputation.com, Inc., cmt. #00385, at 11-12; see also Comment of Center for Democracy & Technology, cmt. #00469, at 25.

[330] Comment of The Centre for Information Policy Leadership at Hunton & Williams, LLP, cmt. #00360, at 7.

[331] As discussed above, in most cases the framework does not require companies to provide consumer choice for first-party marketing, although first parties may choose to provide such choice to meet consumer demand. Outside of the first-party marketing context, however, companies should provide consumers with the ability to suppress the use of their data for marketing.

[332] See Yahoo!, Ad Interest Manager, http://info.yahoo.com/privacy/us/yahoo/opt_out/targeting.

[333] Comment of Consumer Data Industry Ass'n, cmt. #00363, at 4 - 5; Comment of Experian, cmt. #00398, at 10.

[334] 15 U.S.C. §§ 1681g-1681h. See Letter from Maneesha Mithal, Assoc. Dir., Div. of Privacy and Identity Prot., FTC, to Renee Jackson, Counsel for Social Intelligence Corp., (May 9, 2011) (closing letter), available at http://www.ftc.gov/os/closings/110 509socialintelligence letter.pdf .

[335] See Press Release, FTC, FTC Warns Marketers That Mobile Apps May Violate Fair Credit Reporting Act (Feb. 7, 2012), available at http://www.ftc.gov/opa/2012/02/mobileapps.shtm (describing warning letters sent by the FTC to Everify, Inc., InfoPay, Inc., and Intelligator, Inc. on Jan. 25, 2012).

[336] See Laura Landro, Many Pills, Many Not Taken, Wall ST. J., Oct. 10, 2011, available at http://online.wsj.com/article/SB1000 1424052970203388804576616882856318782.html.

[337] Comment of Consumers Union, cmt. #00362, at 16; Comment of CTIA – The Wireless Ass'n, cmt. #00375, at 7; Comment of Microsoft Corp., cmt. #00395, at 15-16.

[338] Comment of Retail Industry Leaders Ass'n, cmt. #00352, at Ex. A.

[339] Comment of Reputation.com, Inc., cmt. #00385, at 11-12. Of course, First Amendment protections would apply to journalists' sources, among other things, and the Commission's recommendations are not intended to apply in that area.

[340] As noted above, companies should pay close attention to the types of eligibility determinations being made to ensure they comply with the FCRA, if warranted.

[341] One commenter noted that when organizations collect and maintain sensitive information about individuals, such as for banking or issuance of credit, they will ask for authenticating information before an individual can access those records. This same commenter then stated that organizations holding less sensitive data may not require similarly rigorous authentication. See Comment of The Centre for Information Policy Leadership at Hunton & Williams, LLP, cmt. #00360, at 7 n.6.

[342] See Comment of Privacy Rights Clearinghouse, cmt. #00351, at 3; Comment of Consumers Union, cmt. #00362, at 11.

[343] See Comment of Consumer Federation of America, cmt. #00358, at 17.

[344] See Comment of Privacy Rights Clearinghouse, cmt. #00351, at 8.

[345] See, e.g., Prepared Statement of the FTC, Identity Theft: Recent Developments Involving the Security of Sensitive Consumer Information: Hearing Before the Senate Comm. on Banking, Housing, and Urban Affairs, 109th Cong. (Mar. 10, 2005), available at http://www.ftc.gov/os/testimony/050310idtheft.pdf; see also FTC Workshop, The Information Marketplace: Merging & Exchanging Consumer Data (Mar. 13, 2001), available at http://www.ftc.gov/bcp/workshops/infomktplace/index. shtml; FTC Workshop, Information Flows: The Costs and Benefits to Consumers and Businesses of the Collection and Use of Consumer Information (June 18, 2003), available at http://www.ftc.gov/bcp/ workshops/infoflows/030618agenda.shtm.

[346] See FTC, Individual Reference Services, A Report to Congress (1997), available at http://www.ftc.gov/bcp/privacy/wkshp97/ irsdoc1.htm.

[347] See Prepared Statement of the FTC, Protecting Consumers' Data: Policy Issues Raised by ChoicePoint: Hearing before H. Comm. on Energy and Commerce, Subcomm. on Commerce, Trade, and Consumer Protection, Comm. on Energy and Commerce, 109th Cong. (Mar. 15, 2005), available at http://www.ftc.gov/os/2005/03/050315protecting consumerdata.pdf.

[348] Data Accountability and Trust Act, H.R. 2221, 111th Congress (as passed by House, Dec. 8, 2009).

[349] See, e.g., Prepared Statement of the FTC, Legislative Hearing on H.R. 2221, the Data Accountability and Protection Act, and H.R. 1319, the Informed P2P User Act: Hearing Before the H. Comm. on Energy and Commerce, Subcomm. on Commerce, Trade, and Consumer Protection, 111th Cong. (May 5, 2009), available at http://www.ftc.gov/os/2009/ 05/P064504peertopeertestimony.pdf.

[350] See, e.g., Prepared Statement of the FTC, Data Security: Hearing Before the H. Comm. on Energy and Commerce, Subcomm. on Commerce, Manufacturing, and Trade, 112th Cong. (May 4, 2011), available at http://www.ftc.gov/opa/2011/05/ pdf/110504datasecurityhouse. pdf; Prepared Statement of the FTC, Data Security: Hearing Before the H. Comm. on Energy and Commerce, Subcomm. on Commerce, Manufacturing, and Trade, 112th Cong.(June 15, 2011), available at http://www.ftc. gov/os/testimony/110615datasecurity house.pdf; Prepared Statement of the FTC, Protecting Consumers in the Modern World: Hearing Before the S. Comm. on Commerce, Science, and Transportation, 112th Cong. (June 29, 2011), available at http://www. ftc.gov/os/testimony/110629privacy testimonybrill.pdf.

[351] See Comment of World Privacy Forum, cmt. #00376, at 6; Comment of Consumer Federation of America, cmt. #00358, at 17-18.

[352] The current website of the Direct Marketing Association (DMA) offers an instructive model for such a mechanism. The DMA – which consists of data brokers, retailers, and others – currently offers a service through which consumers can opt out of receiving marketing solicitations via particular channels, such as direct mail, from DMA member companies. See DMAChoice, http://www.dmachoice.org/dma/member/ home.action.

[353] See Comment of Consumers Union, cmt. #00362, at 13; see also Center for Digital Democracy and U.S. PIRG, cmt. #00338, at 39.

[354] Comment of CNIL, cmt. #00298, at 3.

[355] Do Not Track Kids Act of 2011, H.R. 1895, 112th Congress (2011).

[356] See Facebook, How Do I Remove a Wall Post or Story?, available at http://www.facebook. com/help/?page=174851209237562; LinkedIn, Privacy Policy, http://www.linkedin.com/ static?key=privacy_policy.

[357] See, e.g., FTC, Transcript of March 17, 2010, Privacy Roundtable, Panel 3: Addressing Sensitive Information, 208-215, available at http://www.ftc.gov/bcp/workshops/ privacyrountables/PrivacyRoundtable_March2010_ Transcript.pdf; see also Chris Hoofnagle, Jennifer King, Su Li, & Joseph Turow, How Different Are Young Adults from Older Adults When It Comes to Information Privacy Attitudes & Policies? (Apr. 14, 2010), available at http://papers.ssrn.com/sol3/papers.cfm?abstract_ id=1589864.

[358] While consumers should be able to delete much of the information they place on a particular social media site, there may be First Amendment constraints to requiring third parties to delete the same information. In the FTC's recent proposed settlement with Facebook, the company agreed to implement measures designed to prevent any third party from accessing information under Facebook's control within a reasonable time period, not to exceed thirty days, from the time the user has deleted such information. See In the Matter of Facebook, Inc., FTC File No. 092 3184 (Nov. 29, 2011) (proposed consent order), available at http://ftc.gov/os/caselist/0923184/111129facebookagree.pdf.

[359] See, e.g., Comment of Intuit Inc., cmt. #00348, at 12; Comment of AT&T Inc., cmt. #00420, at 30-31; Comment of Consumers Union, cmt. #00362, at 18.

[360] Comment of Zynga Inc., cmt. #00459, at 4.

[361] See, e.g., Common Sense Media, App Reviews, http://www.commonsensemedia.org/app-reviews (listing reviews that evaluate privacy and safety concerns posed by common mobile applications designed for children); Google, Ad Preferences, Frequently Asked Questions, http://www.google.com/ads/preferences/html/faq.html; Interactive Advertising Bureau, Privacy Matters Campaign, http://www.iab.net/privacymatters/campaign.php; Kashmir Hill, Zynga's PrivacyVille – It's Not Fun, But It Gets the Job Done, FORBES, July 8, 2011, available at http://www.forbes.com/sites/ kashmirhill/2011/07/08/zyngas-privacyville-its-notfun-but-it-gets-the-job-done/.

[362] Comment of United States Council for International Business, cmt. #00366, at 4; Comment of IMS Health, cmt. #00380, at 5; Comment of The Privacy Projects, cmt. #00482, at 2-3.

[363] FTC, Wise Up About Wi-Fi: Tips for Using Public Wireless Networks (2011), http://www.ftc.gov/bcp/edu/pubs/consumer/alerts/ alt193.shtm; FTC, Cookies: Leaving a Trail on the Web, http://onguardonline.gov/articles/0042-cookies-leaving-trail-web; FTC, Understanding Mobile Apps, http://onguardonline.gov/articles/0018-understanding-mobile-apps; FTC Workshop, Stolen Futures: A Forum on Child Identity Theft, (July 12, 2011), http://www.ftc.gov/bcp/workshops/stolenfutures/.

[364] See Press Release, FTC, FTC Seeks Input to Revising its Guidance to Businesses About Disclosures in Online Advertising (May 26, 2011), available at http://www.ftc.gov/opa/2011/05/dotcom.shtm.

[365] See Data Accountability and Trust Act, H.R. 1707, 112th Congress (2011); Data Accountability and Trust Act of 2011, H.R. 1841, 112th Congress (2011); Data Security and Breach Notification Act of 2011, S. 1207, 112th Congress (2011).

End Notes for Appendix C

[1] Protecting Consumer Privacy in an Era of Rapid Change: Recommendations for Businesses and Policymakers ("Report") at 50-52.

[2] Id. at 14, 73.

[3] Id. at 26. I also support the recommendation that such legislation authorize the Commission to seek civil penalties for violations. However, despite its bow to "targeted" legislation, the Report elsewhere counsels that the Commission support privacy legislation generally. See, e.g., id. at 16. To the extent that those recommendations are not defined, or narrowly targeted, I disagree with them.

[4] Id. at 14, 68-70.

[5] See J. Thomas Rosch, Comm'r, Fed. Trade Comm'n, Information and Privacy: In Search of a Data-Driven Policy, Remarks at the Technology Policy Institute Aspen Forum (Aug. 22, 2011), available at http://www.ftc.gov/speeches/ rosch/110822aspeninfospeech.pdf.

[6] See Katy Bachman, Study: Internet User Adoption of DNT Hard to Predict, adweek.com, March 20, 2012, available at http:// www.adweek.com/news/technology/study-internet-user-adoption-dnt-hard-predict-139091 (reporting on a survey that found that what Internet users say they are going to do about using a Do Not Track button and what they are currently doing about blocking tracking on the Internet, are two different things); see also Concurring Statement of Commissioner J. Thomas Rosch, Issuance of Preliminary FTC Staff Report "Protecting Consumer Privacy in an Era of Rapid Change: A Proposed Framework for Businesses and Policymakers" (Dec. 1, 2010), available at http://www.ftc.gov/speeches/ rosch/101201privacyreport.pdf.

[7] See J. Thomas Rosch, Comm'r, Fed. Trade Comm'n, Do Not Track: Privacy in an Internet Age, Remarks at Loyola Chicago Antitrust Institute Forum, (Oct. 14, 2011), available at http://www.ftc.gov/speeches/rosch/111014-dnt-loyola.pdf; see also Report at 9.

[8] Report at 8 and n.37.

9 Id. at 2. The Report seems to imply that the Do Not Call Rule would support this extension of the definition of harm. See id. ("unwarranted intrusions into their daily lives"). However, it must be emphasized that the Congress granted the FTC underlying authority under the Telemarketing and Consumer Fraud and Abuse Prevention Act, 15 U.S.C. §§ 6101-6108, to promulgate the Do Not Call provisions and other substantial amendments to the TSR. The Commission did not do so unilaterally.

10 Id.

11 Id. at 19.

12 Id. at 23, see also id. at 24.

13 Id. at 9-10. This does not mean that I am an isolationist or am impervious to the benefits of a global solution. But, as stated below, there is more than one way to skin this cat.

14 See Letter from the FTC to Hon. Wendell Ford and Hon. John Danforth, Committee on Commerce, Science and Transportation, United States Senate, Commission Statement of Policy on the Scope of Consumer Unfairness Jurisdiction (Dec. 17, 1980), reprinted in International Harvester Co., 104 F.T.C. 949, 1070, 1073 (1984) ("Unfairness Policy Statement") available at http://www.ftc.gov/bcp/policystmt/ad-unfair.htm; Letter from the FTC to Hon. Bob Packwood and Hon. Bob Kasten, Committee on Commerce, Science and Transportation, United States Senate, reprinted in FTC Antitrust & Trade Reg. Rep. (BNA) 1055, at 568-570 ("Packwood-Kasten letter"); and 15 U.S.C. § 45(n), which codified the FTC's modern approach.

15 See Concurring and Dissenting Statement of Commissioner J. Thomas Rosch, In re Intel Corp., Docket No. 9341, (Dec. 16, 2009), available at http://www.ftc.gov/os/adjpro/d9341/ 091216intelstatement.pdf.

16 See Rosch, supra note 7 at 20.

17 See Report at 13.

18 Federal Trade Commission Act Amendments of 1994, Pub. L. No. 103-312.

19 Report at 4, 52.

20 Id. at 53, 54; see esp. id. at 53 n.250.

21 Id. at 5, 54.

22 See Rosch, supra note 7 at 20-21.

23 Tony Romm, "What Exactly Does 'Do Not Track' Mean?," Politico, Mar. 13, 2012, available at http://www.politico.com/news/ stories/0312/73976.html; see also Report at 4 (DAA allows consumer to opt out of "targeted advertising").

24 See Self-Regulatory Principles for Multi-Site Data, Digital Advertising Alliance, Nov. 2011, at 3, 10, 11, available at http:// www.aboutads.info/resource/download/Multi-Site-Data-Principles.pdf; see also Tanzina Vega, Opt-Out Provision Would Halt Some, but Not All, Web Tracking, New York Times, Feb. 26, 2012, available at http://www.nytimes.com/ 2012/02/27/ technology/opt-out-provision-would-halt-some-but-not-all-web-tracking.html? pagewanted=all.

25 See Vega, supra note 24.

26 "Why Johnny Can't Opt Out: A Usability Evaluation of Tools to Limit Online Behavioral Advertising," Carnegie Mellon University CyLab, Oct. 31, 2011, available at http://www.cylab.cmu.edu/files/pdfs/tech_reports/ CMUCyLab11017.pdf; see also Search Engine Use 2012, at 25, Pew Internet & American Life Project, Pew Research Center, Mar. 9, 2012, available at http://pewinternet.org/~/media/Files/Reports/2012/ PIP_Search_ Engine_Use_2012.pdf ("[j]ust 38% of internet users say they are generally aware of ways they themselves can limit how much information about them is collected by a website").

27 See Julie Brill, Comm'r, Fed. Trade Comm'n, Big Data, Big Issues, Remarks at Fordham University School of Law (Mar. 2, 2012) available at http://www.ftc.gov/speeches/ brill/120228fordhamlawschool.pdf.

28 See Bachman, supra note 6.

29 Report at 41.

30 Id. Notwithstanding that Google's prospective conduct seems to fit perfectly the circumstances set forth on this page of the Report (describing a company with multiple lines of business including a search engine and ad network), where the Commission states "consumer choice" is warranted, the Report goes on to conclude on page 56 that Google's practices do not require affirmative express consent because they "currently are not so widespread that they could track a consumer's every movement across the Internet."

31 Id. at 40. See also supra note 30. That observation also applies to "social networks" like Facebook.

32 Id. at 41.

33 See id. at 60 ("Final Principle").

34 Id. at 56 ("the Commission has strong concerns about the use of DPI for purposes inconsistent with an ISP's interaction with a consumer, without express affirmative consent or more robust protection").

35 Id.

[36] Id.

[37] Federal Communications Commission, Connecting America: The National Broadband Plan, Broadband Competition and Innovation Policy, Section 4.1, Networks, Competition in Residential Broadband Markets at 36, available at http://www. broadband.gov/plan/4-broadband-competition-and-innovation-policy/.

[38] Federal Communications Commission Working Paper, Broadband decisions: What drives consumers to switch – or stick with – their broadband Internet provider (Dec. 2010), at 3, 8, available at http://transition.fcc.gov/ Daily_Releases/Daily_ Business/2010/db1206/DOC-303264A1.pdf.

[39] See Rosch, supra note 15.

[40] See, e.g., Report at 56.

[41] Testimony of Jon Leibowitz and J. Thomas Rosch, Chairman and Comm'r, FTC, The FTC in FY2013: Protecting Consumers and Competition: Hearing on Budget Before the H. Comm. on Appropriations Subcomm. on Financial Services and General Government, 112 th Cong. 2 (2012), text from CQ Roll Call, available from: LexisNexis® Congressional.

[42] One notable example is found where the Report discusses the articulation of privacy harms and enforcement actions brought on the basis of deception. The Report then notes "[l]ike these enforcement actions, a privacy framework should address practices that unexpectedly reveal previously private information even absent physical or financial harm, or unwarranted intrusions." Report at 8. The accompanying footnote concludes that "even in the absence of such misrepresentations, revealing previously-private consumer data could cause consumer harm." See also infra note 43.

[43] Id. at 16 ("to the extent Congress enacts any of the Commission's recommendations through legislation"); see also id. at 12- 13 ("the Commission calls on Congress to develop baseline privacy legislation that is technologically neutral and sufficiently flexible to allow companies to continue to innovate").

[44] See Letter from President Barack Obama, appended to White House, Consumer Data Privacy in a Networked World: A Framework for Protecting Privacy and Promoting Innovation in the Global Digital Economy (Feb. 23, 2012), available at http:// www.whitehouse.gov/sites/default/files/privacy-final.pdf.

[45] See FTC Testimony, supra note 41.

In: Consumer Privacy in the 21st Century
Editor: Larry A. Schwartz

ISBN: 978-1-62417-252-6

Chapter 2

CONSUMER DATA PRIVACY IN A NETWORKED WORLD: A FRAMEWORK FOR PROTECTING PRIVACY AND PROMOTING INNOVATION IN THE GLOBAL DIGITAL ECONOMY*

The White House

Washington

February 23, 2012

Americans have always cherished our privacy. From the birth of our republic, we assured ourselves protection against unlawful intrusion into our homes and our personal papers. At the same time, we set up a postal system to enable citizens all over the new nation to engage in commerce and political discourse. Soon after, Congress made it a crime to invade the privacy of the mails. And later we extended privacy protections to new modes of communications such as the telephone, the computer, and eventually email.

Justice Brandeis taught us that privacy is the "right to be let alone," but we also know that privacy is about much more than just solitude or secrecy. Citizens who feel protected from misuse of their personal information feel free to engage in commerce, to participate in the political process, or to seek needed health care. This is why we have laws that protect financial privacy and health privacy, and that protect consumers against unfair and deceptive uses of their information.

This is why the Supreme Court has protected anonymous political speech, the same right exercised by the pamphleteers of the early Republic and today's bloggers.

Never has privacy been more important than today, in the age of the Internet, the World Wide Web and smart phones. In just the last decade, the Internet has enabled a renewal of direct political engagement by citizens around the globe and an explosion of commerce and innovation creating jobs of the future. Much of this innovation is enabled by novel uses of

---

* This is an edited, reformatted and augmented version of The White House, dated February 2012.

personal information. So, it is incumbent on us to do what we have done throughout history: apply our timeless privacy values to the new technologies and circumstances of our times.

I am pleased to present this new Consumer Privacy Bill of Rights as a blueprint for privacy in the information age. These rights give consumers clear guidance on what they should expect from those who handle their personal information, and set expectations for companies that use personal data. I call on these companies to begin immediately working with privacy advocates, consumer protection enforcement agencies, and others to implement these principles in enforceable codes of conduct.

My Administration will work to advance these principles and work with Congress to put them into law. With this Consumer Privacy Bill of Rights, we offer to the world a dynamic model of how to offer strong privacy protection and enable ongoing innovation in new information technologies.

One thing should be clear, even though we live in a world in which we share personal information more freely than in the past, we must reject the conclusion that privacy is an outmoded value. It has been at the heart of our democracy from its inception, and we need it now more than ever.

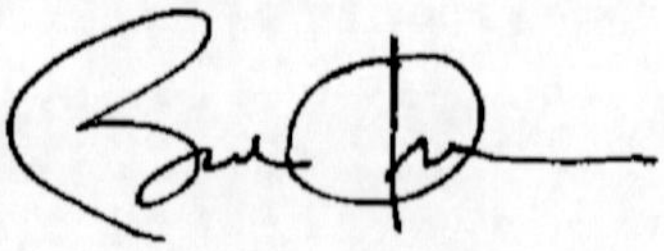

FOREWORD

Trust is essential to maintaining the social and economic benefits that networked technologies bring to the United States and the rest of the world. With the confidence that companies will handle information about them fairly and responsibly, consumers have turned to the Internet to express their creativity, join political movements, form and maintain friendships, and engage in commerce. The Internet's global connectivity means that a single innovator's idea can grow rapidly into a product or service that becomes a daily necessity for hundreds of millions of consumers. American companies lead the way in providing these technologies, and the United States benefits through job creation and economic growth as a result. Our continuing leadership in this area depends on American companies'ability to earn and maintain the trust of consumers in a global marketplace.

Privacy protections are critical to maintaining consumer trust in networked technologies. When consumers provide information about themselves—whether it is in the context of an online social network that is open to public view or a transaction involving sensitive personal data—they reasonably expect companies to use this information in ways that are consistent with the surrounding context. Many companies live up to these expectations, but some do not. Neither consumers nor companies have a clear set of ground rules to apply in the commercial arena. As a result, it is difficult today for consumers to assess whether a company's privacy practices warrant their trust.

The consumer data privacy framework in the United States is, in fact, strong. This framework rests on fundamental privacy values, flexible and adaptable common law protections and consumer protection statutes, Federal Trade Commission (FTC) enforcement, and policy development that involves a broad array of stakeholders. This framework has encouraged not only social and economic innovations based on the Internet but also vibrant discussions of how to protect privacy in a networked society involving civil society, industry, academia, and the government. The current framework, however, lacks two elements: a clear statement of basic privacy principles that apply to the commercial world, and a sustained commitment of all stakeholders to address consumer data privacy issues as they arise from advances in technologies and business models.

To address these issues, the Administration offers *Consumer Data Privacy in a Networked World.* At the center of this framework is a Consumer Privacy Bill of Rights, which embraces privacy principles recognized throughout the world and adapts them to the dynamic environment of the commercial Internet. The Administration has called for Congress to pass legislation that applies the Consumer Privacy Bill of Rights to commercial sectors that are not subject to existing Federal data privacy laws. The Federal Government will play a role in convening discussions among stakeholders—companies, privacy and consumer advocates, international partners, State Attorneys General, Federal criminal and civil law enforcement representatives, and academics—who will then develop codes of conduct that implement the Consumer Privacy Bill of Rights. Such practices, when publicly and affirmatively adopted by companies subject to Federal Trade Commission jurisdiction, will be legally enforceable by the FTC. The United States will engage with our international partners to create greater interoperability among our respective privacy frameworks. This will provide more consistent protections for consumers and lower compliance burdens for companies.

Of course, this framework is just a beginning. Starting now, the Administration will work with and encourage stakeholders, including the private sector, to implement the Consumer Privacy Bill of Rights. The Administration will also work with Congress to write these flexible, general principles into law. The Administration is ready to do its part as a convener to achieve privacy protections that preserve consumer trust and promote innovation.

Executive Summary

Strong consumer data privacy protections are essential to maintaining consumers' trust in the technologies and companies that drive the digital economy. The existing framework in the United States effectively addresses some privacy issues in our increasingly networked society, but additional protections are necessary to preserve consumer trust. The framework set forth in this document will provide these protections while promoting innovation.

The Administration's framework consists of four key elements: A Consumer Privacy Bill of Rights, a multistakeholder process to specify how the principles in the Consumer Privacy Bill of Rights apply in particular business contexts, effective enforcement, and a commitment to increase interoperability with the privacy frameworks of our international partners.

- A Consumer Privacy Bill of Rights

This document sets forth a Consumer Privacy Bill of Rights that, in the Administration's view, provides a baseline of clear protections for consumers and greater certainty for companies. The Administration will encourage stakeholders to implement the Consumer

Privacy Bill of Rights through codes of conduct and will work with Congress to enact these rights through legislation. The Consumer Privacy Bill of Rights applies comprehensive, globally recognized Fair Information Practice Principles (FIPPs) to the interactive and highly interconnected environment in which we live and work today. Specifically, it provides for:

- Individual Control: Consumers have a right to exercise control over what personal data companies collect from them and how they use it.
- Transparency: Consumers have a right to easily understandable and accessible information about privacy and security practices.
- Respect for Context: Consumers have a right to expect that companies will collect, use, and disclose personal data in ways that are consistent with the context in which consumers provide the data.
- Security: Consumers have a right to secure and responsible handling of personal data.
- Access and Accuracy: Consumers have a right to access and correct personal data in usable formats, in a manner that is appropriate to the sensitivity of the data and the risk of adverse consequences to consumers if the data is inaccurate.
- Focused Collection: Consumers have a right to reasonable limits on the personal data that companies collect and retain.
- Accountability: Consumers have a right to have personal data handled by companies with appropriate measures in place to assure they adhere to the Consumer Privacy Bill of Rights.

The Consumer Privacy Bill of Rights provides general principles that afford companies discretion in how they implement them. This flexibility will help promote innovation. Flexibility will also encourage effective privacy protections by allowing companies, informed by input from consumers and other stakeholders, to address the privacy issues that are likely to be most important to their customers and users, rather than requiring companies to adhere to a single, rigid set of requirements.

Enacting the Consumer Privacy Bill of Rights through Federal legislation would increase legal certainty for companies, strengthen consumer trust, and bolster the United States' ability to lead consumer data privacy engagements with our international partners. Even if Congress does not pass legislation, the Consumer Privacy Bill of Rights will serve as a template for privacy protections that increase consumer trust on the Internet and promote innovation.

- Fostering Multistakeholder Processes to Develop Enforceable Codes of Conduct

The Administration's framework outlines a multistakeholder process to produce enforceable codes of conduct that implement the Consumer Privacy Bill of Rights. The Administration will convene open, transparent forums in which stakeholders who share an interest in specific markets or business contexts will work toward consensus on appropriate, legally enforceable codes of conduct. Private sector participation will be voluntary and companies ultimately will choose whether to adopt a given code of conduct. The participation of a broad group of stakeholders, including consumer groups and privacy advocates, will help to ensure that codes of conduct lead to privacy solutions that consumers can easily use and understand. A single code of conduct for a given market or business context will provide consumers with more consistent privacy protections than is common today, when privacy practices and the information that consumers receive about them varies significantly from company to company.

- Strengthening FTC Enforcement

FTC enforcement is critical to ensuring that companies are accountable for adhering to their privacy commitments. Enforcement is also critical to ensuring that responsible companies are not disadvantaged by competitors who would play by different rules. As part of consumer data privacy legislation, the Administration encourages Congress to provide the FTC (and State Attorneys General) with specific authority to enforce the Consumer Privacy Bill of Rights.

- Improving Global Interoperability

The Administration's framework embraces the goal of increased international interoperability as a means to provide consistent, low-barrier rules for personal data in the user-driven and decentralized Internet environment. The two principles that underlie our approach to interoperability are mutual recognition and enforcement cooperation. Mutual recognition depends on effective enforcement and well-defined accountability mechanisms. Multistakeholder processes can provide scalable, flexible means of developing codes of conduct that simplify companies' compliance obligations. Enforcement cooperation helps to ensure that countries are able to protect their citizens' rights when personal data crosses national boundaries. These approaches will guide United States efforts to clarify data protections globally while ensuring the flexibility that is critical to innovation in the commercial world.

The Administration will implement this framework without delay. In the coming months, the Department of Commerce will work with other Federal agencies to convene stakeholders, including our international partners, to develop enforceable codes of conduct that build on the Consumer Privacy Bill of Rights.

I. Introduction: Building on the Strength of the U.S. Consumer Data Privacy Framework

The Internet is integral to economic and social life in the United States and throughout the world. Networked technologies offer individuals nearly limitless ways to express themselves, form social connections, transact business, and organize politically. Networked technologies also spur innovation, enable new business models, and facilitate consumers'and companies'access to information, products, and services markets across the world.

An abundance of data, inexpensive processing power, and increasingly sophisticated analytical techniques drive innovation in our increasingly networked society. Political organizations and candidates for public office build powerful campaigns on data that individuals share about themselves and their political preferences. Data from social networks allows journalists and individuals to report and follow newsworthy events around the world as they unfold. Data plays a key role in the ability of government to stop identity thieves and protect public safety. Researchers use sets of medical data to identify public health issues and probe the causes of human diseases. Network operators use data from communications networks to identify events ranging from a severed fiber optic cable to power outages and the acts of malicious intruders. In addition, personal data fuels an advertising marketplace that brings many online services and sources of content to consumers for free.

Strengthening consumer data privacy protections in the United States is an important Administration priority.[1] Americans value privacy and expect protection from intrusions by both private and governmental actors. Strong privacy protections also are critical to sustaining the trust that nurtures Internet commerce and fuels innovation. Trust means the companies and technical systems on which we depend meet our expectations for privacy, security, and reliability.[2] In addition, United States leadership in consumer data privacy can help establish more flexible, innovation-enhancing privacy models among our international partners.[3]

Preserving trust in the Internet economy protects and enhances substantial economic activity.[4] Online retail sales in the United States total $145 billion annually.[5] New uses of personal data in location services, protected by appropriate privacy and security safeguards, could create important business opportunities.[6] Moreover, the United States is a world leader in exporting cloud computing, location-based services, and other innovative services. To preserve these economic benefits, consumers must continue to trust networked technologies. Strengthening consumer data privacy protections will help to achieve this goal.

Preserving trust also is necessary to realize the full social and cultural benefits of networked technologies. When companies use personal data in ways that are inconsistent with the circumstances under which consumers disclosed the data, however, they may undermine trust. For example, individuals who actively share information with their friends, family, colleagues, and the general public through websites and online social networking sites may not be aware of the ways those services, third parties, and their own associates may use information about them. Unauthorized disclosure of sensitive information can violate individual rights, cause injury or discrimination based on sensitive personal attributes, lead to actions and decisions taken in response to misleading or inaccurate information, and contribute to costly and potentially life-disrupting identity theft.[7] Protecting Americans' privacy by preventing identity theft and prosecuting identity thieves is an important focus for the Administration.

The existing consumer data privacy framework in the United States is flexible and effectively addresses some consumer data privacy challenges in the digital age. This framework consists of industry best practices, FTC enforcement, and a network of chief privacy officers and other privacy professionals who develop privacy practices that adapt to changes in technology and business models and create a growing culture of privacy awareness within companies. Much of the personal data used on the Internet, however, is not subject to comprehensive Federal statutory protection, because most Federal data privacy statutes apply only to specific sectors, such as healthcare, education, communications, and financial services or, in the case of online data collection, to children. The Administration believes that filling gaps in the existing framework will promote more consistent responses to privacy concerns across the wide range of environments in which individuals have access to networked technologies and in which a broad array of companies collect and use personal data. The Administration, however, does not recommend modifying the existing Federal statutes that apply to specific sectors unless they set inconsistent standards for related technologies. Instead, the Administration supports legislation that would supplement the existing framework and extend baseline protections to the sectors that existing Federal statutes do not cover.

The comprehensive consumer data privacy framework set forth here will provide clearer protections for consumers. It will also provide greater certainty for companies while promoting innovation and minimizing compliance costs (consistent with the goals of Executive Order 13563, "Improving Regulation and Regulatory Review"). The framework provides consumers who want to understand and control how personal data flows in the digital economy with better tools to do so. The proposal ensures that companies striving to meet consumers'expectations have more effective ways of engaging consumers and policymakers. This will help companies to determine which personal data practices consumers find unobjectionable and which ones they find invasive. Finally, the Administration's consumer data privacy framework improves our global competitiveness by promoting international policy frameworks that reflect how consumers and companies actually use networked technologies.

As a world leader in Internet innovation, the United States has both the responsibility and incentive to help establish forward-looking privacy policy models that foster innovation and preserve basic privacy rights. The Administration's framework for consumer data privacy offers a path toward achieving these goals. It is based on the following key elements:

- A **Consumer Privacy Bill of Rights**, setting forth individual rights and corresponding obligations of companies in connection with personal data. These consumer rights are based on U.S.-developed and globally recognized Fair Information Practice Principles (FIPPs), articulated in terms that apply to the dynamic environment of the Internet age;
- **Enforceable codes of conduct**, developed through **multistakeholder processes**, to form the basis for specifying what the Consumer Privacy Bill of Rights requires in particular business contexts;
- Federal Trade Commission (FTC) **enforcement** of consumers' data privacy rights through its authority to prohibit unfair or deceptive acts or practices; and
- Increasing **global interoperability** between the U.S. consumer data privacy framework and other countries'frameworks, through mutual recognition, the development of codes of conduct through multistakeholder processes, and enforcement cooperation can reduce barriers to the flow of information.

Consumer Data Privacy in a Networked World builds on the recommendations of the Department of Commerce Internet Policy Task Force's December 2010 report, Commercial Data Privacy and Innovation in the Internet Economy: A Dynamic Policy Framework ("Privacy and Innovation Green Paper").[8] The Internet Policy Task Force developed the recommendations in the Privacy and Innovation Green Paper by engaging with stakeholders—companies, trade groups, privacy advocates, academics, State Attorneys General, Federal civil and criminal law enforcement representatives, and international partners—through a public symposium, written comments, public speeches and presentations, and informal meetings. More than 100 stakeholders subsequently submitted written comments on the Privacy and Innovation Green Paper. These comments provided the Administration with invaluable feedback during the development of Consumer Data Privacy in a Networked World. The Administration gratefully acknowledges the time and resources stakeholders devoted to this issue. Their ongoing engagement will be critical to implementing the framework successfully.

II. DEFINING A CONSUMER PRIVACY BILL OF RIGHTS

Strengthening consumer data privacy protections and promoting innovation require privacy protections that are comprehensive, actionable, and flexible. The United States pioneered the FIPPs in the 1970s, and they have become the globally recognized foundations for privacy protection. The United States has embraced FIPPs by incorporating them into sector-specific privacy laws and applying them to personal data that Federal agencies collect. FIPPs also are a foundation for numerous international data privacy frameworks.[9] These principles continue to provide a solid foundation for consumer data privacy protection, despite far-reaching changes in companies'ability to collect, store, and analyze personal data.

The Consumer Privacy Bill of Rights applies FIPPs to an environment in which processing of data about individuals is far more decentralized and pervasive than it was when FIPPs were initially developed. Large corporations and government agencies collecting information for relatively static databases are no longer typical of personal data collectors and processors. The world is far more varied and dynamic. Companies process increasing quantities of personal data for a widening array of purposes. Consumers increasingly exchange personal data in active ways through channels such as online social networks and personal blogs. The reuse of personal data can be an important source of innovation that brings benefits to consumers but also raises difficult questions about privacy. The central challenge in this environment is to protect consumers' privacy expectations while providing companies with the certainty they need to continue to innovate.[10]

To meet this challenge, the Consumer Privacy Bill of Rights carries FIPPs forward in two ways. First, it affirms a set of consumer rights that inform consumers of what they should expect of companies that handle personal data. The Consumer Privacy Bill of Rights also recognizes that consumers have certain responsibilities to protect their privacy as they engage in an increasingly networked society. Second, the Consumer Privacy Bill of Rights reflects the FIPPs in a way that emphasizes the importance of context in their application.[11] Key elements of context include the goals or purposes that consumers can expect to achieve by using a company's products or services, the services that the companies actually provide, the personal data exchanges that are necessary to provide these services, and whether a company's customers include children and adolescents. Context should shape the balance and relative emphasis of particular principles in the Consumer Privacy Bill of Rights.

The Consumer Privacy Bill of Rights advances these objectives by holding that consumers have a right to:

- Individual Control
- Transparency
- Respect for Context

- Security
- Access and Accuracy
- Focused Collection
- Accountability

The Consumer Privacy Bill of Rights applies to commercial uses of personal data. This term refers to any data, including aggregations of data, which is linkable to a specific individual.[12] Personal data may include data that is linked to a specific computer or other device. For example, an identifier on a smartphone or family computer that is used to build a usage profile is personal data. This definition provides the flexibility that is necessary to capture the many kinds of data about consumers that commercial entities collect, use, and disclose.

The remainder of this section provides the full statement of the Consumer Privacy Bill of Rights and explains the rationale for the rights and obligations under each principle.

1. Individual Control: Consumers have a right to exercise control over what personal data companies collect from them and how they use it. Companies should provide consumers appropriate control over the personal data that consumers share with others and over how companies collect, use, or disclose personal data. Companies should enable these choices by providing consumers with easily used and accessible mechanisms that reflect the scale, scope, and sensitivity of the personal data that they collect, use, or disclose, as well as the sensitivity of the uses they make of personal data. Companies should offer consumers clear and simple choices, presented at times and in ways that enable consumers to make meaningful decisions about personal data collection, use, and disclosure. Companies should offer consumers means to withdraw or limit consent that are as accessible and easily used as the methods for granting consent in the first place.

The Individual Control principle has two dimensions. First, at the time of collection, companies should present choices about data sharing, collection, use, and disclosure that are appropriate for the scale, scope, and sensitivity of personal data in question. For example, companies that have access to significant portions of individuals' Internet usage histories, such as search engines, ad networks, and online social networks, can build detailed profiles of individual behavior over time. These profiles may be broad in scope and large in scale, and they may contain sensitive information, such as personal health or financial data.[13] In these cases, choice mechanisms that are simple and prominent and offer fine-grained control of personal data use and disclosure may be appropriate. By contrast, services that do not collect information that is reasonably linkable to individuals may offer accordingly limited choices.

In any event, a company that deals directly with consumers should give them appropriate choices about what personal data the company collects, irrespective of whether the company uses the data itself or discloses it to third parties. When consumer-facing companies contract with third parties that gather personal data directly from consumers (as is the case with much online advertising), they should be diligent in inquiring about how those third parties use personal data and whether they provide consumers with appropriate choices about collection, use, and disclosure. The Administration also encourages consumer-facing companies to act as stewards of personal data that they and their business partners collect from consumers. Consumer-facing companies should seek ways to recognize consumer choices through mechanisms that are simple, persistent, and scalable from the consumer's perspective.

Third parties should also offer choices about personal data collection that are appropriate for the scale, scope, and sensitivity of data they collect. The focal point for much of the debate about third-party personal data collection in recent years is online behavioral advertising—the practice of collecting information about consumers' online interests in order to deliver targeted advertising to them.[14] This system of advertising revolves around ad networks that can track individual consumers—or at least their devices—across different websites. When organized according to unique identifiers, this data can provide a potentially wide-ranging view of individual use of the Internet. These individual behavioral profiles allow advertisers to target ads based on inferences about individual interests, as revealed by Internet use. Targeted ads are generally more valuable and efficient than purely contextual ads and provide revenue that supports an array of free online content and services.[15] However, many consumers and privacy advocates find tracking and the advertising practices that it enables invade their expectations of privacy.[16]

The Administration recognizes that the ultimate uses of personal data that third parties, such as ad networks, collect affect the privacy interests at stake. As a result, these uses of personal data should help to shape the range of appropriate individual control options. For example, a company that uses personal data only to calculate statistics about how consumers use its services may not implicate significant consumer privacy interests and may not need to provide consumers with ways to prevent data collection for this purpose. Even if the company collects and stores some personal data for some uses, it may not need to provide consumers with a sophisticated array of choices about collection. In the case of online advertising, for instance, verifying ad delivery and preventing a consumer from seeing the same ad many times over may require some personal data collection. But personal data collected only for these statistical purposes may not require the assembly of extensive, long-lived individual profiles and may not require extensive options for control.

Innovative technology can help to expand the range of user control. It is increasingly common for Internet companies that have direct relationships with consumers to offer detailed privacy settings that allow individuals to exercise greater control over what personal data the companies collect, and when. In addition, privacy-enhancing technologies such as the "Do Not Track" mechanism allow consumers to exercise some control over how third parties use personal data or whether they receive it at all. For example, prompted by the FTC,[17] members of the online advertising industry developed self-regulatory principles based on the FIPPs, a common interface to alert consumers of the presence of third party ads and to direct them to more information about the relevant ad network, and a common mechanism to allow consumers to opt out of targeted advertising by individual ad networks.[18] A variety of other actors, including browser vendors, software developers, and standards-setting organizations, are developing "Do Not Track" mechanisms that allow consumers to exercise some control over whether third parties receive personal data. All of these mechanisms show promise. However, they require further development to ensure they are easy to use, strike a balance with innovative uses of personal data, take public safety interests into account, and present consumers with a clear picture of the potential costs and benefits of limiting personal data collection.

As third parties become further removed from direct interactions with consumers, it may be more difficult for them to provide consumers with meaningful control over data collection. Data brokers, for example, aggregate personal data from multiple sources, often without interacting with consumers at all. Such companies face a challenge in providing effective mechanisms for individual control because consumers might not know that these third parties exist. Moreover, some data brokers collect court records, news reports, property records, and other data that is in the public record. The rights of freedom of speech and freedom of the press involved in the collection and use of these documents must be balanced with the need for transparency to individuals about how data about them is collected, used, and disseminated and the opportunity for individuals to access and correct data that has been collected about them.

Still, data brokers and other companies that collect personal data without direct consumer interactions or a reasonably detectable presence in consumer-facing activities should seek innovative ways to provide consumers with effective Individual Control. If it is impractical to provide Individual Control, these companies should ensure that they implement other elements of the Consumer Privacy Bill of Rights in ways that adequately protect consumers' privacy. For example, to provide sufficient privacy protections, such companies may need to go to extra lengths to implement other principles such as Transparency—by providing clear, public explanations of the roles they play in commercial uses of personal data—as well as providing appropriate use controls once information is collected under the Access and Accuracy and Accountability principles to compensate for the lack of a direct consumer relationship.

The second dimension of Individual Control is consumer responsibility. In a growing number of cases, such as online social networks, the use of personal data begins with individuals' decisions to choose privacy settings and to share personal data with others. In such contexts, consumers should evaluate their choices and take responsibility for the ones that they make. Control over the initial act of sharing is critical. Consumers should take responsibility for those decisions, just as companies that participate in and benefit from this sharing should provide usable tools and clear explanations to enable consumers to make meaningful choices.

The Individual Control principle also recognizes that consumers'privacy interests in personal data persist throughout their relationships with a company. Accordingly, this principle includes a right to withdraw consent to use personal data that the company controls. Companies should provide means of withdrawing consent that are on equal footing with ways they obtain consent. For example, if consumers grant consent through a single action on their computers, they should be able to withdraw consent in a similar fashion.'[9]

There are three practical limits to the right to withdraw consent. First, it presumes that consumers have an ongoing relationship with a company. This relationship could be minimal, such as a consumer establishing an account for a single transaction; or it may be as extensive as many financial transactions spanning many years. Nonetheless, the company must have a way to effect a withdrawal of consent to the extent the company has associated and retained data with an individual. Conversely, data that a company cannot reasonably associate with an individual is not subject to the right to withdraw consent. Second, the obligation to respect a consumer's withdrawal of consent only extends to data that the company has under its control. Third, the Individual Control principle does not call for companies to permit withdrawal of consent for personal data that they collected before implementing the

Consumer Privacy Bill of Rights, unless they made such a commitment at the time of collection.

2. TRANSPARENCY: Consumers have a right to easily understandable and accessible information about privacy and security practices. At times and in places that are most useful to enabling consumers to gain a meaningful understanding of privacy risks and the ability to exercise Individual Control, companies should provide clear descriptions of what personal data they collect, why they need the data, how they will use it, when they will delete the data or de-identify it from consumers, and whether and for what purposes they may share personal data with third parties.

Plain language statements about personal data collection, use, disclosure, and retention help consumers understand the terms surrounding commercial interactions. Companies should make these statements visible to consumers when they are most relevant to understanding privacy risks and easily accessible when called for.

Personal data uses that are not consistent with the context of a company-to-consumer transaction or relationship deserve more prominent disclosure than uses that are integral to or commonly accepted in that context. Privacy notices that distinguish personal data uses along these lines will better inform consumers of personal data uses that they have not anticipated, compared to many current privacy notices that generally give equal emphasis to all potential personal data uses.[2°] Such notices will give privacy-conscious consumers easy access to information that is relevant to them. They may also promote greater consistency in disclosures by companies in a given market and attract the attention of consumers who ordinarily would ignore privacy notices, potentially making privacy practices a more salient point of competition among different products and services.

In addition, companies should provide notice in a form that is easy to read on the devices that consumers actually use to access their services. In particular, mobile devices have small screens that make reading full privacy notices effectively impossible. Companies should therefore strive to present mobile consumers with the most relevant information in a manner that takes into account mobile device characteristics, such as small display sizes and privacy risks that are specific to mobile devices.

Finally, companies that do not interact directly with consumers—such as the data brokers discussed above—need to make available explicit explanations of how they acquire, use, and disclose personal data. These companies may need to compensate for the lack of a direct relationship when making these explanations available, for example by posting them on their websites or other publicly accessible locations. Moreover, companies that have first-party relationships with consumers should disclose specifically the purpose(s) for which they provide personal data to third parties, help consumers to understand the nature of those third parties' activities, and whether those third parties are bound to limit their use of the data to achieving those purposes.

This gives consumers a more tractable task of assessing whether to engage with a single entity, rather than trying to understand what personal data third parties—potentially dozens, or even hundreds—receive and how they use it. Similarly, first parties could create greater transparency by disclosing what kinds of personal data they obtain from third parties, who the third parties are, and how they use this data.

This level of transparency may also facilitate the development within the private sector of innovative privacy-enhancing technologies and guidance that consumers can use to protect their privacy.

3. RESPECT FOR CONTEXT: Consumers have a right to expect that companies will collect, use, and disclose personal data in ways that are consistent with the context in which consumers provide the data. Companies should limit their use and disclosure of personal data to those purposes that are consistent with both the relationship that they have with consumers and the context in which consumers originally disclosed the data, unless required by law to do otherwise. If companies will use or disclose personal data for other purposes, they should provide heightened Transparency and Individual Choice by disclosing these other purposes in a manner that is prominent and easily actionable by consumers at the time of data collection. If, subsequent to collection, companies decide to use or disclose personal data for purposes that are inconsistent with the context in which the data was disclosed, they must provide heightened measures of Transparency and Individual Choice. Finally, the age and familiarity with technology of consumers who engage with a company are important elements of context.

Companies should fulfill the obligations under this principle in ways that are appropriate for the age and sophistication of consumers. In particular, the principles in the Consumer Privacy Bill of Rights may require greater protections for personal data obtained from children and teenagers than for adults.

Respect for Context distinguishes personal data uses on the basis of how closely they relate to the purposes for which consumers use a service or application as well as the business processes necessary to provide the service or application.[21] The Respect for Context principle calls on companies that collect data to act as stewards of data in ways that respect their consumers. This principle derives from two principles commonly found in statements of the FIPPs. The first principle, purpose specification, states that companies should specify at the time of collection the purposes for which they collect personal data. Second, the use limitation principle holds that companies should use personal data only to fulfill those specific purposes.

The Respect for Context principle adapts these well-established principles in two ways. First, Respect for Context provides a substantive standard to guide companies' decisions about their basic personal data practices. Generally speaking, companies should limit personal data uses to fulfilling purposes that are consistent with the context in which consumers disclose personal data. Second, while this principle emphasizes the importance of the relationship between a consumer and a company at the time consumers disclose data, it also recognizes that this relationship may change over time in ways not foreseeable at the time of collection. Such adaptive uses of personal data may be the source of innovations that benefit consumers. However, companies must provide appropriate levels of transparency and individual choice—which may be more stringent than was necessary at the time of collection—before reusing personal data.

Applying the Consumer Privacy Bill of Rights in a context-specific manner provides companies flexibility but also requires them to consider carefully what consumers are likely to understand about their data practices based on the products and services they offer, how the companies themselves explain the roles of personal data in delivering them, research on consumers' attitudes and understandings, and feedback from consumers. Context should help to determine which personal data uses are likely to raise the greatest consumer privacy concerns. The company-to-consumer relationship should guide companies'decisions about which uses of personal data they will make most prominent in privacy notices. For example, online retailers need to disclose consumers' names and home addresses to shippers in order to fulfill customers'orders. This disclosure is obvious from the context of the consumer-retailer relationship. Retailers do not need to provide prominent notice of the practice (though they should disclose it in their full privacy notices); companies may infer that consumers have agreed to the disclosure based on the consumers'actions in placing the order and a widespread understanding of the product delivery process.

Several categories of data practices are both common to many contexts and integral to companies' operations. The example above falls into the more general category of product and service fulfillment; companies may infer consent to use and disclose personal data to achieve objectives that consumers have specifically requested, as long as there is a common understanding of the service. Similarly, companies may infer consent to use personal data to conduct marketing in the context of most first-party relationships, given the familiarity of this activity in digital and in-person commerce, the visibility of this kind of marketing, the presence of an easily identifiable party to contact to provide feedback, and consumers'opportunity to end their relationship with a company if they are dissatisfied with it. In addition, companies collect and use personal data for purposes that are common, even if they may not be well known to consumers. For example, analyzing how consumers use a service in order to improve it, preventing fraud, complying with law enforcement orders and other legal obligations, and protecting intellectual property all have been basic elements of doing business and meeting companies' legal obligations.[22] Companies should be able to infer consumer consent to collect personal data for these limited purposes, consistent with the other principles in the Consumer Privacy Bill of Rights.

In other cases, context should guide decisions about which opportunities for consumer control are reasonable for companies to provide and also meaningful to consumers. Information and choices that are meaningful to consumers in one context may be largely irrelevant in others. For example, consider a hypothetical game application for a mobile device that allows consumers to save the game's state, so that they can resume playing after a break. The hypothetical company that provides this game collects the unique identifier of each user's mobile device in order to provide this "save" function. Collecting the mobile device's unique identifier for this purpose may be consistent with the "save" function and consumers' decisions to use it, particularly if the company uses identifiers only for this purpose. If the company provides consumers' unique device identifiers to third parties for purposes such as online behavioral advertising, however, the company should notify consumers and allow them to prevent the disclosure of personal data.

The sophistication of a company's consumers is also a critical element of context. In particular, the privacy framework may require a different degree of protection for children's and teenagers' privacy interests from the protections afforded to adults due to the unique characteristics of these age groups. Children may be particularly susceptible to privacy harms. Currently, the Children's Online Privacy Protection Act (COPPA) and the FTC's implementing regulations provide strong protections by requiring online services that are directed to children, or that know that they are collecting personal data from children, to obtain verifiable parental consent before they collect such data.[23] Online services that are "directed to" children must meet this same standard. The Administration looks forward to exploring with stakeholders whether more stringent applications of the Consumer Privacy Bill of Rights—such as an agreement not to create individual profiles about children, even if online services obtain the necessary consent to collect personal data—are appropriate to protect children's privacy.

The terms governing a company-to-consumer relationship are another key element of context. In particular, advertising supports innovative new services and helps to provide consumers with free access to a broad array of online services and applications. The Respect for Context principle does not foreclose any particular ad-based business models. Rather, the Respect for Context principle requires companies to recognize that different business models based on different personal data raise different privacy risks. A company should clearly inform consumers of what they are getting in exchange for the personal data they provide. The Administration also encourages companies engaged in online advertising to refrain from collecting, using, or disclosing personal data that may be used to make decisions regarding employment, credit, and insurance eligibility or similar matters that may have significant adverse consequences to consumers. Collecting data for such sensitive uses is at odds with the contextually well-defined purposes of generating revenue and providing consumers with ads that they are more likely to find relevant. Such practices also may be at odds with the norm of responsible data stewardship that the Respect for Context principle encourages.

Consider, for example, an online social networking service whose users disclose biographical information when creating an account and provide information about their social contacts and interests by including friends, business associates, and companies in their networks. As consumers use the service, they may generate large amounts of information that is associated with their identity on the online social network, including written updates, photos, videos, and location information. Consumers make affirmative choices to share this information with members of their online social networks. These disclosures are all integral to the company providing its social networking service. Furthermore, it is reasonable for the company to reveal at least some of these details to other members in order to help them form new connections.

Whether the online social networking service provider will use this information, and for what purposes, may be less clear from the context that consumers experience. The personal data that consumers generate may be valuable for improving the service, selling online advertising, or assembling individual profiles that the company provides to third parties. These uses fall along a continuum that starts at the core context of consumers engaging online with a group of associates. Consumers expect the company to improve its services. The company does not need to seek affirmative consent each time it uses existing data to improve a service, or even creates a new service, provided that these new uses of personal data are consistent with what users come to expect in a social networking context.

Suppose that the company leases individual profile information to third parties, such as information brokers. Respect for Context may not require the company to specify each use that a recipient might make of this data, but, at a minimum, it may require the company to state prominently and explicitly that it discloses personal data to third parties who may further aggregate and use this data for other purposes. The Respect for Context principle, in combination with other principles in the Consumer Privacy Bill of Rights, also calls on the company to provide consumers with meaningful opportunities to prevent these disclosures.

4. SECURITY: Consumers have a right to secure and responsible handling of personal data. Companies should assess the privacy and security risks associated with their personal data practices and maintain reasonable safeguards to control risks such as loss; unauthorized access, use, destruction, or modification; and improper disclosure.

Technologies and procedures that keep personal data secure are essential to protecting consumer privacy. Security failures involving personal data, whether resulting from accidents or deliberate attacks, can cause harms that range from embarrassment to financial loss and physical harm. Companies that lose control of personal data may suffer reputational harm as well as financial losses if business partners or consumers end their relationships after a security breach. These consequences provide companies with significant incentives to keep personal data secure. The security precautions that are appropriate for a given company will depend on its lines of business, the kinds of personal data it collects, the likelihood of harm to consumers, and many other factors.

The Security principle recognizes these needs. It gives companies the discretion to choose technologies and procedures that best fit the scale and scope of the personal data that they maintain, subject to their obligations under any applicable data security statutes, including their duties to notify consumers and law enforcement agencies if the security of data about them is breached, and their commitments to adopt reasonable security practices.

5. ACCESS AND ACCURACY: Consumers have a right to access and correct personal data in usable formats, in a manner that is appropriate to the sensitivity of the data and the risk of adverse consequences to consumers if the data is inaccurate. Companies should use reasonable measures to ensure they maintain accurate personal data. Companies also should provide consumers with reasonable access to personal data that they collect or maintain about them, as well as the appropriate means and opportunity to correct inaccurate data or request its deletion or use limitation. Companies that handle personal data should construe this principle in a manner consistent with freedom of expression and freedom of the press. In determining what measures they may use to maintain accuracy and to provide access, correction, deletion, or suppression capabilities to consumers, companies may also consider the scale, scope, and sensitivity of the personal data that they collect or maintain and the likelihood that its use may expose consumers to financial, physical, or other material harm.

An increasingly diverse array of entities uses personal data to make decisions that affect consumers in ways ranging from the ads they see online to their candidacy for employment. Outside of sectors covered by specific Federal privacy laws, such as the Health Insurance Portability and Accountability Act (HIPAA) and the Fair Credit Reporting Act, consumers do not currently have the right to access and correct this data. The Administration is committed to publishing data on the Internet in machine-readable formats to advance the goals of innovation, transparency, participation, and collaboration. For example, to promote innovation and efficiency in the delivery of electricity, the Administration supports providing consumers with timely access to energy usage data in standardized, machine-readable formats over the Internet.[24] Similarly, the expanded use of health IT, including patients'access to health data through electronic health records, is a key element of the Administration's innovation strategy.[25] Comprehensive privacy and security safeguards, tailored for both contexts, are fundamental to both strategies.

Providing consumers with access to information about them in usable formats holds similar promise in the commercial arena. To help consumers make more informed choices, the Administration encourages companies to make personal data available in useful formats to the properly authenticated individuals over the Internet.[26]

The Access and Accuracy principle recognizes that the use of inaccurate personal data may lead to a range of harms. The risk of these harms, in addition to the scale, scope, and sensitivity of personal data that a company retains, help to determine what kinds of access and correction facilities may be reasonable in a given context. As a result, this principle does not distinguish between companies that are consumer-facing and those that are not. In all cases, however, the mechanisms that companies use to provide consumers with access to data about them should not create additional privacy or security risks.

United States Constitutional law has long recognized that privacy interests co-exist alongside fundamental First Amendment rights to freedom of speech, freedom of the press, and freedom of association. Individuals and members of the press exercising their free speech rights may well speak about other individuals and include personal information in their speech. The Access and Accuracy principle should therefore be interpreted with full respect for First Amendment values, especially for non-commercial speakers and individuals exercising freedom of the press.

6. FOCUSED COLLECTION: Consumers have a right to reasonable limits on the personal data that companies collect and retain. Companies should collect only as much personal data as they need to accomplish purposes specified under the Respect for Context principle. Companies should securely dispose of or de-identify personal data once they no longer need it, unless they are under a legal obligation to do otherwise.

The Focused Collection principle holds that companies should engage in considered decisions about the kinds of data they need to collect to accomplish specific purposes. For example, the hypothetical game company referenced above that collects the unique identifier of each user's mobile device in order to provide a "save" function should consider whether it must use the mobile device identifier or whether a less broadly linkable identifier would work as well. Nevertheless, as discussed under the Respect for Context principle, companies may find new uses for personal data after they collect it, provided they take appropriate measures of transparency and individual choice. The Focused Collection principle does not relieve companies of any independent legal obligations, including law enforcement orders, that require them to retain personal data.

Wide-ranging data collection may be essential for some familiar and socially beneficial Internet services and applications. Search engines are one example. Search engines gather detailed data about the contents and structure of the World Wide Web. Consumers understand and depend on search engines to collect this broad range of data and make it available for a wide range of end uses. Search engines also log search queries to improve their services. Search engines may collect such data, which includes personal data, in a manner that is consistent with the Focused Collection principle, so long as their purposes for collecting personal data are clear, and they do not retain personal data beyond the time they need it to achieve any of these purposes.

7. ACCOUNTABILITY: Consumers have a right to have personal data handled by companies with appropriate measures in place to assure they adhere to the Consumer Privacy Bill of Rights. Companies should be accountable to enforcement authorities and consumers for adhering to these principles. Companies also should hold employees responsible for adhering to these principles. To achieve this end, companies should train their employees as appropriate to handle personal data consistently with these principles and regularly evaluate their performance in this regard. Where appropriate, companies should conduct full audits. Companies that disclose personal data to third parties should at a minimum ensure that the recipients are under enforceable contractual obligations to adhere to these principles, unless they are required by law to do otherwise.

Privacy protection depends on companies being accountable to consumers as well as to agencies that enforce consumer data privacy protections. The Accountability principle, however, goes beyond external accountability to encompass practices through which companies prevent lapses in their privacy commitments or detect and remedy any lapses that may occur. Companies that can demonstrate that they live up to their privacy commitments have powerful means of maintaining and strengthening consumer trust. A company's own evaluation can prove invaluable to this process. The appropriate evaluation technique, which could be a self-assessment and need not necessarily be a full audit, will depend on the size, complexity, and nature of a company's business, as well as the sensitivity of the data involved. In recent years, chief privacy officers—experts who raise awareness of privacy issues in companies that face rapid changes in technologies, consumer expectations, and regulations—have emerged as a valuable source of guidance and internal evaluation. Chief privacy officers are likely to provide a continuing source of guidance within companies throughout the development of products and services.

To be fully effective, however, companies should link evaluations to the enforcement of pre-established internal expectations; evaluations are not an end in themselves. Audits—whether conducted by the company or by an independent third party—may be appropriate under some circumstances, but they are not always necessary to fulfill the Accountability principle.

Moreover, accountability must attach to data transferred from one company to another. From the perspective of the Consumer Privacy Bill of Rights, the emphasis is not on the disclosures themselves, but on whether a disclosure leads to a use of personal data that is inconsistent within the context of its collection or a consumer's expressed desire to control the data. Thus, if a company transfers personal data to a third party, it remains accountable and thus should hold the recipient accountable—through contracts or other legally enforceable instruments—for using and disclosing the data in ways that are consistent with the Consumer Privacy Bill of Rights.

III. IMPLEMENTING THE CONSUMER PRIVACY BILL OF RIGHTS: MULTISTAKEHOLDER PROCESSES TO DEVELOP ENFORCEABLE CODES OF CONDUCT

Implementing the general principles in the Consumer Privacy Bill of Rights across the wide range of innovative uses of personal data requires a process to establish more specific practices. The Administration encourages individual companies, industry groups, privacy advocates, consumer groups, crime victims, academics, international partners, State Attorneys General, Federal civil and criminal law enforcement representatives, and other relevant groups to participate in multistakeholder processes to develop codes of conduct that implement these general principles.

In consumer data privacy, as in other areas affecting Internet policy, the Administration believes that multistakeholder processes underlie many of the institutions responsible for the Internet's success. This reflects the Administration's abiding commitment to preserving the Internet as anopen, decentralized, user-driven platform for communication, innovation, and economic growth.[27]

The Administration supports open, transparent multistakeholder processes because, when appropriately structured, they can provide the flexibility, speed, and decentralization necessary to address Internet policy challenges. A process that is open to a broad range of participants and facilitates their full participation will allow technical experts, companies, advocates, civil and criminal law enforcement representatives responsible for enforcing consumer privacy laws, and academics to work together to find creative solutions to problems. Flexibility in the deliberative process is critical to allowing stakeholders to explore the technical and policy dimensions—which are often intertwined—of Internet policy issues. Moreover, the United States will need to confront a broad, complex, and global set of consumer data privacy issues for decades to come. A process that works efficiently and on a global scale is therefore essential.

Another key advantage of multistakeholder processes is that they can produce solutions in a more timely fashion than regulatory processes and treaty-based organizations. In the Internet standards world, for example, working groups frequently form around a specific problem and make significant progress toward a solution within months, rather than years. These groups frequently function on the basis of consensus and are amenable to the participation of individuals and groups with limited resources. These characteristics lend legitimacy to the groups and their solutions, which in turn can encourage rapid and effective implementation. Finally, multistakeholder processes do not rely on a single, centralized authority to solve problems. Specific multistakeholder institutions address specific kinds of Internet policy challenges. This kind of specialization not only speeds up the development of solutions but also helps to avoid the duplication of stakeholders' efforts.

Due in part to its reliance on multistakeholder processes, United States Internet policy has generally avoided fragmented, prescriptive, and unpredictable rules that frustrate innovation and undermine consumer trust. The United States has also refrained from adopting legal requirements that prescribe specific technical requirements, which could fragment the global market for information technologies and services and inhibit innovation. Instead, the United States generally defers to the expert bodies that produce Internet technical standards. In addition, the Administration continues its support for Internet policy processes that are open, transparent, and promote cooperation within a legal framework that sets appropriate performance requirements for individuals and companies.

Consumer data privacy issues exemplify the need for multistakeholder processes that develop the practices and technologies necessary to implement general policy principles. Experience in the United States has shown that both companies and consumers benefit when companies commit to the task of innovating privacy practices. In the early days of commercial activity on the Internet (mid-1990s to early 2000s), for example, the Department of Commerce, the FTC, and the White House convened stakeholders to gather information about privacy issues in this rapidly evolving marketplace. These efforts yielded a flexible, voluntary privacy framework that provided meaningful privacy protections while fostering dynamic innovations in technologies and business models.[28]

Even without legislation, the Administration intends to convene and facilitate multistakeholder processes to produce enforceable codes of conduct. In an open forum, stakeholders with an interest in a specific market or business context will work toward consensus on a legally enforceable code of conduct that implements the Consumer Privacy Bill of Rights. Multistakeholder processes are different from traditional agency rulemakings. The Federal Government will work with stakeholders to establish operating procedures for an open, transparent process. Ultimately, however, the stakeholders themselves will control the process and its results. There is no Federal regulation at the end of the process, and codes will not bind any companies unless they choose to adopt them. The incentive for stakeholders to participate in this process is twofold. Companies will build consumer trust by engaging directly with consumers and other stakeholders during the process. Adopting a code of conduct that stakeholders develop through this process would further build consumer trust. Second, in any enforcement action based on conduct covered by a code, the FTC will consider a company's adherence to a code favorably.

A. Building on the Successes of Internet Policymaking

The Internet provides several successful examples of the kind of multistakeholder policy development the Administration envisions. Private-sector standards-setting organizations, for example, are at the forefront of setting Internet-related technical standards. Groups such as the Internet Engineering Task Force (IETF) and the World Wide Web Consortium (W3C) use transparent processes to set Internet-related technical standards.

These processes are successful, in part, because stakeholders share an interest in developing consensus-based solutions to the underlying challenges. The success of the resulting standards is evident in the constantly growing range of services and applications—as well as the trillions of dollars in global commerce—they support. Similarly, the Internet Corporation for Assigned Names and Numbers (ICANN), a nonprofit corporation, coordinates the technical management of the domain name system, which maps domain names to unique numerical addresses. ICANN is also a multistakeholder organization that includes representatives from a broad array of interests, including generic top level domain registries, registrars and registrants, country code top level domain registries, the Regional Internet Registries, root server operators, national governments, and Internet users at large.

With this structure, ICANN coordinates the technical management of an important function of the Internet—mapping names that people can remember to numerical addresses that computers can use—and does so in a manner that allows for a wide range of stakeholder input. Government-convened policymaking efforts, such as the Executive Branch-led privacy discussions of the 1990s and early 2000s, continue to be central to advancing consumer data privacy protections in the United States. The framework in this document is a direct result of the Department of Commerce Internet Policy Task Force's extensive engagement with stakeholders—companies, trade groups, privacy advocates, academics, civil and criminal law enforcement representatives, and foreign government officials.

In addition, the FTC has encouraged multistakeholder efforts to develop a "Do Not Track" mechanism, which would afford greater consumer control over personal data in the context of online behavioral advertising.

B. Defining the Multistakeholder Process for Consumer Data Privacy

The Department of Commerce's National Telecommunications and Information Administration (NTIA) has the necessary authority and expertise, developed through its role in other areas of Internet policy, to convene multistakeholder processes that address consumer data privacy issues.[29] NTIA will lead the Department of Commerce's convening of stakeholders in a deliberative process that develops codes of conduct and allows stakeholders to adapt the codes to protect consumers' privacy as technologies and market conditions change.[30]

Figure 1. The principal stages of the multistakeholder process for consumer data privacy.

1. Deliberation

- **Identifying Issues.** Stakeholder groups, with the assistance of NTIA, will identify markets and industry sectors that involve significant consumer data privacy issues and may be ripe for an enforceable code of conduct. The process will be open, but the focus of a given process likely will not appeal equally to all stakeholders.
- **Initiating and Facilitating Deliberations.** NTIA will take steps to enlist the participation of stakeholders to develop an enforceable code of conduct. As convener, NTIA will open meetings to all stakeholders, including international partners, the FTC, Federal civil and criminal law enforcement representatives, and State Attorneys General, that have an interest in defining an appropriate code of conduct and express a willingness to work in good faith toward reaching consensus on the code's provisions.
- As their first order of business, stakeholders will establish operating processes and procedures. The Administration is committed to a process that is open, transparent, and accommodates participation by groups that have limited resources; however the deliberative process must meet the needs of its participants, who determine and abide by its outcome.[31]

- **Conclusion.** A code that reflects the agreement of all stakeholders is ready for companies to consider adopting. The Administration expects, however, that consensus will emerge on parts of a code, and that stakeholders are likely to resolve the most difficult issues later in the process. At this stage, NTIA may need to work intensively with stakeholders to help them resolve their differences. NTIA's role will be to help the parties reach clarity on what their positions are and whether there are options for compromise toward consensus, rather than substituting its own judgment. To minimize the possibility that some stakeholders may draw inflexible lines that prevent consensus, the parties should discuss and set out rules or procedures at the outset of the process to govern how the group will reach an orderly conclusion, even if there is not complete agreement on results.

2. Adoption

Once a code of conduct is complete, companies to which the code is relevant may choose to adopt it. The Administration expects that a company's public commitment to adhere to a code of conduct will become enforceable under Section 5 of the FTC Act (15 U.S.C. § 45), just as a company is bound today to follow its privacy statements.[32] Enforceability is essential to assuring consumers that companies' practices match their commitments and thus to strengthening consumer trust.

3. Evolution

A key goal of the multistakeholder process is to enable stakeholders to modify privacy protections in response to rapid changes in technology, consumer expectations, and market conditions, to assure they sufficiently protect consumer data privacy. The multistakeholder process offers several ways to keep codes of conduct current. Stakeholders may decide at any time that a code of conduct no longer provides effective consumer data privacy protections, in light of technological or market changes. NTIA might also draw this conclusion and seek to re-convene stakeholders. As with the initial development of a code of conduct, however, stakeholder participation in the process to revise a code of conduct would be voluntary. The Federal Government would not revise a code of conduct; rather, stakeholder groups will make these changes with Federal Government input. Finally, under the legislative safe harbor framework discussed in the following section, Congress could prescribe a renewal period for codes of conduct, so that the FTC periodically reviews codes that are the basis of enforcement safe harbors.

IV. Building on the FTC's Enforcement Expertise

A. Protecting Consumers through Strong Enforcement

Enforcement is critical to ensuring that the privacy commitments companies make by adopting a code of conduct are meaningful. Self-regulatory bodies, which develop and administer voluntary guidelines for member companies, can provide a first line of enforcement, though they are not necessary for the framework described here. Enforcement through self-regulatory bodies can help to detect and remedy compliance issues at an early stage. As a result, this kind of enforcement can strengthen trust in a code of conduct and the companies that commit to the code.

Government agencies also play a vital role in enforcing the privacy protections in codes of conduct. The FTC is the Federal Government's leading consumer privacy enforcement authority.[33] Enforcement actions by the FTC (and State Attorneys General) have established that companies' failures to adhere to voluntary privacy commitments, such as those stated in privacy policies, are actionable under the FTC Act's (and State analogues) prohibition on unfair or deceptive acts or practices.[34] In addition, the FTC brings cases against companies that allegedly failed to use reasonable security measures to protect personal information about consumers.[35] Using this authority, the FTC has brought cases that effectively protect consumer data privacy within a flexible and evolving approach to changing technologies and markets. The same authority would allow the FTC to enforce the commitments of companies under its jurisdiction to adhere to codes of conduct developed through the multistakeholder process.[36] Thus, companies that adopt codes of conduct will make commitments that are legally enforceable under existing law.

B. Providing Incentives to Develop Enforceable Codes of Conduct

The FTC has significant enforcement and policy expertise to offer all stakeholders on consumer data privacy issues codes of conduct. With or without consumer data privacy legislation, the FTC should provide assistance and advice regarding development of the codes. In the absence of legislation, the FTC, Federal civil and criminal law enforcement representatives, and States should participate in the multistakeholder deliberations by providing advice on substance and process. Once stakeholders have developed a code, a company may voluntarily adhere to the code in order to gain greater certainty and assure its customers that its practices protect their privacy. Companies may choose to adopt multiple codes of conduct to cover different lines of business; the common baseline of the Consumer Privacy Bill of Rights should help ensure that the codes are consistent. Then, in any investigation or enforcement action related to the subject matter of one or more codes, the FTC should consider the company's adherence to the codes favorably.

V. Promoting International Interoperability

The Internet helps U.S. companies expand across borders. As a result, cross-border data flows are a vital component of the domestic and global economies. Differences in national privacy laws create challenges for companies wishing to transfer personal data across national borders. Complying with different privacy laws is burdensome for companies that transfer personal data as part of well-defined, discrete data processing operations because legal standards may vary among jurisdictions, and companies may need to obtain multiple regulatory approvals to conduct even routine operations.

Services that cater to individual users face steeper compliance challenges because they handle data flows that are more complex and varied. Further complicating matters is the proliferation of cloud computing systems.[37] This globally distributed architecture helps deliver cost-effective, innovative new services to consumers, companies, and governments. It also allows consumers and companies to send the personal data they generate and use to recipients all over the world. Consumer data privacy frameworks should not only facilitate these technologies and business models but also adapt rapidly to those that have yet to emerge. Though governments may take different approaches to meeting these challenges, it is critical to the continued growth of the digital economy that they strive to create interoperability between privacy regimes. The Administration believes flexible multistakeholder processes that address novel uses and transfers of data facilitate interoperable privacy regimes. The United States is committed to engaging with its international partners to increase interoperability in privacy laws by pursuing mutual recognition, the development of codes of conduct through multistakeholder processes, and enforcement cooperation. It is also committed to including international counterparts in these multistakeholder processes, to enable global consensus on emerging privacy issues.

A. Mutual Recognition

Mutual recognition of commercial data privacy frameworks is a means to achieve meaningful global data protection. A starting point for mutual recognition is the embrace of common values surrounding privacy and personal data protection. Two principles should determine whether the conditions for mutual recognition between specific privacy frameworks exist: effective enforcement and mechanisms that allow companies to demonstrate accountability. Where companies are under comparable legal requirements, mutual recognition means that all parties can enforce the companies' obligations. Effective enforcement, conducted according to publicly announced policies, is therefore critical to establishing interoperability. Enforcement authorities and mechanisms vary from country to country, and the United States recognizes that a variety of approaches can be effective. The United States relies primarily upon the FTC's case-by-case enforcement of general prohibitions on unfair or deceptive acts and practices. This approach helps develop evolving standards for handling personal data in the private sector. In the context of mutual recognition, accountability refers to a company's capacity to demonstrate the implementation of enforceable policies and procedures relating to privacy (whether adopted voluntarily or as a result of legal obligations). Accountability mechanisms include self-assessments, evaluations, and audits.[38] The Administration encourages stakeholders to work together to identify globally accepted accountability mechanisms when developing codes of conduct. One example of an initiative to facilitate transnational mutual recognition is the Asia-Pacific Economic Cooperation's (APEC) voluntary system of Cross Border Privacy Rules (CBPR), which is based on the APEC Privacy Framework and includes privacy principles that APEC member economies have agreed to recognize.[39] Codes of conduct based on these principles could streamline the data privacy policies and practices of companies operating throughout the vast APEC region.[40] Upon implementation, APEC's CBPR system will require interested applicants to demonstrate that they comply with a set of CBPR program requirements based on the APEC Privacy Framework. Moreover, the commitments an applicant makes during this process, while voluntary, must be enforceable under laws in member economies. Successful CBPR certification will entitle participating companies to represent to consumers that they are accountable and meet stringent and globally recognized standards, thereby facilitating the transfer of personal data throughout the APEC region. In Europe, Article 27 of European Union (EU) Directive 95/46/EC on the protection of individuals with regard to the processing of personal data and on the free movement of such data, commonly known as the EU Data Protection Directive, encourages the development of codes of conduct to help implement the law. Like the Administration's framework, which proposes industry-specific codes of conduct, the Data Protection Directive recognizes that codes of conduct that implement general privacy principles may differ in their details, according to the needs of the relevant industry. The Administration is committed to working with organizations at the EU level as well as with member states to make codes of conduct the basis of mutually recognized privacy protections.

The Safe Harbor Frameworks that the United States developed with the EU and Switzerland are early examples of global interoperability that have had a meaningful impact on transatlantic data flows. The United States, the EU, and Switzerland negotiated these Frameworks to accomplish the objectives of protecting personal information while also ensuring that companies could transfer information in a way that did not disrupt their global business operations. These Frameworks allow companies to self-certify that they comply with requirements under the EU Data Protection Directive, subject to FTC enforcement of these representations.[41] The more than 2,700 companies that participate in the Safe Harbor Frameworks may transfer personal data from the EU to the United States. As a result, the Safe Harbor Frameworks have effectively reduced barriers to personal data flow and thereby support trade and economic growth.

B. An International Role for Multistakeholder Processes and Codes of Conduct

The attributes of speed, flexibility and decentralized problem-solving in well-structured multistakeholder consultations offer certain advantages over traditional government regulation when it comes to establishing globally applicable rules and guidelines that promote innovation and protect consumers. Multistakeholder-developed codes of conduct, combined with existing mutual recognition frameworks, hold the promise of greatly simplifying companies'compliance burdens. While the Safe Harbor Frameworks have proven to be valuable in facilitating transatlantic trade, they are not perfect solutions for all U.S. entities. Sectors not regulated by the FTC, such as financial services, telecommunications common carriers, and insurance, are not covered by the Safe Harbor Frameworks. Some companies in these sectors have indicated that they would like to see an improved environment for transatlantic data transfers. To build on the success of the Safe Harbor Frameworks, the Administration, through the Departments of Commerce and State, plans to develop additional mechanisms—such as jointly developed codes of conduct—that support mutual recognition of legal regimes, facilitate the free flow of information, and address emerging privacy challenges. The Administration hopes to include international stakeholders in the multistakeholder processes. The Safe Harbor Frameworks could one day be supplemented by codes of conduct reflecting transatlantic consensus on important, emerging privacy issues.

C. Enforcement Cooperation

To realize global interoperability in data protection, mutual recognition must be accompanied by robust enforcement cooperation. Such collaboration, whether bilateral or multilateral, is necessary to address information sharing among data protection authorities. Empowered by legislation that grants it greater authority to cooperate with foreign counterparts, the FTC helped to create the Global Privacy Enforcement Network ("GPEN"). GPEN aims to further the development of privacy enforcement priorities, sharing of best practices, and support for joint enforcement initiatives. The FTC is involved in a number of other international organizations, including the OECD, APEC, the Asia-Pacific Privacy Authorities forum, and the International Conference of Data Protection and Privacy Commissioners. The work of the United States Government in GPEN, the OECD, APEC, and other venues is increasing collaboration in privacy investigations and enforcement actions globally. Given that Internet-based services reach individuals in jurisdictions around the world, it is neither effective nor wise policy for governments to enforce national data privacy legislation in isolation.

VI. Enacting Consumer Data Privacy Legislation

The Administration urges Congress to pass legislation adopting the Consumer Privacy Bill of Rights. Legislation would promote trust in the digital economy by providing a basic set of privacy rights throughout areas of the commercial sector that are not currently subject to specific Federal data privacy legislation. The flexible approach that the Administration supports will allow companies to implement the Consumer Privacy Bill of Rights in ways that fit the context in which they do business.

A. Codify the Consumer Privacy Bill of Rights

Congress should act to protect consumers from violations of the rights defined in the Administration's proposed Consumer Privacy Bill of Rights. These rights provide clear protection for consumers and define rules of the road for the rapidly growing marketplace for personal data.[42] The legislation should permit the FTC and State Attorneys General to enforce these rights directly. The legislation will need to state companies'obligations under the Consumer Privacy Bill of Rights with greater specificity than this document provides. The Consumer Privacy Bill of Rights is a guide for the Administration to work collaboratively with Congress on statutory language.[43]

To provide greater legal certainty and to encourage the development and adoption of industry-specific codes of conduct, the Administration also supports legislation that authorizes the FTC to review codes of conduct and grant companies that commit to adhere—and do adhere—to such codes forbearance from enforcement of provisions of the legislation.

In addition, consumer data privacy legislation should avoid:

- Adding duplicative or overly burdensome regulatory requirements to companies that are already adhering to legislatively adopted privacy principles.
- Prescribing technology-specific means of complying with the law's obligations.
- Precluding new business models that are consistent with the Consumer Privacy Bill of Rights in general but may involve new uses of personal information not contemplated at the time the statute is written.
- Altering existing statutory or regulatory authorities pursuant to which the government may obtain information that is necessary to assist in conducting border searches, investigating criminal conduct or other violations of law, or protecting public safety and national security.
- Contravening the ability of law enforcement to investigate and prosecute criminal acts, and ensure public safety.
- Altering existing statutory, regulatory, or policy authorities that apply to the government's information practices or address privacy issues outside of a purely commercial, consumer-oriented context.

B. Grant the FTC Direct Enforcement Authority

The Administration encourages Congress to grant the FTC the authority to enforce each element of the statutory Consumer Privacy Bill of Rights.[44] This authority would provide greater certainty to consumers and companies both. Companies would begin with a clearer roadmap to their privacy obligations. Consumers would benefit from knowing that Congress has empowered the FTC to enforce a comprehensive set of privacy protections in the commercial marketplace. At the same time, a statute that allows the FTC to enforce the Consumer Privacy Bill of Rights directly would provide flexibility and permit the FTC to address emerging privacy issues through specific enforcement actions governed by applicable procedural safeguards. Companies seeking even greater certainty under such legislation should use the multistakeholder process and enforcement safe harbor discussed below to develop context-specific codes of conduct in a timely fashion. The Administration recommends that Congress grant the same authority to State Attorneys General. So long as they coordinate with the FTC in their enforcement actions, States could provide additional enforcement resources and a considerable source of consumer data privacy expertise. In domains involving rapid changes in technology and business practices, Congress has chosen to create flexible standards rather than tailoring them to technologies and practices that exist at the time it passes a law. In the realm of antitrust, for example, the Sherman Act prohibits agreements "in restraint of trade."[45] The Copyright Act defines basic terms such as "copies," "devices," and "processes" with reference to technologies "now known or later developed."[46] And, in the realm of data privacy, the FTC has brought numerous enforcement actions under the FTC Act Section 5's prohibition on "unfair or deceptive acts or practices." A combination of agency guidelines, judicial interpretation, and industry practices provides interpretations of these terms to allow individuals and companies to determine with greater certainty whether their conduct complies with these general laws. The Administration encourages Congress to follow a similar path with baseline consumer data privacy legislation. It is important that a baseline statute provide a level playing field for companies, a consistent set of expectations for consumers, and greater clarity and transparency in the basis for FTC enforcement actions. The FTC also could engage the public to clarify how it will enforce the statutory Consumer Privacy Bill of Rights. The primary mechanisms to clarify the statute's requirements should be the multistakeholder process and enforcement safe harbor, based on enforceable codes of conduct, as discussed below. The more traditional modes of clarifying general statutory requirements, however, could also play a helpful role.

C. Provide Legal Certainty through an Enforcement Safe Harbor

The Administration supports authorizing the FTC to provide greater assurance to companies that adopt enforceable codes of conduct than is possible under current law. Two legislative structures would help to accomplish this goal. First, the FTC should have explicit authority to review codes of conduct against the Consumer Privacy Bill of Rights, as they are set forth in legislation. Legislation should require the FTC to review codes submitted for review within a reasonable amount of time (e.g., 180 days), require the FTC to consider public comments on a code, limit its review authority to approving or rejecting a code that reflects the consensus of all participants in the multistakeholder process, and establish a period for reviewing approved codes to ensure that they sufficiently protect consumer privacy in light of technological and market changes. The record from the multistakeholder process that produced a code—and particularly the presence of general consensus on its provisions—would help to guide the FTC's assessment of whether a code sufficiently implements the Consumer Privacy Bill of Rights. Because the outcome of FTC review will likely influence companies' decisions to adopt codes of conduct—the end result of the multistakeholder process—it is appropriate to determine the details of FTC review through a process that is open to all stakeholders. These details, however, need to be legally binding. Accordingly, the Administration recommends that Congress grant the FTC authority under the Administrative Procedure Act (5 U.S.C. § 552 *et seq.*) to issue rules that establish a fair and transparent process for reviewing and approving codes of conduct. The second element that the Administration recommends is giving the FTC the authority to grant a "safe harbor"—that is, forbearance from enforcement of the statutory Consumer Privacy Bill of Rights—to companies that follow a code of conduct that the FTC has reviewed and approved. Companies that decline to adopt a code of conduct, or choose not to seek FTC review of a code that they do adopt, would simply be subject to the general obligations of the legislatively adopted Consumer Privacy Bill of Rights.

D. Balance Federal and State Roles in Consumer Data Privacy Protection

Federal legislation that enacts a Consumer Privacy Bill of Rights should provide a national standard for protecting consumer data privacy where existing Federal data privacy statutes do not apply. Nationally uniform consumer data privacy rules are necessary to create certainty for companies and consistent protections for consumers. These rules should take into consideration the need for certain information to be available for law enforcement-related purposes. Moreover, national uniformity is crucial to preserving the incentives that the

Administration's framework provides through the multistakeholder process. Stakeholders'incentives to participate in the multistakeholder process, and companies'incentives to adopt codes of conduct, would be diminished if States enacted laws with more stringent requirements. The Administration therefore recommends that Congress preempt State laws to the extent they are inconsistent with the Consumer Privacy Bill of Rights as enacted and applied. The Administration also recommends that Congress provide forbearance from enforcement of State laws against companies that adopt and comply with FTC-approved codes of conduct. The Administration's proposed approach preserves important policymaking and enforcement roles for the States. States can and should play a highly constructive role in the multistakeholder process. The Administration also supports granting State Attorneys General with the authority to enforce the Consumer Privacy Bill of Rights. Taken together, these mechanisms will provide States means to address consumer data privacy issues that States identify while maintaining uniformity at the national level. The Administration will also work with Congress, States, the private sector, and other stakeholders to determine whether there are specific sectors in which States could enact laws that would not disrupt the broader uniformity the Administration seeks in consumer data privacy protections. For example, it may be appropriate to allow States to enact laws that apply the Consumer Privacy Bill of Rights to personal data in sectors they closely regulate, such as retail electricity distribution.[47]

E. Preserve Effective Protections in Existing Federal Data Privacy Laws

Consumer data privacy legislation should preserve existing sector-specific Federal laws that effectively protect personal data, minimize the duplication of legal requirements, and provide consumers with a clear sense of what protections they have and who enforces them. Where existing Federal laws do not meet these guidelines, however, the Administration encourages Congress to consider how consumer data privacy legislation could simplify existing requirements, to the benefit of consumers and companies. In general, the sector-specific Federal data privacy laws establish legal obligations that are tailored to the sensitivity of personal data used and the prevailing practices in those sectors.[48] For instance, HIPAA and the HIPAA Privacy and Security Rules regulate the collection, use, and disclosure of personal health information by healthcare providers, insurers, and health information clearinghouses. HIPAA permits by default personal health information practices that are necessary or commonly accepted in the healthcare context, such as disclosures of personal health information between two healthcare providers in order to treat a patient. Federal data privacy laws that apply to education, credit reporting, financial services, and the collection of children's personal data are examples of similarly well-tailored requirements.

1. Create Comprehensive Privacy Protection without Duplicating Burdens

To avoid creating duplicative regulatory burdens, the Administration supports exempting companies from consumer data privacy legislation to the extent that their activities are subject to existing Federal data privacy laws. However, activities within such companies that do not fall under an existing data privacy law would be covered by the legislation that the Administration proposes. The alternative— exempting entire entities that are subject to an existing Federal data privacy law—could allow the exception to swallow the rule. For example, the Gramm-Leach-Bliley Act (GLB) requires financial institutions to take certain privacy and security precautions with nonpublic personal information. If entities that are subject to GLB were exempt from a baseline consumer data privacy law for non-GLB-covered personal data, the baseline statute's effectiveness could be significantly diminished.

2. Amend Laws That Create Inconsistent or Confusing Requirements

Because existing Federal laws treat similar technologies within the communications sector differently,[49] the Administration supports simplifying and clarifying the legal landscape and making the FTC responsible for enforcing the Consumer Privacy Bill of Rights against communications providers.

F. Set a National Standard for Security Breach Notification

In the specific area of security breaches, the Administration supports creating a national standard under which companies must notify consumers of unauthorized disclosures of certain kinds of personal data. Security breach notification (SBN) laws effectively promote the protection of sensitive personal data. They require companies in certain situations to notify consumers whose personal data was exposed to unauthorized recipients. Notice helps consumers protect themselves against harms such as identity theft. It also provides companies with incentives to establish better data security in the first place. The SBN model is also gaining acceptance internationally as a performance-based requirement that effectively protects consumers. Currently, 47 States, the District of Columbia, and several U.S. Territories, have SBN laws. Variations in States have allowed a sense of the most effective approaches to emerge, but the need for national uniformity is now evident. The patchwork of State laws creates significant burdens for companies without much countervailing benefit for consumers. As part of its comprehensive cybersecurity legislative package, the Administration recommended creating a national standard for notifying consumers in the event that there are unauthorized disclosures of certain types of personal data.[50] This national standard would replace the various State standards that exist today and preempt future State legislation in this area.

VII. FEDERAL GOVERNMENT LEADERSHIP IN IMPROVING INDIVIDUAL PRIVACY PROTECTIONS

In areas other than consumer data privacy, the Administration is continuing the Federal government's long history of championing data privacy protections in the public and private spheres. This history stems from the early days of computerized data processing. In 1973, the Department of Health, Education, and Welfare (HEW) Advisory Committee on Automated Personal Data Systems issued a report entitled Records, Computers, and the Rights of Citizens. This landmark report provided an early statement of the FIPPs that provide a foundation for the Administration's Consumer Privacy Bill of Rights. Since then, the Federal government has led the way in demonstrating that protecting privacy is integral to conducting the Nation's business. No single event or policy need has spurred this activity. In some cases,

Federal agencies consider privacy issues in response to specific Congressional mandates. In other cases, Federal agencies integrate privacy into innovative initiatives that advance their core missions. The activities of Federal agencies with duties that range across a broad array of economic sectors—including healthcare, financial services, and education—illustrate the Administration's commitment to promoting best practices, enabling new services, providing tools to address many different privacy issues, and enforcing individual privacy rights.

A. Enabling New Services

Like the private sector, Federal agencies must confront data privacy issues when delivering services to the public. A particularly challenging set of privacy issues arises in connection with delivering healthcare to the Nation's veterans. The Department of Veterans Affairs (VA) provides healthcare for 8.3 million enrolled veterans through more than 1,400 facilities distributed across the Nation. To help manage a healthcare operation of this scale and scope efficiently and cost-effectively, the VA is continuing to incorporate information technology into its healthcare delivery system. Protecting the privacy of veterans' health information is essential to the success of this endeavor. VA recently launched an initiative that demonstrates how careful attention to privacy and security protections for personal health information can lead to significant advances in how healthcare is delivered. VA incorporated privacy and security protections into its "My HealtheVet Personal Health Record." This system is a gateway to information that helps veterans to enable their caregivers to deliver better care and provides other Internet-based tools that empower veterans to become active partners in their health care. The VA's Blue Button service allows veterans to download an electronic copy of their HealtheVet information in a secure manner.

How Administration Action Is Enabling Privacy in Other Areas

- Integrating Privacy into Cybersecurity Initiatives. Protecting privacy is a priority in the Administration's efforts to secure online environments for continuing increases in productivity, innovation, and support for new business ventures. Led by the National Institute of Standards and Technology (NIST), the *National Strategy for Trusted Identities in Cyberspace* calls for a partnership with the commercial sector to develop more standardized, secure, and privacy-enhancing ways to authenticate individuals online.
- Enhancing Transparency in Credit Markets. The Administration is ensuring that privacy protections keep pace with developments in uses of personal data in setting the terms of consumer credit. The Federal Reserve Board, together with the FTC, issued a rule that requires creditors to provide a consumer with notice when, based on the consumer's credit report, the creditor provides credit to the consumer on less favorable terms than it provides to other consumers. This rule also entitles consumers who are notified of such "risk-based pricing" to obtain a free credit report, so that they can check whether the information creditors use is accurate.

B. Protecting Privacy through Effective Enforcement

The FTC has used its civil enforcement authority against those commercial enterprises that fail to follow Commission rules or act in an unfair or deceptive manner.

Since 2009, the FTC has taken actions against companies that have failed to exercise reasonable care to secure sensitive personal and medical information, represented that they abide by the U.S.-EU or U.S.-Swiss Safe Harbor agreements when they do not or they have allowed these certifications to lapse, or that misrepresent the use of tracking software.

The FTC also prosecuted actions involving deceptive practices by online seal providers, social media companies, and companies claiming to protect identities. In addition, the FTC prosecuted cases under the Telemarketing Sales Rule, the COPPA Rule, the Fair Credit Reporting Act, and the GLB Safeguards Rule.

The Administration also takes enforcing statutory privacy rights seriously. Federal agencies with law enforcement authority have taken action against those who violate privacy rights.

For example, the Department of Justice (DOJ) aggressively prosecutes cases involving identity theft—the use of misappropriated personal data that can cause life-disrupting and economically devastating harm to its victims.

In 2010 alone, DOJ's United States Attorneys'Offices prosecuted nearly 1300 cases involving identity theft, and U.S. Attorneys have brought nearly 700 identity theft cases in the current fiscal year.

DOJ, assisted by investigators from the Federal Bureau of Investigation and Department of Homeland Security (DHS) components such as United States Secret Service and U.S. Immigration and Customs Enforcement, also vigorously prosecutes individuals who obtain personal data (and other information) by breaking into computers.

Taken together, these efforts help protect the confidentiality of personal data and bring justice for victims of identity theft and other crimes that involve the misuse of personal data.

C. Guidance for Protecting Privacy

Federal agencies are also devoting resources to producing guidance on data privacy that has broad applicability in the private sector. The Department of Health and Human Services (HHS), for example, has issued guidance that analyzes some of the fundamental issues surrounding responses to security breaches that involve personally identifiable information.

In 2009, the Department of Health and Human Services Office for Civil Rights (OCR) issued guidance on when health information is considered to be secure (and therefore exempt from breach notification requirements) by specifying the technologies and methodologies that render protected health information unusable, unreadable, or indecipherable.

In 2010, OCR also issued guidance on conducting a risk analysis under the HIPAA Security Rule. OCR plans to issue additional guidance on the HIPAA Privacy Rule's "minimum necessary" standard and on de-identification of health information under the HIPAA Privacy Rule.

Federal agencies are also providing guidance on how to make more effective use of existing privacy-protecting measures.

In 2009, eight Federal agencies released a model privacy notice form that financial institutions can opt to use for their privacy notices to consumers required by GLB. Use of the model form provides a legal safe harbor for compliance with the GLB Privacy Rule, though the model form is not required.

The agencies conducted extensive consumer research and testing in developing the model form to ensure that consumers can easily understand what financial institutions do with their personal information and compare different institutions' information sharing practices.

Other Significant Administration Guidance on Privacy:

- Raising Public Awareness of Privacy and Data Security. DHS is leading a national public awareness effort called *Stop. Think. Connect.* to inform the American public of the need to strengthen cybersecurity and to provide practical tips to help Americans increase their safety and security online.
- In addition, the FTC has issued guides explaining measures that consumers and companies can take to protect children's privacy online, minimize the risk of medical identity theft, and prevent the loss of sensitive data through peer-to-peer file sharing applications.
- Applying Privacy Principles to New Technologies. The Administration is demonstrating that the same privacy principles that inform the general consumer data privacy framework developed here also apply to specific, emerging contexts. The "Smart Grid"—the incorporation of information technologies to make the electric grid more efficient, more accommodating of clean sources of energy, and a source of new jobs and innovation—provides an excellent example. Over the past two years, the Department of Energy and the National Institute of Standards and Technology engaged with stakeholders to understand privacy issues that could arise from this promising new technology.
- This work culminated in the Administration's *Policy Framework for The 21st Century Grid: Enabling Our Secure Energy Future*, which recommends that States make comprehensive FIPPs the starting point for protecting the detailed energy usage data that the Smart Grid will generate.

D. Integrating Privacy into the Structure of Federal Agencies

Finally, Federal agencies are leading the way in incorporating privacy into their structure and operations and in developing accountable organizations.

Some of these accountability-enhancing practices and tools have diffused to the private sector and across the globe. For example, the Internal Revenue Service and DHS pioneered the use of privacy impact assessments (PIAs), which provide for structured assessments of the potential privacy issues arising from new information systems and, under the E-Government Act of 2002, are now required of Federal agencies under some circumstances.

Building on efforts of previous Administrations, this Administration has extended the use of PIAs to social media.

Since their initial development within the Federal government, PIAs have become widely used in the private sector and within the European Union.

Federal agencies also continue to make privacy professionals part of their senior leadership structures. Many Federal agencies have full-time, professional chief privacy officers, who engage on privacy issues within their agencies, in broader discussions within the Federal government, and with the general public.

CONCLUSION

The United States is committed to protecting privacy. It is an element of individual dignity and an aspect of participation in democratic society. To an increasing extent, privacy protections have become critical to the information-based economy. Stronger consumer data privacy protections will buttress the trust that is necessary to promote the full economic, social, and political uses of networked technologies.

The increasing quantities of personal data that these technologies subject to collection, use, and disclosure have fueled innovation and significant social benefits. We can preserve these benefits while also ensuring that our consumer data privacy policy better reflects the value that Americans place on privacy and bolsters trust in the Internet and other networked technologies. The framework set forth in the preceding pages provides a way to achieve these goals. The Consumer Privacy Bill of Rights should be the legal baseline that governs consumer data privacy in the United States.

The Administration will work with Congress to bring this about, but it will also work with private-sector stakeholders to adopt the Consumer Privacy Bill of Rights in the absence of legislation. To encourage adoption, the Department of Commerce will convene multistakeholder processes to encourage the development of enforceable, context-specific codes of conduct.

The United States Government will engage with our international partners to increase the interoperability of our respective consumer data privacy frameworks. Federal agencies will continue to develop innovative privacy-protecting programs and guidance as well as enforce the broad array of existing Federal laws that protect consumer privacy.

A cornerstone of this framework is its call for the ongoing participation of private-sector stakeholders. The views that companies, civil society, academics, and advocates provided to the Administration through written comments, public symposia, and informal discussions have been invaluable in shaping this framework. Implementing it, and making progress toward consumer data privacy protections that support a more trustworthy networked world, will require all of us to continue to work together.

APPENDIX A: THE CONSUMER PRIVACY BILL OF RIGHTS

Consumer Privacy Bill if Rights

The Consumer Privacy Bill of Rights applies to *personal data*, which means any data, including aggregations of data, which is linkable to a specific individual. Personal data may include data that is linked to a specific computer or other device. The Administration supports Federal legislation that adopts the principles of the Consumer Privacy Bill of Rights.

Even without legislation, the Administration will convene multistakeholder processes that use these rights as a template for codes of conduct that are enforceable by the Federal Trade Commission.

These elements—the Consumer Privacy Bill of Rights, codes of conduct, and strong enforcement—will increase interoperability between the U.S. consumer data privacy framework and those of our international partners.

1) **INDIVIDUAL CONTROL:** Consumers have a right to exercise control over what personal data companies collect from them and how they use it. Companies should provide consumers appropriate control over the personal data that consumers share with others and over how companies collect, use, or disclose personal data. Companies should enable these choices by providing consumers with easily used and accessible mechanisms that reflect the scale, scope, and sensitivity of the personal data that they collect, use, or disclose, as well as the sensitivity of the uses they make of personal data.
   Companies should offer consumers clear and simple choices, presented at times and in ways that enable consumers to make meaningful decisions about personal data collection, use, and disclosure. Companies should offer consumers means to withdraw or limit consent that are as accessible and easily used as the methods for granting consent in the first place.
2) **TRANSPARENCY:** Consumers have a right to easily understandable and accessible information about privacy and security practices. At times and in places that are most useful to enabling consumers to gain a meaningful understanding of privacy risks and the ability to exercise Individual Control, companies should provide clear descriptions of what personal data they collect, why they need the data, how they will use it, when they will delete the data or de-identify it from consumers, and whether and for what purposes they may share personal data with third parties.
3) **RESPECT FOR CONTEXT:** Consumers have a right to expect that companies will collect, use, and disclose personal data in ways that are consistent with the context in which consumers provide the data. Companies should limit their use and disclosure of personal data to those purposes that are consistent with both the relationship that they have with consumers and the context in which consumers originally disclosed the data, unless required by law to do otherwise.
   If companies will use or disclose personal data for other purposes, they should provide heightened Transparency and Individual Control by disclosing these other purposes in a manner that is prominent and easily actionable by consumers at the time of data collection.
   If, subsequent to collection, companies decide to use or disclose personal data for purposes that are inconsistent with the context in which the data was disclosed, they must provide heightened measures of Transparency and Individual Choice.
   Finally, the age and familiarity with technology of consumers who engage with a company are important elements of context. Companies should fulfill the obligations under this principle in ways that are appropriate for the age and sophistication of consumers.

In particular, the principles in the Consumer Privacy Bill of Rights may require greater protections for personal data obtained from children and teenagers than for adults.

4) **SECURITY:** Consumers have a right to secure and responsible handling of personal data. Companies should assess the privacy and security risks associated with their personal data practices and maintain reasonable safeguards to control risks such as loss; unauthorized access, use, destruction, or modification; and improper disclosure.
5) **ACCESS AND ACCURACY:** Consumers have a right to access and correct personal data in usable formats, in a manner that is appropriate to the sensitivity of the data and the risk of adverse consequences to consumers if the data is inaccurate. Companies should use reasonable measures to ensure they maintain accurate personal data. Companies also should provide consumers with reasonable access to personal data that they collect or maintain about them, as well as the appropriate means and opportunity to correct inaccurate data or request its deletion or use limitation.

   Companies that handle personal data should construe this principle in a manner consistent with freedom of expression and freedom of the press.

   In determining what measures they may use to maintain accuracy and to provide access, correction, deletion, or suppression capabilities to consumers, companies may also consider the scale, scope, and sensitivity of the personal data that they collect or maintain and the likelihood that its use may expose consumers to financial, physical, or other material harm.
6) **FOCUSED COLLECTION:** Consumers have a right to reasonable limits on the personal data that companies collect and retain. Companies should collect only as much personal data as they need to accomplish purposes specified under the Respect for Context principle. Companies should securely dispose of or de-identify personal data once they no longer need it, unless they are under a legal obligation to do otherwise.
7) **ACCOUNTABILITY**: Consumers have a right to have personal data handled by companies with appropriate measures in place to assure they adhere to the Consumer Privacy Bill of Rights. Companies should be accountable to enforcement authorities and consumers for adhering to these principles. Companies also should hold employees responsible for adhering to these principles. To achieve this end, companies should train their employees as appropriate to handle personal data consistently with these principles and regularly evaluate their performance in this regard.

   Where appropriate, companies should conduct full audits. Companies that disclose personal data to third parties should at a minimum ensure that the recipients are under enforceable contractual obligations to adhere to these principles, unless they are required by law to do otherwise.

Appendix B: Comparison of the Consumer Privacy Bill of Rights to Other Statements of the Fair Information Practice Principles (FIPPs)

Consumer Privacy Bill of Rights	OECD Privacy Guidelines (excerpts)	DHS Privacy Policy (generalized)	APEC Principles (excerpts)
Individual Control.Consumers have a right to exercise control over what personal data that companies collect from them and how they use it.	Use Limitation Principle. Personal data should not be disclosed . . . except "with the consent of the data subject or by the authority of law."	Individual Participation. Organizations should involve the individual in the process of using PII [personally identifiable information] and, to the extent practicable, seek individual consent for the collection, use, dissemination, and maintenance of PII.	Choice. Where appropriate, individualsshould be provided with clear, prominent, easily understandable, accessible and affordable mechanisms to exercisechoice in relation to the collection, use and disclosure of their personal information.
Transparency. Consumers have a right to easily understandable information about privacy and security practices.	Openness Principle. There should be a general policy of openness about developments, practices and policies with respect to personal data.	Transparency. Organizations should be transparent and notify individuals regarding collection, use, dissemina-tion, and maintenance of PII.	Notice. Personal information control-lers should provide clear and easily accessible statements about their practices and policies . . . .
Respect for Context. Consumers have a right to expect that companies will collect, use, and disclose personal data in ways that are consistent with the context in which consumers provide the data.	Purpose Specification Principle.The purposes for which personal data are collected should be specified not later than at the time of data collection and the subsequent use limited to the fulfillment of those purposes or such others as are not incompatible with those purposes and as are specified on each occasion of change of purpose.	Purpose Specification. Organizations should specifically articulate the authority that permits the collection of PII and specifically articulate the purpose or purposes for which the PII is intended to be used.	Notice.All reasonably practicable steps shall be taken to ensure that such notice is provided either before or at the time of collection of personal information. Otherwise, such notice should be provided as soon after as is practicable.
	Use Limitation Principle. Personal data should not be disclosed, made available or otherwise used for purposes other than those specified in accordance with Paragraph 9 [purpose specification] except . . . (a) with the consent of the data subject; or (b) by the authority of law.	Use Limitation. Organizations should use PII solely for the purpose(s) speci-fied in the notice. Sharing PII should be for a purpose compatible with the pur-pose for which the PII was collected.	Uses of Personal Information. Personal information collected should be used only to fulfill the purposes of collection and other compatible or related purposes except: a) with the consent of the individual whose personal information is collected; b) when necessary to provide a service or product requested by the individual;or, c) by the authority of law and other legal instruments, proclamations and pronouncements of legal effect.

(Continued)

Consumer Privacy Bill of Rights	OECD Privacy Guidelines (excerpts)	DHS Privacy Policy (generalized)	APEC Principles (excerpts)
Security. Consumers have a right to secure and responsible handling of personal data.	Security Safeguards Principle.Personal data should be protected by reasonable security safeguards against such risks as loss or unauthorized access, destruction, use, modification or disclosure of data.	Security. Organizations should protect PII (in all media) through appropriate security safeguards against risks such as loss, unauthorized access or use, destruction, modification, or unintended or inappropriate disclosure.	Security Safeguards. Personal information controllers should protect personal information that they hold with appropriate safeguards against risks, such as loss or unauthorized access to personal information, or unauthorized destruction, use, modification or disclosure of information or other misuses.
Access and Accuracy. Consumers have a right to access and correct personal data in usable formats, in a manner that is appropriate to the sensitivity of the data and the risk of adverse consequences to consumers if the data is inaccurate.	Individual Participation Principle.An individual should have the right: a) to obtain from a data controller, or otherwise, confirmation of whether or not the data controller has data relating to him; b) to have communicated to him, data relating to him within a reasonable time; at a charge, if any, that is not excessive; in a reasonable manner; and in a form that is readily intelligible to him; c) to be given reasons if a request made under subparagraphs(a) and (b) is denied, and to be able to challenge such denial; d) to challenge data relating to him and, if the challenge is successful to have the data erased, rectified, completed or amended.	Data Quality and Integrity.Organizations should, to the extent practicable, ensure that PII is accurate, relevant, timely, and complete.	Access and Correction. Individuals should be able to: a) obtain from the personal information controller confirmation of whetheror not the personal information controller holds personal information about them; b) have communicated to them, after having provided sufficient proof of their identity, personal information about them; i. within a reasonable time ii. at a charge, if any, that is not excessive; iii. in a reasonable manner; iv. in a form that is generally understandable; and, c) challenge the accuracy of information relating to them and, if possible and as appropriate, have the information rectified, completed, amended or deleted.
	Data Quality Principle.Personal data should be relevant to the purposes for which they are to be used, and, to the extent necessary for those purposes, should be accurate, complete and kept up-to-date.		Integrity of Personal Information. Personal information should be accurate, complete and kept up-to-date to the extent necessary for the purposes of use.

Consumer Privacy Bill of Rights	OECD Privacy Guidelines (excerpts)	DHS Privacy Policy (generalized)	APEC Principles (excerpts)
			Preventing Harm. Recognizing the interests of the individual to legitimate expectations of privacy, personal information protection should be designed to prevent the misuse of suchinformation.
Focused Collection: Consumers have a right to reasonable limits on the personal data that companies collect and retain.	Collection Limitation Principle.There should be limits to the collection of personal data and any such data should be obtained by lawful and fair means and, where appropriate, with the knowledge or consent of the data subject.	Data Minimization: Organizations should only collect PII that is directly relevant and necessary to accomplish the specified purpose(s) and only retain PII for as long as is necessary to fulfill the specified purpose(s).	Collection Limitation.The collection of personal information should be limited to information that is relevant to the purposes of collection and any such information should be obtained by lawful and fair means, and where appropriate, with notice to, or consent of, the individual concerned.
Accountability. Consumers have a right to have personal data handled by companies with appropriate measures in place to assure they adhere to the Consumer Privacy Bill of Rights.	Accountability Principle.A data controller should be accountable for complying with measures which give effect to the principles stated above.	Accountability and Auditing: Organizations should be accountable for complying with these principles, providing training to all employees and contractors who use PII, and auditing the actual use of PII to demonstrate compliance with these principles and all applicable privacy protection requirements.	Accountability.A personal information controller should be accountable for complying with measures that give effect to the Principles stated above. When personal information is to be transferred to another person or organization, whether domestically or internationally, the personal information controller should obtain the consent of the individual or exercise due diligence and take reasonable steps to ensure that the recipient person or organization will protect theinformation consistently with these Principles.

End Notes

[1] This framework is concerned solely with how private-sector entities handle personal data in commercial settings. A separate set of constitutional and statutory protections apply to the government's access to data that is in the possession of private parties. In addition, the Privacy Act of 1974, Pub. L. No. 93-579 (5 U.S.C. § 552a), and implementing guidance from the Office of Management and Budget, *available at* http://www.whitehouse.gov/omb/ privacy_general, govern the Federal government's handling of personally identifiable information. Both of these areas are beyond the scope of this document.

[2] Throughout this document, "company" means any organization, corporation, trust, partnership, sole proprietorship, unincorporated association, or venture established to make a profit, or nonprofit entity, that collects, uses, discloses, stores, or transfers personal data in interstate commerce, to the extent such organizations are not subject to existing Federal data privacy laws.

[3] *See, e.g.*, Remarks of Secretary of State Hillary Rodham Clinton, Release of Administration's International Strategy for Cyberspace (May 2011) ("Many of you representing the governments of other countries, as well as the private sector or foundations or civil society groups, share our commitment to ensuring that the Internet remains open, secure, free, not only for the 2 billion people who are now offline, but for the billions more who will be online in the years ahead.").

[4] President Barack Obama, *International Strategy for Cyberspace*, at 8, May 2011, http://www.whitehouse.gov/ sites/default/files/rss_viewer/international_strategy_for_cyberspace.pdf.

[5] U.S. Census Bureau, *E-Stats*, May 26, 2011, http://www.census.gov/econ/estats/2009/ 2009 reportfinal.pdf, at 1.

[6] McKinsey Global Institute, *Big Data: The Next Frontier for Innovation, Competition, and Productivity*, at 94-95, May 2011, http://www.mckinsey.com/mgi/publications/ big_data/ pdfs/MGI_big_data_full_report.pdf. The National Institute of Standards and Technology (NIST) has identified five essential characteristics of cloud computing: on-demand self-service, broad network access, resource pooling, rapid elasticity, and measured service. Peter Mell and Tim Gance, The NIST Definition of Cloud Computing, version 15, Oct. 7, 2009, http://csrc.nist.gov/groups/SNS/cloud-computing/cloud-def-v15.doc.

[7] Recently, identity theft alone was estimated to cause economic losses of more than $15 billion in a single year. Fed. Trade Comm'n, 2006 Identity Theft Survey Report (2007), *available at* http://www.ftc.gov/os/2007/11/ SynovateFinalReportIDTheft2006.pdf.

[8] Department of Commerce, *Commercial Data Privacy and Innovation in the Internet Economy: Dynamic Policy Framework*, Dec. 2010, *available* at http://www.ntia.doc.gov/report/2010/ commercial-data-privacy-and-innovationinternet-economy-dynamic-policy-framework.

[9] As noted in the Privacy and Innovation Green Paper (p. 11):

In 1973, the Department of Health, Education, and Welfare (HEW) released its report, *Records, Computers, and the Rights of Citizens*, which outlined a Code of Fair Information Practices that would create "safeguard requirements" for certain "automated personal data systems" maintained by the Federal Government. This Code of Fair Information Practices, now commonly referred to as fair information practice principles (FIPPs), established the framework on which much privacy policy would be built.

Examples of FIPPs-based international frameworks include the Organisation for Economic Co-operation and Development *Guidelines on the Protection of Privacy and Transborder Flows of Personal Data* and the Asia-Pacific Economic Cooperation *Privacy Framework*. The Privacy and Innovation Green Paper proposed for consideration the following set of FIPPs: transparency, individual participation, purpose specification, data minimization, use limitation, data quality and integrity, security, and accountability and auditing.

[10] As the Privacy and Innovation Green Paper noted, "New devices and applications allow the collection and use of personal information in ways that, at times, can be contrary to many consumers' privacy expectations." Department of Commerce, Privacy and Innovation Green Paper, at i (statement of Commerce Secretary Gary Locke).

[11] For a comparison of the Consumer Privacy Bill of Rights to other statements of the FIPPs, see Appendix B.

[12] This definition is similar to the Federal Government's definition of "personally identifiable information":

[I]nformation that can be used to distinguish or trace an individual's identity, either alone or when combined with other personal or identifying information that is linked or linkable to a specific individual. The definition of PII is not anchored to any single category of information or technology. Rather, it requires a case-by-case assessment of the specific risk that an individual can be identified.

Peter R. Orszag, Memorandum for the Heads of Executive Departments and Agencies, Guidance for Agency Use of Third-Party Websites and Applications, at 8 (Appendix), June 25, 2010, http://www.whitehouse.gov/ sites/default/files/omb/assets/memoranda_2010/m10-23.pdf.

[13] "Scope" refers to the range of activities or interests as well as the time period that is reflected in a dataset. "Scale" refers to the number of individuals whose activities are in a dataset.

[14] *See* FTC, *Self-Regulatory Principles for Online Behavioral Advertising* (staff report), at 2, Feb. 2009 (stating that online behavioral advertising "involves the tracking of consumers' online activities in order to deliver tailored advertising").

[15] According to one study, behaviorally targeted ads are worth significantly more than non-targeted ads. *See* Howard Beales, *The Value of Behavioral Targeting*, at 3, Mar. 24, 2010 (finding, based on data provided by ad networks, that behaviorally targeted ad rates in 2009 were 2.68 times greater than non-targeted ad rates), http://www.networkadvertising.org/ pdfs/Beales_NAI_Study.pdf; FTC, *Protecting Consumer Privacy in an Era of Rapid Change: A Proposed Framework for Businesses and Policymakers* (preliminary staff report), at 24, Dec. 2010 (reporting that FTC privacy roundtable participants discussed that "the more information that is known about a consumer, the more a company will pay to deliver a precisely-targeted advertisement to him") ("FTC Staff Report").

[16] See Aleecia M. McDonald and Lorrie Faith Cranor, *Americans' Attitudes About Internet Behavioral Advertising Practices*, Proceedings of the 9th Annual ACM Workshop on Privacy in the Electronic Society (WPES) (2010).

[17] *See generally* FTC, *Self-Regulatory Principles for Online Behavioral Advertising* (staff report), Feb. 2009.

[18] *See* AboutAds.info, *Self-Regulatory Principles for Online Behavioral Advertising,* http://www.aboutads.info/ resource/download/seven-principles-07-01-09.pdf (July 2009); Interactive Advertising Bureau, Comment on the Privacy and Innovation Green Paper (Attachment B) (explaining online advertisers' system for directing users to ad networks' privacy policies and opt-outs).

[19] The obligation to provide these choices should be read in conjunction with the Access and Accuracy principle discussed below.

[20] *See* Assistant Secretary for Communications and Information Lawrence E. Strickling, Testimony Before the Senate Committee on Commerce, Science, and Transportation, Mar. 16, 2011, at 2-3.

[21] Several commenters on the Privacy and Innovation Green Paper emphasized the importance of context in applying FIPPs. *See, e.g.*, AT&T Comment on the Privacy and Innovation Green Paper, at 7, Jan. 28, 2011 ("FIPPs are usefully expressed as generalized policy guides that should shape the multi-stakeholder collaborative processes to develop flexible and contextualized codes of practice for particular industries."); Centre for Information Policy Leadership Comment on the Privacy and Innovation Green Paper, at 3, Jan. 28, 2011 ("Principles of fair information practices should be applied within a contextual framework, and not in a rigid or fixed way."); Google Comment on the Privacy and Innovation Green Paper, at 6, Jan. 28, 2011 ("In particular, FIPPs must be flexible enough to take account of the spectrum of identifiability, linkability, and sensitivity of various data in various contexts."); Intel Comment on the Privacy and Innovation Green Paper, at 4 ("[M]any of the issues present in a privacy regulatory scheme are highly contextual."); Intuit Comment on the Privacy and Innovation Green Paper, at 9 ("It is the use of the information as well as its characteristics that should inform our treatment of it. Context is crucial."); Helen Nissenbaum, Kenneth Farrall, and Finn Brunton, Comment on the Privacy and Innovation Green Paper, at 2-3 (recommending consideration of context as a source of "baseline substantive constraints on data practices following the model of current US sectoral privacy regulation"); Online Publishers Association Comment on the Privacy and Innovation Green Paper, at 6 ("Online publishers share a direct and trusted relationship with visitors to their sites. In the context of this relationship, OPA members sometimes collect and use information to target and deliver the online advertising that subsidizes production of quality digital content."); TRUSTe Comment on the Privacy and Innovation Green Paper, at 2 ("We view privacy as inherently contextual; disclosure obligations will differ depending on the context of the interaction."). Current scholarship also emphasizes the importance of the relationship between context and privacy. *See* Helen Nissenbaum, *Privacy in Context: Technology, Policy, and the Integrity of Social Life* (2009).

[22] This list of practices that are common to many contexts is similar to the "commonly accepted practices" that FTC staff identified in its 2010 report. *See* FTC Staff Report at 53-54. In the Administration's view, protecting intellectual property is so widespread and necessary to many companies that they should be able to infer consent to achieve this objective. Several commenters on the Department of Commerce's Privacy and Information Green Paper encouraged the Administration to recognize such practices in order to provide certainty for companies and to give greater prominence to choices that consumers are more likely to find meaningful.

[23] *See* Children's Online Privacy Protection Act, Pub. L. 105-277 (codified at 15 U.S.C. §§ 6501-6506) *and* FTC, Children's Online Protection Rule, 16 C.F.R. Part 312. COPPA defines "child" to mean "an individual under the age of 13." 15 U.S.C. § 6501(1).

[24] National Science and Technology Council, *A Policy Framework for the 21st Century Grid: Enabling Our Secure Energy Future*, at 41, 46, June 2011, *available* at http://www.whitehouse.gov/sites/default/files/microsites/ostp/nstcsmart-grid-june2011.pdf.

[25] See The White House, *A Strategy for American Innovation: A Strategy for American Innovation: Securing Our Economic Growth and Prosperity,* Feb. 2011, http://www.whitehouse.gov/innovation/strategy; Department of Health and Human Services, Final Rule on Electronic Health Record Incentive Program, 75 Fed. Reg. 44314, July 28, 2010.

[26] *See* Memorandum for the Heads of Executive Departments and Agencies, "Informing Consumers Through Smart Disclosure," *available at* http://www.whitehouse.gov/sites/ default/files/omb/inforeg/for-agencies/informing-consumers-through-smart-disclosure.pdf ("To the extent practicable and subject to valid restrictions, agencies should publish information online in an open format that can be retrieved, downloaded, indexed, and searched by commonly used Web search applications. An open format is one that is platform independent, machine readable, and made available to the public without restriction that would impede the re-use of that information."); M-10-06, Memorandum for the Heads of Executive Departments and Agencies, "Open Government Directive," *available at* http://www.whitehouse.gov/sites/default/files/omb/assets/memoranda_2010/ m10-06.pdf ("Machine readable data are digital information stored in a format enabling the information to be processed and analyzed by computer. These formats allow electronic data to be as usable as possible.").

[27] The United States recently joined the other members of the Organisation for Economic Co-operation and Development (OECD) in recognizing the economic and social importance of the Internet. *See* OECD, Communiqué on Principles for Internet Policy-Making, OECD High-Level Meeting on The Internet Economy: Generating Innovation and Growth, June 28-29, 2011, http://www.ntia.doc.gov/legacy/ntiahome/privwhitepaper.html.

[28] For example, the combined efforts of the Department of Commerce, FTC, and the White House produced the consumer data privacy framework of notice and choice, which protected privacy in the context of rapidly developing technologies and markets. *See* FTC, *Privacy Online: Fair Information Practices in the Electronic Marketplace: A Federal Trade Commission Report to Congress, at* http://www.ftc.gov/reports/privacy2000/privacy2000.pdf (2000); White House, *Framework for Global Electronic Commerce, at* § 5, http://clinton4.nara.gov/WH/New/Commerce/ (1997); National Telecommunications and Information Administration, *Privacy and the NII: Safeguarding Telecommunications-Related Personal Information* (Oct. 1995), http://www.ntia.doc.gov/legacy/ntiahome/ privwhitepaper.html.

[29] NTIA is designated by statute as the "President's principal adviser on telecommunications policies pertaining to the Nation's economic and technological advancement . . . ." 47 U.S.C. § 902(b)(2)(D).

[30] Other Federal agencies may play this convening role if consumer data privacy issues arise in their areas of expertise. Alternatively, private-sector organizations could convene stakeholders, though the dearth of private sector-led code development efforts is precisely the reason that the Administration proposes to serve as convener.

[31] The Administration's guidelines for increasing transparency, participation, and collaboration in public policy development could prove useful here. See President Barack Obama, Memorandum to the Heads of Executive Departments and Agencies: Transparency and Open Government, http://www.whitehouse.gov/the_press_office/Transparencyand OpenGovernment/; Peter R. Orszag, Memorandum for the Heads of Executive Departments and Agencies: Open Government Directive, Dec. 8, 2009, http://www.whitehouse.gov/open/documents/open-government-directive.

[32] The FTC brings cases based on violations of commitments in its privacy statements under its authority to prevent deceptive acts or practices. In addition, the FTC brings data privacy cases under its unfairness jurisdiction, which will remain an important source of consumer data privacy protection.

[33] Note, however, the FTC does not currently have authority to enforce Section 5 of the FTC Act, 15, U.S.C. § 45, against certain corporations that operate for profit.

[34] *See* FTC Act § 5, 15 U.S.C. § 45. In addition to using its Section 5 authority to protect consumer data privacy, the FTC has brought dozens of cases under sector-specific statutes, such as the Children's Online Privacy Protection Act, the Fair Credit Reporting Act, the Gramm-Leach-Bliley Act, and the Do Not Call Rule. For a review of these cases, see FTC Staff Report at 9-13.

[35] *See* FTC Staff Report at 10 (reviewing enforcement actions that include counts based on unfair acts or practices).

[36] The FTC's jurisdiction over nonprofits and certain other types of entities under FTC Act § 5 may be limited.

[37] NIST has identified five essential characteristics of cloud computing: on-demand self-service, broad network access, resource pooling, rapid elasticity, and measured service. *See supra* note 6.

[38] Auditing is not a requirement under the Accountability principle stated in the Consumer Privacy Bill of Rights. This section discusses the potential use of audits by companies that seek to take advantage of global interoperability in privacy laws. Not all organizations, however, fit this description.

[39] The nine principles are collection limitation, integrity of personal information, notice, uses of personal information, choice, security safeguards, access and correction, accountability, and harm prevention. *See* http://publications.apec.org/publication-detail.php?pub_id=390.

[40] Currently, APEC includes 21 members: Australia, Brunei Darussalam, Canada, Chile, the People's Republic of China, Hong Kong, Indonesia, Japan, the Republic of Korea, Malaysia, Mexico, New Zealand, Papua New Guinea, Peru, the Philippines, Russia, Singapore, Chinese Taipei, Thailand, the United States, and Vietnam. APEC, Member Economies, http://www.apec.org/About-Us/About-APEC/Member-Economies.aspx (last visited Sept. 7, 2011).

[41] For a summary of the FTC's enforcement of the U.S.-EU Safe Harbor Framework, see FTC, FTC Settles with Six Companies Claiming to Comply with International Privacy Framework, Oct. 6, 2009, http://www.ftc.gov/opa/2009/10/safeharbor.shtm. *See also In re* Google, Inc., Complaint, at 7 File No. 102 3136, Mar. 30, 2011 (alleging "respondent did not adhere to the US Safe Harbor Privacy Principles of Notice and Choice").

[42] The Administration is separately considering the need to amend laws pertaining to the government's access to data in the possession of private parties, including the Electronic Communications Privacy Act, to address changes in technology.

[43] In the absence of legislation, the Consumer Privacy Bill of Rights set forth in this document provides guidance for stakeholders and does not alter the FTC's existing enforcement authority under FTC Act § 5.

[44] The FTC refers civil penalty actions to the Department of Justice, which may bring an action within 45 days. If the Department of Justice declines to litigate, the FTC may prosecute the case itself. *See, e.g.,* 15 U.S.C. § 56(a).

[45] 15 U.S.C § 1.

[46] 17 U.S.C. § 101.

[47] Indeed, the Administration recently called for State public utilities commissions to follow privacy principles that are very similar to those in the Consumer Privacy Bill of Rights in order to protect personal data associated with the "smart" electric grid. *See supra* note 23.

[48] This limitation also means that the laws that regulate the Federal government's collection, use, and disclosure of personal data are beyond the framework's scope.

[49] *See*, e.g., 47 U.S.C. §§ 222, 338 & 551 (requiring telecommunications carriers, satellite carriers, and cable services, respectively, to protect customers' personal information).

[50] The White House, Data Breach Notification Legislative Language, May 2011, http://www.whitehouse.gov/sites/default/files/omb/legislative/letters/data-breach-notification.pdf.

In: Consumer Privacy in the 21st Century
Editor: Larry A. Schwartz

ISBN: 978-1-62417-252-6

Chapter 3

MOBILE APPS FOR KIDS: CURRENT PRIVACY DISCLOSURES ARE DISAPPOINTING*

Federal Trade Commission

FTC STAFF REPORT

Overview

The market for mobile applications has experienced explosive growth over the past three and a half years. When Apple's iTunes App Store and Google's Android Market first launched in 2008, smartphone users could choose from about 600 apps.[2] Today, there are more than 500,000 apps in the Apple App store[3] and 380,000 apps in the Android Market,[4] which consumers can access from a variety of mobile devices, including smartphones and tablets. Consumers have downloaded these apps more than 28 billion times,[5] and young children and teens are increasingly embracing smartphone technology for entertainment and educational purposes.[6] As consumers increasingly rely on their mobile devices for multiple activities, the quantity and diversity of mobile apps continue to expand.

This rapidly growing market provides enormous opportunities and benefits for app users of all ages, but raises questions about users' privacy, especially when the users are children and teens. Mobile apps can capture a broad range of user information from the device automatically – including the user's precise geolocation, phone number, list of contacts, call logs, unique device identifiers, and other information stored on the mobile device – and can share this data with a large number of possible recipients. These capabilities can provide beneficial services to consumers – for example, access to maps and directions, and the ability to play interactive games with other users – but they also can be used by apps to collect detailed personal information in a manner parents cannot detect.

* This is an edited, reformatted and augmented version of Federal Trade Commission, dated February 2012.

Protecting children's privacy is one of the Commission's top priorities. In order to better understand and evaluate the emerging app market and the products and services it offers to children, Federal Trade Commission staff designed and conducted a survey of the apps offered for children in the two largest U.S. app stores, the Android Market and the Apple App store. Staff focused in particular on the types of apps offered to children; the age range of the intended audience; the disclosures provided to users about the apps' data collection and sharing practices; the availability of interactive features, such as connecting with social media; and the app store ratings and parental controls offered for these systems. This report highlights the lack of information available to parents prior to downloading mobile apps for their children, and calls on industry to provide greater transparency about their data practices.[7]

Staff searched the app stores using the word "kids," and examined hundreds of pages promoting apps, which ranged from alphabet and word games, math and number games, and memory games to books and stories, flash cards, and puzzles. Most of the apps' descriptions specifically indicated that the apps were intended for use by children, and some promoted use by children of certain ages, stating, for example, "teach young children, ages 2 to 5." Prices ranged from free to $9.99, but most apps were $0.99 or less, and free apps were overwhelmingly the most frequently downloaded.

While staff encountered a diverse pool of apps for kids created by hundreds of different developers, staff found little, if any, information in the app marketplaces about the data collection and sharing practices of these apps. Staff found almost no relevant language regarding app data collection or sharing on the Apple app promotion pages,[8] and minimal information (beyond the general "permission" statements required on the Android operating system[9]) on just three of the Android promotion pages. In most instances, staff was unable to determine from the promotion pages whether the apps collected any data at all, let alone the type of data collected, the purpose of the collection, and who collected or obtained access to the data.

As part of its mission to protect children, the Commission vigorously enforces the Children's Online Privacy Protection Act ("COPPA") and the FTC's implementing Rule, which require operators of online services (including interactive mobile apps) directed to children under age 13 to provide notice and obtain parental consent before collecting items of "personal information" from children.[10] Since collecting the data for this survey, the FTC settled its first COPPA enforcement action against a mobile app developer[11] and issued a Notice of Proposed Rulemaking to amend the Commission's COPPA Rule.[12] Those initiatives, along with this report, are a warning call to industry that it must do more to provide parents with easily accessible, basic information about the mobile apps that their children use.

Most of the apps in the study appear to be intended for children's use, and many may, in fact, be "directed to children" within the meaning of COPPA.[13] This survey focused on the disclosures provided to users regarding their data practices; it did not test whether the selected apps actually collected, used, or disclosed personal information from children. Over the next six months, staff will conduct an additional review to determine whether there are COPPA violations and whether enforcement is appropriate.[14] Staff also will evaluate whether the industry is moving forward to address the disclosure issues raised in this report.

Recommendations

FTC staff believes that all members of the kids app ecosystem – the app stores, developers, and third parties providing services within the apps – should play an active role in providing key information to parents who download apps. The mobile app marketplace is growing at a tremendous speed, and many consumer protections, including privacy and privacy disclosures, have not kept pace with this development. Parents need easy access to basic information so they can make informed decisions about the apps they allow their children to use.[15] App developers should provide this information through simple and short disclosures or icons that are easy to find and understand on the small screen of a mobile device. Parents should be able to learn what information an app collects, how the information will be used, and with whom the information will be shared.[16] App developers also should alert parents if the app connects with any social media, or allows targeted advertising to occur through the app. Third parties that collect user information through apps also should disclose their privacy practices, whether through a link on the app promotion page, the developers' disclosures, or another easily accessible method. The app stores also should do more to help parents and kids. The two major app stores provide the basic architecture for communicating information about the kids apps they offer, such as pricing and category information. However, the app stores should provide a more consistent way for developers to display information regarding their app's data collection practices and interactive features. For example, app stores could provide a designated space for developers to disclose this information. The app stores also could provide standardized icons to signal features, such as a connection with social media services. Although the app store developer agreements require developers to disclose the information their apps collect, the app stores do not appear to enforce these requirements.[17] This lack of enforcement provides little incentive to app developers to provide such disclosures and leaves parents without the information they need. As gatekeepers of the app marketplace, the app stores should do more. This recommendation applies not just to Apple and Google, but also to other companies that provide a marketplace for kids mobile apps. Additional work is needed to identify the best means and place for conveying data practices in plain language and in easily accessible ways on the small screens of mobile devices. Staff encourages industry members, privacy groups, academics, and others to develop and test new ways to provide information to parents – for example, by standardizing language, creating icons, or using a layered approach. To this end, the Commission currently is engaged in a project to update its existing business guidance, "Dot Com Disclosures," about online advertising disclosures.[18] As part of this project, the agency will host a public workshop in 2012 to gain input from interested parties, including industry representatives, consumer groups, and consumer disclosure experts. One of the topics that will be addressed is mobile privacy disclosures, including how they can be short, effective, and accessible to consumers on small screens. Staff anticipates that the workshop discussion will spur further development in this area.

Methodology

In July 2011, FTC staff searched on the desktop version of Apple's App Store and the browser-based version of the Android Market for the term "kids."[19] The search yielded over

8,000 results in the Apple App Store and over 3,600 in the Android Market. Staff collected the app promotion pages for the first 480 results returned by each app store,[20] for a total of 960 apps. Both app stores provide a promotion page for each app offered, which typically lists the name of the app developer directly under the app title and includes a textual description of the app.

The app promotion page also displays information such as the app's price, publication date, app store category, content maturity rating, user feedback ratings, number of user feedback ratings, screenshot previews, developer contact information, and, in many instances, a link to a developer website.[21]

Staff then conducted a closer review of the promotion pages for 200 Android apps and 200 Apple apps chosen randomly from each pool of the 480 "kids" results. Staff examined the information listed on the app store promotion page and the first page ("landing" page) of the associated developer's website. On the app store promotion page, staff looked for language and terms in the app description in order to sort the apps by type and intended audience. Staff also looked to see if the app linked to any social media, allowed users to make purchases ("in-app" purchases), included advertising, displayed developer contact information, and provided information about the app's data collection practices. On the landing page of the developer website, staff looked for additional information about the app, as well as contact and data collection information for the developer.[22]

Staff notes two additional points with respect to the methodology. First, staff did not download any of the apps surveyed, and did not test the apps' information collection, use, or disclosure practices. Rather, staff reviewed the information that a consumer easily could access either from the app store or from the developer's website prior to downloading the app.

Information provided to parents after downloading an app is, in staff's view, less useful in the parent's decision-making since, by then, the child may already be using the app and the parent already could have been charged a fee.[23]

Second, staff reviewed only the app store pages made available to desktop computer visitors, which allowed staff to electronically collect and preserve the app promotion pages at a specific moment in time. Staff recognizes that there are a few differences between the content offered through the desktop interface and the content offered through the mobile device interface, but does not believe these differences are material or change the conclusions of this report.[24]

I. Range of Apps Offered

Staff found a wide range of kids apps offered at low prices by hundreds of developers.

Types of Apps for Kids

To get a sense of the types of apps available for kids, staff categorized each of the 400 apps based on language contained in the app name or description.[25] For example, a multiplication flash card app would fall into the "educational," "math," and "flash cards" categories. Staff found that education, games, math, spelling, and animals were the most popular app categories.

The percentage of apps found by subject category is listed in Table 1.

Table 1. Categories of "Kids" Apps

	Apple App Store	Android Market
Category	**% of Apps**	**% of Apps**
Educational	51.0%	50.0%
Game	49.5%	41.0%
Animal-related	22.0%	23.0%
Alphabet/Spelling/Words	20.5%	17.0%
Math/Numbers	20.0%	16.5%
Matching	16.0%	9.5%
Memory	14.0%	15.5%
Book/Story	12.5%	6.5%
Coloring	9.0%	17.0%
Musical	7.0%	6.0%
Puzzle	6.5%	8.0%
Learning a language	6.5%	11.0%
Flash Cards	3.5%	3.5%
Photo-related	2.5%	4.0%
Quiz/Test	1.5%	3.5%
Jokes	1.0%	1.0%
Other[26]	8.5% n=200	14.5% n=200

Intended Audience

Staff also reviewed the app descriptions for cues to the intended audience, looking for both general and specific age groups. Almost all of the apps reviewed appeared to be intended for use by kids, and many provided specific age ranges. Staff looked for words in app names or descriptions suggesting that the apps were recommended for, or were appropriate for, certain general groups, such as "infants," "toddlers," "preschoolers," "children," "kids," "parents" and "teachers."[27] Table 2 lists the percentage of apps on each platform promoted for use by certain age groups.

Table 2. Intended Audience – General Age Groups

Apple App Store	Android Market		Combined
General Age Group	% of Apps	% of Apps	% of Apps
Infant/Toddler	11.5%	4.0%	89.75%
Child	56.0%	40.5%	
Kid	63.5%	76.5%	
Preschool	7.5%	10.5%	
Elementary School	1.5%	1.5%	
Parent	17.5%	20.0%	24.25%
Teacher	3.5%	2.5%	
Adult	7.5%	2.5%	
Family	6.0%	4.5%	5.25%
Everyone	5.0%	1.0%	3.00%
No Indication	8.0%	2.0%	5.00%
	n=200	n=200	n=400

Most of the app promotion pages suggested that the apps were for kids (or some subset of kids, such as infants) as shown in Table 2. Twenty-four percent of the 400 app descriptions contained language suggesting that the apps were intended for use by an adult, such as a parent or teacher, but most of those apps indicated they were for use by kids too. While 5% (twenty) of the 400 app descriptions did not include language suggesting any intended audience, all but two of these apps appeared to include content that kids may enjoy, such as games like checkers, table tennis, and basketball. Overall, staff estimates that about 95% of the 400 apps reviewed in detail were apps intended for kids' use.[28]

Twenty three percent of the 400 apps specified a particular age range or school grade level. For these apps, staff recorded the recommended age ranges, converting any grade levels to ages.[29] Over 50% of the apps that listed an age or grade range listed a range beginning at 2 years old or younger; over 80% listed a range beginning at age four or younger; and over 90% specified an age range starting at 6 years old or younger.[30] Conversely, over 75% of the apps that specified an age range specified one ending at 12 years old or younger, and roughly 45% specified an age range ending at 6 years old or younger. Table 3 lists the number of apps for specified age ranges.

Table 3. Intended Audience – Specific Age Ranges

		Maximum recommended age					**% of apps with this min. age**
		3-4	**5-6**	**7-8**	**9-12**	**13+**	
Minimum recommended age	**0-2**	9	27	6	2	11	60%
	3-4		1	8	5	9	25%
	5-6		4	1	1	1	8%
	7-8			3	2		5%
	13					1	1%
% of apps with this max. age		10%	35%	20%	11%	24%	n=91

Most Kids Apps Are Inexpensive

While prices ranged from free to $9.99, most of the 960 app store promotion pages listed a price of $0.99 or less. Indeed, 77% of the apps in the survey listed an install price of $0.99 or less, and 48% were free.[31] Free apps appeared to be the most frequently downloaded.

The Android Market provides a "download range" and a "feedback" field on the promotion page of each app. The "download range" is an estimate of the number of times a particular app has been downloaded (such as "100 – 500" or "10,000 – 50,000") while the "feedback" field reveals the number of app users that have provided comments or feedback regarding their experience with the app. Staff used the download ranges to estimate the relative popularity of apps in each price category.[32]

Using this indicator, staff found that the free Android apps accounted for 99% of all downloads in the Android survey results, even though they accounted for only 62% of the apps returned by the "kids" search. Staff then compared these findings to the results obtained by using the "feedback" information to infer app popularity. As shown in Table 4, the "feedback" method closely tracked the "download" method.

Apple's App Store does not provide download ranges for its apps, but it does display the number of users that have provided feedback for each app. As with Android, staff used the number of feedback ratings to infer the relative popularity of the Apple apps.

Staff found that free Apple apps appeared to be more popular than paid apps, accounting for 68% of all "ratings," even though they only accounted for 35% of the search results (see Table 5).

Table 4. Android Market Price and Popularity

Price	% of Apps	% of Downloads[33]	% of Feedback Ratings
Free	61.7%	99.43%	97.64%
$0.01 to $0.99	14.0%	0.13%	0.19%
$1 to $1.99	9.2%	0.09%	0.27%
$2 to $2.99	2.9%	0.23%	1.43%
$3 to $3.99	1.6%	0.09%	0.37%
$4.00+	1.6%	0.01%	0.03%
Foreign	9.0%	0.02%	0.07%
	n=480		

Table 5. Apple App Store Prices and Popularity

Price	% of Apps	% of Ratings
Free	34.80%	68.29%
$0.99	43.95%	22.08%
$1.99	14.58%	9.15%
$2.99	3.75%	0.19%
$3.99	1.04%	0.10%
$4.99	1.88%	0.19%
	n=480	

Number of Developers

Staff found that hundreds of developers were responsible for the apps in the study. Staff encountered 441 unique developers in this study, only twelve of which had apps on both platforms. Table 6 presents the number of developers responsible for the apps in the search results.

Table 6. Number of Apps Per Developer and Popularity Indicators

		Apple App Store			Android Market	
# of Apps Per Developer	**# of Developers**	**% All Apps**	**% Feedback Ratings**	**# of Developers**	**% All Apps**	**% of Downloads**
1	142	29.6%	49.8%	150	31.3%	50.2%
2	43	17.9%	18.8%	48	20.0%	9.7%
3	11	6.9%	6.0%	11	6.9%	2.2%
4	5	4.2%	4.4%	6	5.0%	9.1%
5-9	13	17.7%	19.8%	14	16.9%	7.3%
10+	5	23.8%	1.1%	5	20.0%	21.4%
		n=480			n=480	

Only a handful of app developers were responsible for more than 10 apps in our sample. Developers with one app in our sample were popular, accounting for about 50% of all downloads/feedback ratings, even though they were responsible for only about 30% of the apps. In contrast, those developers with more than 10 apps in our sample accounted for about 1% of the feedback ratings for Apple, (and 20% of the downloads for Android) despite accounting for about 20% of all of the apps in the survey. This finding illustrates the broad and diverse nature of the mobile app marketplace.

Contact Information

Many of the developers provided some type of contact information directly on their app's promotion page, or linked to a developer website that contained contact information. Staff found that 13% of the 400 kids apps listed an email address somewhere on the promotion page.[34] Eighty-one percent of the 400 app promotion pages linked to a functioning English-language developer website, a number of which provided contact information.[35] Sixty-five percent (of the 400) linked to a functioning developer website whose landing page contained either some form of contact information or a link to contact information.[36] Within this group, 23% (of the 400) linked to a developer website that listed an email address on the landing page, 8% linked to a landing page providing a phone number, 6% linked to a landing page with a mailing address, 2% provided all three types of contact information on the landing page, and 38% linked to a landing page containing a link that appeared to lead to contact information.[37]

II. Data Collection and Sharing Practices

The survey findings regarding data collection and sharing were of greatest concern to FTC staff. Indeed, across the wide range of "kids" apps examined in the survey, staff found very little information about the data collection or sharing practices of these apps. Apple's and Google's mobile operating systems and app stores provide limited notice to users regarding app capabilities, and leave the bulk of disclosure to individual app developers. In most instances, staff was unable to determine from the information on the app store page or the developer's landing page whether an app collected *any* data, let alone the type of data collected, the purpose for such collection, and who collected or obtained access to such data.[38] This is troubling given the ability of mobile apps to access users' information on devices automatically and to transmit this information invisibly to a wide variety of entities.

The Mobile App Stores and Operating Systems

Apple's iOS and Google's Android operating systems offer powerful capabilities to the mobile applications that run on them.[39] For example, they enable mobile apps to determine the user's precise geolocation and communicate with other devices via the Internet. For mobile gaming apps, these systems may allow a child to identify and connect with others playing the same game nearby. The operating systems also may provide apps with access to sensitive information such as a user's call logs, contacts, and unique device identifiers, or enable the app to use the phone service on the mobile device to make or answer calls or send text messages. Depending on the type of service the app provides and how the app has been configured, this broad access to data may or may not be necessary to provide the service and may occur without the user's knowledge.

The app stores and operating systems take different approaches to managing the information and capabilities that apps may access. Android requires its apps to declare any potentially sensitive capabilities on a "permissions" screen, which displays just before installing the app.[40] While helpful, these disclosures do not explain clearly (or provide an easy means for consumers to learn) why an app has the permissions it does, what the app does with such access, or whether the app shares any information with third parties. Providing clear and accessible information is especially important in the kids app space, where any data accessed and collected would likely be from a mobile device used by a child, and could reveal information that a parent may not want shared with unknown third parties, such as a child's precise geolocation or phone number. Faced with concerns about what data an app may or may not collect, a parent may be forced to choose between downloading the app, and running the risk that the child's sensitive information will be shared with unknown third parties, or not downloading the app, and depriving the child of an enjoyable game or activity.

Of the 182 Android apps indicating they were intended for use by kids, only 24% specified that the app required "no special permissions to run" – *i.e.,* that a child could use the app without the app accessing any information or capabilities from the mobile device. Conversely, 76% indicated that the app required at least one "permission" to run. In fact, staff found that over half of the Android app promotion pages listed a "permission" for "full Internet access," meaning that the "permission" enables the app to access and receive a wide variety of content while the app is running.[41] Table 7 lists the percentage of Android apps that contained some of the more potentially sensitive permissions.[42]

Table 7. Android Market "Kids" Apps Permissions

Permission	% of Apps	% of Free Apps	% of Paid Apps
Network communication: full Internet access	60.99%	78.81%	28.13%
Phone calls: read phone state and identity[43]	20.88%	29.66%	4.69%
Modify/delete SD card[44]	15.93%	16.95%	14.06%
Your location -	8.24%	11.02%	3.13%
Fine (GPS) location	6.04%	7.63%	3.13%
Coarse (network-based) location	5.49%	7.63%	1.56%
Both fine and coarse location	3.30%	4.24%	1.56%
Hardware controls: take pictures and videos	3.85%	4.24%	3.13%
Services that cost you money: directly call phone numbers	2.20%	3.39%	0.00%
Modify global system settings	2.75%	3.39%	1.56%
Hardware controls: record audio	1.65%	2.54%	0.00%
Your personal information: read sensitive log data	0.55%	0.85%	0.00%
No special permissions	24.18%	13.56%	43.75%
	n=182	n=118	n=64

In contrast to Android's "permissions" approach, Apple states that it relies on an app review process in which it screens and approves apps before permitting them to be offered in Apple's app store.[45] Because Apple's App Store does not require its apps to display "permissions" to users prior to download, staff could not measure the degree to which the Apple kids apps were capable of accessing device information.[46] Apple states that it reviews every application "in order to protect consumer privacy" and "safeguard children from inappropriate content,"[47] and that "any App that targets minors for data collection will be rejected."[48] The details of this screening process are not clear.

Location information is treated differently from other information by each system but follows essentially an "on/off" model. Both operating systems can signal the user when an app requests the user's location by displaying a specific icon.[49] Both systems also provide a global setting that allows users to turn off their devices' location capabilities.[50] As described above, Android's operating system requires developers to declare a "permission" for access to location information. After an app is downloaded, Apple's operating system provides: 1) a notice the first time that an app attempts to acquire the user's location; and 2) an on/off switch in the device's settings allowing users to permit an app to access their location information on an app-by-app basis.[51] These additional protections offered by Apple apply only to an app requesting location information.

Beyond the basic technological models, both app stores require developers by agreement to disclose the information their apps collect,[52] though neither store specifies how or where such information should be provided. Both stores' privacy policies also state that the privacy policies of the app developers control the practices of a mobile app offered in the app stores.[53] Under this model, the information provided by developers is critical for transparency. Nevertheless, as described below, such information is rarely provided.

Disclosure of App Data Collection and Sharing

Staff's review of both the app store promotion pages and developer websites of the 400 closely examined apps in the survey revealed very little information about the apps' data practices.

Indeed, the Apple app promotion pages that staff examined provided almost no information on individual developers' data collection and sharing practices. Similarly, the Android app promotion pages that staff examined provided little information other than the mandatory "permissions." Only three (1.5%) of the 200 Android apps even attempted to convey information about the purpose for the "permissions." These three apps made the following disclosures (respectively) on their promotion pages:

- "Needs Location permission for Ads. If you prefer, get the AD FREE version."
- "Permissions are required by the Ad networks, which keep the app free."
- "All requested permissions are for ads only."

All three statements put the user on notice that the app provides information to an ad network, but do not identify what information is collected, by whom, how it is used, and whether it is shared with others.

Staff also looked for information about the apps' data collection and sharing practices on the landing pages of the developers' websites.[54] As with the app promotion pages, staff found very little information. Sixteen percent of the 400 kids app promotion pages linked to a developer landing page that contained or linked to disclosure information. Within this group, 13% (of the 400) linked to a landing page that displayed a link labeled "privacy policy," and the remaining 3% linked to developer sites that provided links to some other disclosures. These other disclosures had labels such as "terms of use," "terms and conditions," "terms of service," "Legal Notices," and "disclaimers." [55] Out of the entire set of 400 app promotion pages examined, only two (0.5%) linked to a developer landing page that disclosed information about data collection and sharing on the landing page itself.

Disclosure of Additional Interactive Features

Staff also examined the app store promotion pages for features that may serve as a platform for data collection, such as the ability to make purchases within the app, connect with social media, and serve targeted advertising. These features often are provided to the app developer by various third parties, who may gain access to kids' data as a result.

In-App Purchase Mechanism

Some developers offer app users the ability to purchase additional content via an in-app purchase mechanism. For example, a storybook application may come with a single story, but then allow the app user to purchase additional stories without having to leave the app. The ability of children to purchase items within mobile applications has been a subject of concern in media reports and by members of Congress, as parents may not know about such capabilities prior to download.[56]

Staff found that 11.0% of the 200 Apple App Store promotion pages, and 0.5% of the 200 Android pages indicated that the app had some form of in-app purchase mechanism. While Apple includes a box disclosing "Top In-App Purchases" on the promotion page for apps with in-app purchase mechanisms, Android appears to require only those developers that use Android's own in-app purchasing mechanism to display a permission discussed above.[57] In light of the significant concerns raised by in-app purchase capabilities in apps for children, staff is evaluating what types of protections should apply to these capabilities. It is clear, however, that confusing and hard-to-find disclosures do not give parents the control that they need in this area.

Staff believes that parents need consistent, easily accessible, and recognizable disclosures regarding in-app purchase capabilities so that they can make informed decisions about whether to allow their children to use apps with such capabilities.

Social Network Integration and Other Social Features

Staff found that 5% of the 400 app promotion pages indicated that the app was integrated with a social network – that is, a user could access a social network, and thus share information, through the app. Staff found that 3.5% of the 400 promotion pages indicated integration with Facebook, 2% with Twitter, and 2% with various other social networks.[58] Because the app stores do not appear to require disclosure of these social features on the promotion page, it is likely that the survey numbers understate the prevalence of social functionality. In addition, some apps have their own internal sharing functions – for example, automatically sharing game results, usernames, and other information with unknown users on the app's scoreboard or news feed. Staff believes that the presence of social features within an app is highly relevant to parents selecting apps for their children, and that such functionality should be disclosed prior to download.

In-App Advertising

The existence of advertising within an app may be significant to parents for several reasons. First, parents may want to limit the data collected by advertisers and ad networks about their children.[59] Second, even if the advertising is not based on any information collected by the user, parents may want to limit their children's exposure to ads. Finally, ads running inside an app may incorporate various capabilities allowing the user to do things like directly call phone numbers or visit websites appearing in the ad, and parents may not want these options available to their children.

Staff found that about 7% of the 400 app store promotion pages indicated that the app contained advertising. As above, this number is likely to understate the number of apps containing advertising because app stores do not appear to require developers to disclose in-app advertising on their promotion pages, and because advertising is a common way to monetize apps.[60] Some of the disclosures appeared to be designed to warn parents about the potential exposure of their children to ads. For example, one promotion page indicated that the app would only display ads during the initial download, when parents would be the likely audience. Other statements attempted to address the information collection aspect of targeted in-app advertising. As previously discussed, three of the Android apps attempted to explain (though fairly cryptically) that a permission to access certain information was related to in-app advertising.

Still others included language addressing the "click-to" functionality often found within advertisements – for example, stating that the developer had moved the placement of banner ads to the top of the screen within the app in order "to avoid accidental clicks by the little fingers." Some app developers appeared to be offering certain protections to users as a selling-point in the competitive app market. For example, several app promotion pages included language indicating that the app was "ad free," and one disclosed that, "[f]or security reasons," the app switched the device to "airplane mode" when in use in order to "protect you [sic] children from any risk."

The presence of these statements to parents and other users suggests that certain developers are aware of parents' concerns and are taking some steps to respond. However, parents need clear, easy-to-read, and consistent disclosures regarding the advertising that their children may view on apps, especially when that advertising is personalized based on the child's in-app activities. And to the extent that third parties providing the advertising (or other interactive features) gain access to kids' data in providing these services, they also must ensure that their data practices are disclosed to parents in a clear and meaningful way.

App Rating Systems and Parental Controls

Both app stores and operating systems offer rating systems and controls that can provide parents with useful tools to manage their children's access to and use of mobile apps. The systems allow parents to restrict access to mobile content and features, and can limit the collection of data from the mobile device, such as limiting the sharing of geolocation information. These systems are not designed, however, to provide specific information about the data collected and shared by apps.[61]

Rating Systems[62]

The Apple App Store and the Android Market assign various content ratings to the apps they offer indicating a recommended level of maturity. Some of the parent controls rely on these content ratings to screen out inappropriate material.[63] Apple's and Android's content ratings are unique to the particular app store, and the methods for evaluating content and assigning ratings rely largely on the app developer to supply the initial rating.[64]

Apple's content ratings consist of four different age indicators ("4+," "9+," "12+," and "17+") that are assigned to apps as part of Apple's approval process. Prior to submitting an app to Apple for approval, app developers must fill out a ratings matrix.[65] The matrix requires the developer to select the frequency (e.g., "none," "infrequent/mild," or "frequent/intense") of different types of content ("Cartoon or Fantasy Violence," "Sexual Content or Nudity," "Profanity or Crude Humor," etc.), and assigns a rating based on the developer's input.[66] Staff did not evaluate the appropriateness of any of the ratings assigned, but notes that nearly all of the Apple apps reviewed in this survey contained the lowest content rating of "4+." See Table 8.

Table 8. Content Ratings for Apple App Store "Kids" Apps

Apple Content Rating	Apple App Store
"4+"	97.5%
"9+"	1.5%
"12+"	1.0%
"17+"	0% n=200

Content ratings in the Android Market also are largely determined by the app developer, and consist of four different maturity indicators ("Everyone," "Low maturity," "Medium maturity," and "High maturity").[67] Android's ratings do not map directly to specific ages but, like Apple's, are tied to violent or mature content. Android provides content-based guidelines to developers, and requires that maturity ratings be tied to the app's functionality.[68] For example, the guidelines state that "Apps rated 'Everyone' must not ask users for their location." [69] As shown in Table 9, an overwhelming majority of the Android apps reviewed by staff contained the lowest content rating of "Everyone." A number of the Android apps involved in this survey did not contain a maturity rating because they pre-dated Android's introduction of the content rating requirement in November 2010. Twenty-two such apps appeared in staff's review and are not included in the percentages presented in Table 9.

Table 9. Content Ratings for Android Market "Kids" Apps[70]

Android Content Rating	Android Market
"Everyone"	83%
"Low maturity"	12%
"Medium maturity"	2%
"High maturity"	2%
	n=178

Parental Controls

Both app stores provide various controls allowing parents to restrict which apps may be downloaded onto their children's mobile devices, based on app content ratings.[71] In addition, Apple's mobile operating system incorporates controls that allow parents to password-protect access to a number of specific applications, such as Apple's Internet browser (Safari), the online video website YouTube, the iTunes App Store itself, the device's camera application, as well as some device capabilities, such as location sharing and in-app purchase mechanisms.[72] Although the Android operating system does not have such built-in parental controls, a number of available apps allow parents to password-protect access to various content and device capabilities.[73]

On both systems, parents can set the device settings to limit the flow of some information – for example, blocking GPS location sharing or setting the device on "airplane mode" in order to restrict the interactive features of an app. However, a parent needs to set these limits each time the child uses an app, and taking such actions may adversely limit desirable app functionality.[74] Further, while these types of controls may help parents manage the use of the device by their children, they do not provide information about the data practices associated with the apps that run on them. Thus, parents may be forced to choose between allowing their child to use an app, with all the unknown risks associated with such use, and cutting off their child's use of the app altogether. With better information about the data practices of these apps, parents can make informed decisions about which apps their children can use safely, and which apps parents wish to avoid.

Conclusion

The mobile apps marketplace is a constantly evolving new media that offers parents many new options for entertaining and educating their children. Staff's survey shows, however, that parents generally cannot determine, before downloading an app, whether the app poses risks related to the collection, use, and sharing of their children's personal information. Although the two major U.S. mobile app stores provide some information and controls governing apps, all members of the mobile app ecosystem – the app stores, the developers, and the third parties providing services within the apps – must do more to ensure that parents have access to clear, concise and timely information about the apps they download for their children. Parents should be able to learn, before downloading an app for their children, what data will be collected, how the data will be used, and who will obtain access to the data. Armed with such information, parents can make knowledgeable decisions about the apps they choose for their children, and embrace these technologies with more confidence. Staff is committed to working with all stakeholders on these issues, and also plans to continue its vigorous enforcement of the COPPA statute and Rule. Staff hopes that this report will spur greater transparency and meaningful disclosure about the data collection practices in apps for children.

APPENDIX

Methodology

This section provides additional information about the data collected and reviewed in the attached FTC Staff Report on Kids Apps.

Apple Data Collection

On July 14, 2011, staff used a desktop computer with the Windows 7 operating system to locate and copy the app store promotion pages for 960 mobile applications using the following steps. Staff first searched on the term "kids" in the desktop version of Apple's iTunes app store and noted that each app had its own nine-digit unique identifier number and its own app store promotion page describing the app. The app store promotion page for each app was viewable by typing in the specific web address within the itunes.apple.com website, which contained the unique app identifier number, into the Internet Explorer browser on the desktop computer. Thus, staff could locate the unique web address for each app store promotion page using the following convention "http://itunes.apple.com/us/app/id[9-digit-unique-appidentification-number]?mt=8." Staff then used software to visit and copy the browser-viewable app promotion pages for the first 480 apps returned by the "kids" search in the Apple app store.

Android Data Collection

On July 14, 2011, staff used the same desktop computer with the Internet Explorer browser to access the desktop version of the Android Market, available at https://market.android.com. Staff searched on the term "kids" and noted that each app had its own unique identifier and its own app store promotion page describing the app. Like Apple, the Android Market app promotion page for each app was viewable by typing in the specific web address within the market.android.com website, which contained the unique app identifier, into the browser. Staff could locate the unique web address for each app store promotion page using the following convention, "https://market.android.com/details?id=[unique-app-id]&feature=search_result." Staff then used software to visit and copy the app promotion pages for the first 480 Android Market apps returned by the "kids" search.

Data Extraction

Staff saved each app store promotion page as a .txt file and as an .html file. Staff identified the relevant fields, such as price, developer, and number of ratings, found within the copied app promotion pages and extracted that data into an electronic database. This automated extraction was the source of all of the n=480 tables in the report.

Reviewing the Random Sample of App Store Promotion Pages

Staff completed a review of 400 randomly selected app store promotion pages. For each of the pools of the 480 app promotion pages, staff used a random number generator to select 200 unique numbers and created a separate database that contained only the 200 app store promotion pages that corresponded with the 200 randomly selected numbers. Reviewers were instructed to examine the electronically captured app promotion pages (that had been saved as .html files), and to answer a series of questions about things like app topic, age range, and disclosures related to their review of the app promotion page using the database form. The specific instructions related to this review are detailed below. Once staff completed the review, two additional reviewers rated the sample, and found almost complete agreement between the first and second review, suggesting that the application of staff's criteria was relatively unambiguous.

Reviewers were also instructed to click on the website address listed on the app promotion page in the field for "[developer's] website." Staff then saved and reviewed the resulting webpage (the "landing page" of the developer's website), and entered the answers to a series of questions using the database form. Tables containing calculations that list "n=200" specify that the calculations were obtained from one of the two random samples.[1]

App Store Desktop Interface v. Mobile Device Interface

Staff collected the information in this report only from the content offered in the desktop interface of the two app stores. There are two relevant differences between this content and the content available through the mobile device interface, but staff does not believe these differences change the conclusions of this report.

App store promotion pages viewed in the Android Market using a mobile device include a field that displays a developer email address. At the time staff collected the information for the survey, this field was not found on the desktop version of the Android Market, and, thus, was not captured in the survey. Therefore, more email addresses were likely available for the Android apps in this survey than staff collected.

Similarly, app store promotion pages viewed in the desktop version of Apple's App Store included a field that displayed a web address labeled "[Developer Name] Support," even though this field was not found in promotion pages viewed from an iPhone. As noted in the report, staff did not review these additional web addresses and does not know if they contained additional contact information or disclosure information. Staff did note that 61% of the promotion pages listed the same address for both the developer's website and the support website.

Categorizing Apps based on Type

Staff categorized the apps in the random sample based on a number of categories according to words found within the app descriptions and titles. The following is a list of the categories and any additional words used to classify an app into the categories: Educational ("learn," "teach," or any variation of the word "educate"); Game ("play"); Animal-related ("animal," "creatures," or the names or icons of different types of animals); Alphabet/Spelling/Words ("letters"); Math/Numbers ("arithmetic," "counting," "addition," "subtraction," "multiplication," or "division"); Matching ("match," or "find 2 of the same"); Memory; Book/Story ("chapters"); Coloring ("paint" or "draw"); Musical ("music" or "song"); Puzzle; Learning a language[2]; Flash Cards; Photo-related ("photo" or "picture"); Quiz/Test; Jokes; and other. Apps could fall into more than one category. For example, a matching game that involved pictures of animals would be categorized under "Game," "Matching," and "Animal-related."

Categorizing Apps based on Intended User

Staff categorized the 400 apps in the random sample based on whether the app title or description identified any one of the following groups as an audience for whom the app was intended or recommended: Infant; Toddler; Child; Kid; Teen; Adult; Parent; Teacher; Family; Mature; Everyone; Preschool; Elementary; Middle School; High School; Age Range; Grade Range; Other; and No Indication. Grade and age range information have been presented separately from the qualitative categories in the report. Simply containing one of these audience groups in the app title or description was not sufficient to trigger an intended use category. The app title or description had to indicate in some way that the app was for one or more of these groups' use. For example, one of the promotion pages described an app containing recipes for child-friendly meals. Although the description included the term "child," the app was intended for use by parents or caretakers to make meals for children and therefore was not included in the "child" category.

Price Level Popularity

To estimate price level popularity for the Android apps in the survey, staff summed the lower bound of the download range for each app within a given price level. Next, staff divided these price level sums by the sum of the lower bound of the download ranges for all 480 Android apps. Using this method, staff found that the free Android apps returned by the "kids" search, which accounted for 62% of the search results, accounted for 99% of all downloads. Table 7 of the report contains the results obtained using the lower bound method.

Staff then repeated its calculations using the upper bound and midpoint of each download range. Staff found that the results returned by each method were nearly indistinguishable from the results obtained using the lower bound of the download ranges.

Both the Android Market and the Apple App Store display the number of users that have provided feedback for a particular app. Staff used this feature to estimate price level popularity for the Apple apps, and as a second estimate of app popularity for the Android apps, by repeating the calculations described above substituting the number of feedbacks for downloads.

Developer Websites

Both the Apple App Store and the Android Market provide a specified field on the app store promotion page for developers to list their website. Although some app store promotion pages additionally listed web addresses in other places (such as the text of the app description), staff restricted its review to the landing page of the developer website address listed in the developer web address field. Staff found that a sizeable number of the website addresses listed in the developer web address field did not lead to relevant or functioning websites.

Of the 400 randomly selected "kids" app promotion pages reviewed by staff, 43 (11%) did not list a web address in the specified field for developer website; 17 (4%) listed a web address that staff was unable to examine; and 10 (3%) listed a web address that either led back to the app promotion page, or was not related to the app or developer in any apparent way. Staff was unable to examine websites when they encountered problems including: error messages (such as "site not found" or "site under construction" messages); never-ending redirects; "access forbidden" messages; and one Facebook page that required the visitor to be logged into Facebook in order to access the webpage. In addition, 5 (1%) of the web addresses led to websites that were entirely in a foreign language (even though staff used an English language browser and browsed US app stores), and therefore were not counted. In the end, 324 (81%) of the 400 "kids" app promotion pages listed a web address in the specified field that led to a functioning and relevant English language webpage.

Web Addresses in the Standardized Locations in the Apple App Store

The Apple App Store desktop version provides developers with standardized locations on each app's promotion page for placing links to the developer's website, a support site, and an application license agreement. Most Apple app store promotion pages in the survey contained a link to a developer website (469 out of 480, or 97.7%), and all of the pages contained a link to a support website. A few contained a link to an application license agreement (6 out of 480, or 1.3%). As stated above, 61% of the promotion pages listed the same address for both the developer's website and the support website. Staff did not look at the remaining 39%; it is possible that more of the pages linked to additional privacy disclosures or developer contact information.

Other Websites

Reviewers also noted any web addresses listed on the app promotion pages outside of the app store standardized locations. While a number of developers used their app description space on the page to encourage readers to like them on Facebook, or follow them on Twitter, only 8% of the 400 app promotion pages reviewed by staff provided an address to an additional website.

Android Permissions Language

Below is a list of the Android disclosures identified in Table 7 of the report, taken verbatim from the app promotion pages encountered in this survey. While each disclosure is reported in its entirety, the list is not exhaustive of those used in the Android Market or found in the samples associated with this report.

- "Network communication > full Internet access > Allows an application to create network sockets."
- "Phone calls > read phone state and identity > Allows the application to access the phone features of the device. An application with this permission can determine the phone number and serial number of this phone, whether a call is active, the number that call is connected to and the like."
- "Modify/delete SD card contents > Allows an application to write to the USB storage. Allows an application to write to the SD card."
- "Your location > coarse (network-based) location > Access coarse location sources such as the cellular network database to determine an approximate device location, where available. Malicious applications can use this to determine approximately where you are."
- "Your location > fine (GPS) location > Access fine location sources such as the Global Positioning System on the device, where available. Malicious applications can use this to determine where you are, and may consume additional battery power."
- "Hardware controls > take pictures and videos > Allows application to take pictures and videos with the camera. This allows the application at any time to collect images the camera is seeing."
- "Services that cost you money > directly call phone numbers > Allows the application to call phone numbers without your intervention. Malicious applications may cause unexpected calls on your phone bill. Note that this does not allow the application to call emergency numbers."
- "System tools > modify global system settings > Allows an application to modify the system's settings data. Malicious applications can corrupt your system's configuration."
- "Hardware controls > record audio > Allows application to access the audio record path."

- "Your personal information > read sensitive log data > Allows an application to read from the system's various log files. This allows it to discover general information about what you are doing with the device, potentially including personal or private information."

Implications of Methodology and Interpretation of Results

Survey designs inevitably make tradeoffs; presenting evidence in ways that shed the most light on some questions necessarily leave other issues unaddressed. Searching the app stores using the word "kids" is a transparent methodology that works in both app stores and generates a diverse and relevant set of results; however, it is important to bear in mind the following implications of the survey design:

The first 480 apps returned by each query[3] were given both equal importance and equal likelihood of inclusion in the random sample. This means that the report's findings relate to overall performance from the field of apps for kids, rather than giving extra weight to those with more downloads.

Staff did not remove the small handful of apps from the random sample that may not be intended for kids. However, these non-kid apps are rare enough that excluding them would not significantly change the report's findings.

The algorithms responsible for returning search results differ between the Android Market and the Apple App Store, which likely rely on keywords and other information to render search results.[4] Staff is not privy to the precise formulas, and using other search terms or selecting apps in different ways might generate somewhat different results.

These issues suggest exercising caution in claiming that the percentages found in the report extend to samples of apps beyond that used by this report. However, none of these issues change the conclusion that kids' app promotion pages that make few disclosures are widespread and easy to find.

End Notes

[1] The primary authors of this FTC staff survey and report are Patricia Poss and Andrew Hasty of the FTC's Bureau of Consumer Protection. They received valuable assistance from Andrew Bristow, a Princeton student on temporary staff at the FTC, and staff from throughout the Bureau of Consumer Protection. Robert Letzler and Michael Shores of the Bureau of Economics provided valuable assistance with presentation of the empirical results.

[2] Apple offered 552 apps at launch in July 2008. Michael Arrington, *iPhone App Store Has Launched (Updated),* TechCrunch (July 10, 2008), http://techcrunch.com/2008/07/10/app-store-launches-upgradeitunes-now/. Google's Android Market offered 50 apps when it launched in October 2008. Dean Takahashi, *Google Releases Details on Android Market Launch,* VentureBeat (Oct. 22, 2008), http://venturebeat.com/2008/10/22/google-releases-details-on-android-market-launch/.

[3] Press Release, Apple, *Apple's Mac App Store Downloads Top 100 Million* (Dec. 12, 2011), http://www.apple.com/pr/library/2011/12/12Apples-Mac-App-Store-Downloads-Top-100-Million.html.

[4] *Google Android Market,* Distimo, http://www.distimo.com/appstores/app-store/19-Google_Android_ Market (last updated Dec. 30, 2011).

[5] *See* Press Release, Apple, *Apple's Mac App Store, supra* note 3 (more than 18 billion downloads from Apple App Store); Eric Chu, *10 Billion Android Market Downloads and Counting* (Dec. 6, 2011), http://android-developers.blogspot.com/2011/12/10-billion-android-market-downloads-and.html.

[6] Common Sense Media reported that half (52%) of all children in the United States have access to a smartphone (41%), a video iPod (21%), or an iPad or other tablet device (8%). Common Sense Media, *Zero to Eight:*

Children's Media Use in America 9 (Fall 2011), *available at* www.commonsensemedia.org/sites/default/files/research/zerotoeightfinal2011. pdf. Another study indicated that two-thirds of the children ages 4-7 stated they had used an iPhone, often one owned by a family member and handed back to them while riding in an automobile. Cynthia Chiong & Carly Shuler, Joan Ganz Cooney Center, *Learning: Is there an App for that?* 15 (Nov. 2010), *available at* www.joanganzcooneycenter.org/upload_kits/ learningapps_final_110410.pdf. In addition, recent research states that "In the third quarter of 2011, teens age 13-17 used an average of 320 MB of data per month on their phones, increasing 256 percent over last year and growing at a rate faster than any other age group." *New Mobile Obsession: U.S. Teens Triple Data Usage,* Nielsen (Dec. 15, 2011), http://blog.nielsen.com/nielsenwire/online_mobile/new-mobile-obsession-u-s-teenstriple-data-usage/.

[7] These recommendations are consistent with the FTC staff's preliminary privacy report that called on companies to be more transparent as to their data collection practices and encouraged companies to offer short, easy-to-read disclosures (or icons) that consumers are likely to see, read, and understand. *See* FTC Preliminary Staff Report, *Protecting Consumer Privacy in an Era of Rapid Change: A Proposed Framework for Businesses and Policymakers* 69-71 (Dec. 1, 2010), *available at* http://ftc.gov/ os/2010/12/101201privacy report.pdf.

[8] A promotion page is the screen in the app store where a developer provides certain basic information about its app.

[9] As discussed further below, "permissions" are phrases describing an app's capabilities that appear on the mobile screen prior to downloading an app in the Android app store.

[10] The Commission's COPPA Rule was promulgated pursuant to the Children's Online Privacy Protection Act of 1998, 15 U.S.C. §§ 6501-6506. The text of the COPPA Rule can be found at 16 C.F.R. Part 312.

[11] *United States v. W3 Innovations, LLC,* No. CV-11-03958 (N.D. Cal. Sept. 8, 2011) (FTC consent order with developer of child-directed mobile apps for alleged violations of the COPPA Rule), *available at* http://ftc.gov/os/caselist/1023251/110908w3order.pdf.

[12] Children's Online Privacy Protection Rule, 76 Fed. Reg. 59,804 (proposed Sept. 27, 2011) (stating that "online services" currently covered by the COPPA Rule "includes mobile applications that allow children to play network-connected games, engage in social networking activities, purchase goods or services online, receive behaviorally targeted advertisements, or interact with other content or services."), *available at* http://www.gpo.gov/fdsys/pkg/FR-2011-09-27/pdf/2011-24314.pdf.

[13] *See* 16 C.F.R. § 312.2 (defining "[w]ebsite or online service directed to children").

[14] FTC investigations are nonpublic until the Commission takes a public action such as issuing a complaint or announcing a settlement.

[15] A number of organizations have issued guidance for app developers. *See* Press Release, Future of Privacy Forum, *FPF and CDT Release Best Practices for Mobile Apps Developers* (Dec. 21, 2011), http://www.applicationprivacy.org/?p=1947; Press Release, Mobile Marketing Association, *Mobile Marketing Association Releases New Privacy Policy Guidelines for Mobile Apps for Public Comment* (Oct. 17, 2011), http://mmaglobal.com/news/mobile-marketing-association-releases-new-privacy-policy-guidelinesmobile-apps-public-comment; Privacy Choice, *PrivacyChoice Challenges Developers to "Get Their Apps in Gear"* (Oct. 18, 2011), *available at* http://blog.privacychoice.org/2011/10/18/get-your-apps-in-gear/.

[16] If the app is directed to children and in fact collects information from children, the app must provide a notice and obtain parental consent prior to collection pursuant to COPPA. *See* 16 C.F.R. § 312.3. In addition, Commission staff has stated more generally that when companies collect sensitive information about children and precise geolocation data, companies should seek affirmative express consent before the data is collected or shared. *See* FTC Preliminary Staff Report, *supra* note 7, at 61.

[17] *See Best Practices for Mobile Applications Developers,* Future of Privacy Forum, 3, http://www.futureofprivacy.org/wp-content/uploads/Apps-Best-Practices-v-beta.pdf (last visited Jan. 24, 2012) (citing section 3.3.10 of the iOS Developer Program License Agreement, stating that "Developers must provide clear and complete information to users regarding collection, use and disclosure of user or device data."); Android Market Developer Distribution Agreement, 4.3, http://www.android.com/us/developerdistribution-agreement.html (last visited Oct. 31, 2011) ("If the users provide you with, or your Product accesses or uses, user names, passwords, or other login information or personal information, you must make the users aware that the information will be available to your Product, and you must provide legally adequate privacy notice and protection for those users."); *see also* Scott Thurm & Yukari Iwatani Kane, *Your Apps are Watching You,* Wall St. J., Dec. 18, 2010, *available at* http://online.wsj.com/article/SB10001424052748704694004576020083 703574602.html (reporting that numerous Apple and Android applications transmitted user information, and numerous apps did not provide privacy policies on their websites or inside the apps at the time of testing).

[18] *See* Press Release, FTC, FTC Seeks Input to Revising its Guidance to Business About Disclosures in Online Advertising (May 26, 2011), *available at* http://www.ftc.gov/opa/ 2011/05/dotcom.shtm.

[19] The report focuses on the information available to parents selecting apps for children, who would in most instances be under 13 years of age. Parents of teens, however, may have similar concerns about the collection of information from apps their older children use.

[20] Staff does not know what factors the app stores use to determine the rank order of the apps returned from their search functions. The apps appeared relevant to the search term "kids."

[21] The Android Market also provides an estimated range of the number of times an app has been downloaded and a list of "permissions" associated with every app.

[22] As shown in the tables below, some of the findings in the survey are based on an analysis of the 960 apps while others are based on the more detailed analysis of the subset of 400 apps.

[23] Most apps are not expensive but all sales are final in the Apple App store (*see* iTunes Store Terms and Conditions, http://www.apple.com/legal/itunes/us/terms.html#GIFTS (last visited Jan. 17, 2012)) and refunds for apps obtained through the Android Market must be made within 15 minutes from download (*see Returning Apps,* Android Market Help Articles, http://support.google.com/androidmarket/bin/answer. py?hl=en& answer=134336 (last visited Jan. 17, 2012)).

[24] *See* Appendix, pages A2-A3 for additional information about the differences; *see also* Armando Rodriquez, PC World, "Web-based Android Market Looks Good" (Feb. 2, 2011), http://www.pcworld.com/article/ 218532/webbased_android_market_looks_gocd.html ("Essentially it is the same information you would get from browsing the Market on your phone only in a much nicer-looking package.").

[25] *See* Appendix, page A3-A4 for more information about how staff categorized the apps.

[26] The "Other" category mostly included apps offering parenting guides, and children's television or movie recommendations. Staff also encountered three apps for parents to use to monitor their child's geolocation.

[27] *See* Appendix, page A3-A4 for additional information.

[28] In total, 5% of the 400 apps closely reviewed by staff were likely not intended to be used by kids, based on the apps' descriptions. Except where noted, staff did not remove these apps from the analysis in this report. *See* Appendix, page A7.

[29] Staff converted the grade kindergarten to the age 5, first grade to the age 6, second grade to the age 7, etc.

[30] A recent study looking at the paid apps in the Apple App Store's Education category found 58% of the apps were for toddlers and preschool age children. Carly Shuler, Joan Ganz Cooney Center, *iLearn II: An Analysis of the Education Category of Apple's App Store,* 13-14 (Jan. 2012), *available at* http:// joanganzcooneycenter.org/ Reports-33.html.

[31] Developers do not receive compensation from the app stores when a user downloads a free app. Developers can still make money from such apps, however. As discussed below, one of the common business models is to partner with a mobile ad network that will pay a developer to include code in the app software that allows the ad network to serve ads.

[32] Several apps in the study appeared to be quite popular. One Android app appeared to have been downloaded between 5,000,000 and 10,000,000 times; six Android apps showed 1,000,000 to 5,000,000 downloads; five Android apps showed 500,000 to 1,000,000 downloads; and 19 Android apps showed that they had been downloaded 100,000 to 500,000 times.

[33] The percentages reported were calculated using the lower values of the download ranges. *See* Appendix, page A4 for more information about the download calculation.

[34] Currently, both the mobile and desktop versions of the Android Market include an email contact on the app promotion pages. At the time staff collected the information for this report, however, only the mobile version of the Android Market included this information. Therefore, the 13% figure would likely be higher if staff had captured the mobile version of the app promotion pages, or if staff were to repeat the information collection today. *See* Appendix, page A2.

[35] Staff used an English language configured browser to visit developer websites, but nevertheless encountered five foreign language websites.

[36] Because staff only reviewed the landing page of the associated websites, there may have been apps that included contact information on subsequent pages of the associated site. *See* Appendix, page A4-A5.

[37] These percentages do not add up to the 65% total because the landing pages contained different combinations of contact information.

[38] As noted, staff encountered a significant number of apps for very young children. These children are unlikely to be able to type sensitive personal information into the mobile device. Nevertheless, the app may collect and

share information about the device and/or child, such as the device's location or phone number, or other information stored on the device by the user.

[39] *See Press Release, Future of Privacy Forum, supra* note 15 ("Application developers can access a considerably broader range of information about users than traditional web developers"); Lookout Mobile Security, *App Genome Report* (Feb. 2011), *available at* www.mylookout.com/appgenome/ (finding that 28% of the free apps in the Android Market and 34% of the free apps in the Apple App Store have the capability to access user location information, and 7.5% of the free apps in the Android Market and 11% of the free apps in the Apple App Store have the capability to access user contacts); Thurm & Kane, *supra* note 17 (documenting the data collection that occurred through many popular smartphone apps).

[40] *See, e.g., Consumer Privacy and Protection in the Mobile Marketplace: Hearing before the Subcomm. on Consumer Protection, Product Safety and Insurance of the S. Comm. on Commerce, Science and Transportation.* 112th Cong. 6-7 (May 10, 2011) (prepared statement of Alan Davidson, Director of Public Policy, Google Inc.), *available at* http://commerce.senate.gov/public/?a=Files.Serve&File_id=517bc26fab89-4339-ad0f-441879598ed1 (the user may choose to trust the application by completing the installation or the user may choose to cancel the installation).

[41] Android provides consumers with a very technical description of this permission stating that it allows "an application to create network sockets." *See* Appendix, page A5.

[42] For purposes of Table 7, staff removed any apps determined by staff not to be for kids.

[43] "Phone calls: read phone state and identity" allows the app to determine if the mobile device is currently making a telephone call – presumably so that it can avoid interrupting the call. It can also determine the mobile device's telephone number. A more descriptive list of the Android operating system permissions found in this survey is provided on pages A5-A6 of the Appendix.

[44] "Modify/delete SD card" means the app would have the ability to save and erase data on the mobile device's memory card. *See* Appendix, pages A5-A6.

[45] *See Apple Answers the FCC's Questions*, Apple Inc. (Aug. 21, 2009), *available at* http://www.apple.com/hotnews/apple-answers-fcc-questions (stating that it provides guidelines to developers that are used in considering whether to approve applications, and describing Apple's review process).

[46] At least one survey of free apps in the Apple App Store and the Android Market, however, found little difference between the two stores in the prevalence of access to sensitive data. Lookout Mobile Security, *supra* note 39, Figs 9-10; *see also* Thurm & Kane, *supra* note 17, (documenting the data collection that occurred through many popular smartphone apps).

[47] *Apple Answers the FCC's Questions, supra* note 45.

[48] *See Consumer Privacy and Protection in the Mobile Marketplace: Hearing before the Subcomm. on Consumer Protection, Product Safety and Insurance of the S. Comm. on Commerce, Science and Transportation,* 112th Cong. 3 (May 19, 2011) (prepared statement of Catherine Novelli, Vice President, Worldwide Government Affairs, Apple Inc.), *available at* http://commerce.senate.gov/public/?a=Files.Serve&File_id=4e365814- c929-4785-9d39-596052ab3a7d (stating "we make it very clear in our App Store Review Guidelines that any App that targets minors for data collection will be rejected.").

[49] *See* Statement of Catherine Novelli, *supra* note 48, at 4-5 ("An arrow icon alerts iOS 4 users that an application is using or has recently used location-based information"); *Understanding the LocationListener in Android,* DoityourselfAndroid.com (Dec. 25, 2010) http://blog.doityourselfandroid.com/2010/12/25/ understanding-locationlistener-android/ (discussing the GPS icon on Android and stating that "No GPS icon will be shown in the title bar, unless a certain application (like Google Maps) triggers it to request a location.").

[50] *See* Statement of Catherine Novelli, *supra* note 48, at 4; Statement of Alan Davidson, *supra* note 40, at 5-6.

[51] *See* Statement of Catherine Novelli, *supra* note 48, at 4.

[52] *See Best Practices for Mobile Applications Developers,* Future of Privacy Forum, 3, http://www.futureofprivacy.org/wp-content/uploads/Apps-Best-Practices-v-beta.pdf (last visited Jan. 24, 2012) (citing section 3.3.10 of the iOS Developer Program License Agreement, stating that "Developers must provide clear and complete information to users regarding collection, use and disclosure of user or device data."); Android Market Developer Distribution Agreement, 4.3, http://www.android.com/us/developerdistribution-agreement.html (last visited Oct. 31, 2011) ("If the users provide you with, or your Product accesses or uses, user names, passwords, or other login information or personal information, you must make the users aware that the information will be available to your Product, and you must provide legally adequate privacy notice and protection for those users.").

[53] Apple Privacy Policy, http://www.apple.com/privacy (last visited Jan. 17, 2012) ("Information collected by third parties, which may include such things as location data or contact details, is governed by their privacy

practices. We encourage you to learn about the privacy practices of those third parties."); Android Privacy Policy, http://www.android.com/privacy. html (last visited Jan. 17, 2012) ("Information collected by the third party application provider is governed by their privacy policies.").

[54] The desktop version of the Apple App Store provides standardized locations on each app's preview page for placing links to the developer's website, a support site, and an application license agreement. Staff only reviewed the developer website link. *See* Appendix, pages A4-A5.

[55] As noted in the FTC staff's preliminary privacy report, consumers are unlikely to read disclosures buried in privacy policies or "terms of service" agreements because they are not easily accessible and are invariably long, legalistic, and difficult to understand. These concerns are heightened in the mobile space, where consumers are interacting with very small screens. The privacy report encouraged companies to offer short, easy-to-read, "just in time" disclosures (or icons) that consumers are likely to see, read, and understand. *See* FTC Preliminary Staff Report, *supra* note 7, at 69-71.

[56] *See* Cecilia Kang, *Lawmakers urge FTC to investigate free kids games on iPhone*, Washington Post, Feb. 8, 2011, *available at* http://www.washingtonpost.com/wp-dyn/content/article/ 2011/02/08/AR2011020805721.html.

[57] *See Administering In-app Billing,* Android Developers Guide, http://developer.android.com/ guide/market/billing/billing_integrate.html (last visited Jan. 17, 2012).

[58] A few applications indicated integration with more than one social network.

[59] In-app advertising typically involves a relationship between the app developer and an ad network, where the ad network pays the developer to incorporate the ad network's code into the developer's application. When the app is running, the ad software allows the ad network to send ads to the user's device. Depending on how the ad network software is configured, the ad network may collect information from the user to provide targeted ads. *See* Thurm & Kane, *supra* note 17 ("[M]any ad networks offer software 'kits' that automatically insert ads into an app. The kits track where users spend time inside the app."); *see generally Google Ads for Mobile FAQ,* http://code.google.com/mobile/afma_ads/kb/ (last visited Jan. 17, 2012) (describing the integration of ad software for targeted advertising); iAd, http://developer.apple.com/iad/ (last visited Jan. 17, 2012) (describing the integration of ad features in iOS).

[60] *See* Jolie O'Dell, *The Rise of Mobile In-App Ads* (July 16, 2011), http://mashable.com/2011/07/ 16/in-appads/ (43% of the app developers used in-app advertising in 2011).

[61] Other organizations review mobile apps and provide ratings and recommendations to help parents select content appropriate apps for kids. *See, e.g.,* Common Sense Media, *Best apps: Our recommendations for families,* http://www.commonsensemedia.org/mobile-app-lists (last visited Jan. 17, 2012).

[62] While reviewing the app promotion pages in the survey, staff did not encounter any references to the age and content ratings found on many computer and video games, which are assigned by the Entertainment Software Rating Board (ESRB). Staff also notes that the ESRB and the wireless trade association CTIA have recently created a new mobile app rating system that uses its traditional icons to inform users. *See* Press Release, ESRB, *CTIA-The Wireless Association and ESRB Announce Mobile Application Rating System* (Nov. 29, 2011), *available at* http://www.esrb.org/about/news/downloads/CTIA_ESRB_ Release_11.29.11.pdf. Like the Apple and Android rating systems, this new ratings system considers whether the app contains violence, language, or sexual content. It also considers whether the app has a minimum age requirement, allows the exchange of user-generated content, or enables users to share their location with other app users. However, this system also relies on developer provided information. Apple and Google are not currently participating in this initiative. *See* Kevin Fitchard, *Apple, Google Absent From ESRB's New Mobile App Rating System,* Gigaom (Nov. 29, 2011), http://gigaom.com/2011/11/29/apple-google-absent-from-esrbs-new-mobileapp-rating-system/.

[63] *See, e.g.,* Statement of Catherine Novelli, *supra* note 48, at 2; *iTunes: Using Parental Controls,* Apple, http://support.apple.com/kb/ht1904 (last modified Sept. 23, 2011). The Android Market allows users to filter apps displayed in the market based on app content ratings. *Application Content Ratings,* Android Market, http://support.google.com/androidmarket/ bin/answer.py?hl=en&answer=1075738 (last visited Jan. 17, 2012).

[64] *See* Apple, *iTunes Connect Developer Guide, Version 7.2* 52-53 (Oct. 17, 2011), *available at* https:// itunesconnect.apple.com/docs/iTunesConnect_DeveloperGuide.pdf; Statement of Alan Davidson, *supra* note 40, at 7.

[65] *See iTunes Connect Developer Guide, supra* note 64, at 52.

[66] *Id.*

[67] *Rating Your Application Content for Android Market*, Android Market for Developer, http://support.google. com/androidmarket/developer/bin/answer.py?hl=en&answer=188189 (last visited Jan. 17, 2012).

[68] *Id.*

[69] *Id.*

[70] Staff did not evaluate the appropriateness of the Android ratings, but noticed that four of the Android "kids" apps listed a "medium maturity" rating, and four others listed a "high maturity" rating. Upon further review of these app descriptions, only five of these eight apps appeared to be intended for a child to use. These five apps consisted of three flashcard games, one painting game, and one "animal sounds" game. Based on the information available, staff could not determine why these five apps had such high maturity ratings.

[71] *See* Apple, *iOS: Understanding Restrictions*, *available at* http://support.apple.com/kb/ht4213 (last modified Oct. 24, 2011); Kids and Media, *Parental Controls for Android* (Dec. 5, 2011), www.kidsandmedia.org/ parent-controls-for-android/; *see also Application Content Ratings*, Android Market, *supra* note 63.

[72] *See* Apple, *iOS: Understanding Restrictions*, *supra* note 71.

[73] *See* Kids and Media, *Parental controls for Android, supra* note 71; iKid Apps, *How to Setup Parental Controls on Android* (July 22, 2011) *available at* http://www.ikidapps.com/2011/ 07/how-to-setup-parentalcontrols-on-android.html.

[74] For example, a child may not be able to access higher levels of a game or additional content if the internet connection has been blocked.

End Notes for Appendix

[1] The specific random sample used is identified by the column heading under which the "n=200" specification is found.

[2] This category only included apps that had the word "learn" plus a language in the title or description.

[3] Searches on the Android Market only yield 480 accessible results. Staff considered all 480 Android Market results, and truncated the results from the Apple App Store to 480 in order to make the samples comparable.

[4] For this reason, it is not surprising that only 61.5% of the Apple app promotion pages and 72.5% of the Android app promotion pages indicated they were intended to be used by "kids."

INDEX

D

K

L

M

N

O

S

T